THE EARLY GRADE READING ASSESSMENT:
Applications and Interventions to Improve Basic Literacy

Edited by Amber Gove and Anna Wetterberg

RTI Press

Library of Congress Control Number: 2001012345
ISBN 978-1-934831-08-3

RTI Press publication No. BK-0007-1109
doi:10.3768/rtipress.2011.bk.0007.1109
www.rti.org/rtipress.

Cover photos

Top: Swadchet Sankey administers an early grade reading assessment in Hausa to a student in Sokoto State as part of the USAID-supported Nigeria Northern Education Initiative project. Photographer: Alison Pflepsen, RTI International

Middle: Liberian teacher Patience Sieh, trained under the USAID-supported EGRA Plus project, leads a class in an early literacy activity. Photographer: Medina Korda, RTI International

Bottom: Liberian students enjoy early reading materials provided by the USAID-supported EGRA Plus project. Photographer: Medina Korda, RTI International

The RTI Press mission is to disseminate information about RTI research, analytic tools, and technical expertise to a national and international audience. RTI Press publications are peer-reviewed by at least two independent substantive experts and one or more Press editors.

RTI International is an independent, nonprofit research organization dedicated to improving the human condition by turning knowledge into practice. RTI offers innovative research and technical services to governments and businesses worldwide in the areas of health and pharmaceuticals, education and training, surveys and statistics, advanced technology, international development, economic and social policy, energy and the environment, and laboratory testing and chemistry services.

This publication is part of the RTI Press Book series.
RTI International
3040 Cornwallis Road, PO Box 12194, Research Triangle Park, NC 27709-2194 USA
rtipress@rti.org
www.rti.org

Contents

Foreword:
Learning for All

After 14 years of conflict, Liberia's children now fill our schools. Seeing them on their way to class each morning is one of my greatest pleasures, and a reassuring sign that Liberia has regained stability. But we need more than schools filled with children and teachers; our country's hopes for sustained peace and economic development depend, instead, on learning and on an educated citizenry.

When I became President in 2006, one of my biggest challenges was to respond to the expectations of a people long denied the opportunity to learn. During the years of our civil conflict, schools were destroyed, and teachers either fled or were killed. Our Administration responded by building schools, recruiting certificated teachers, and making public primary education free and compulsory. Students responded in the hundreds of thousands, filling our classrooms. The recent signing into law of the Education Reform Act of 2011 extends free education through grade 9, and is aimed at keeping more children in school, especially girls.

Despite our efforts, a recent assessment of early reading shows that many teachers are ill-equipped to teach reading—the foundation of learning. Sobering statistics from 2008 reveal that 34 percent of Liberian students who were tested at the end of grade 2 could not read a single word. As shocking as these data are, they are not unique to Liberia. Similar assessments of early reading throughout sub-Saharan Africa have shown that many children spend two, four, and even six years in school without learning to read.

A promise of "Education for All," proclaimed in Dakar, to ensure that by 2015 all children "have access to a complete free and compulsory primary education," is an empty pledge if learning is absent. Leaders throughout the region have made great strides in ensuring that children have access to school, and enrolment in some countries has increased by hundreds of percent. But access is not enough. Learning has long been a neglected promise of "Education for All." What we need is a renewed commitment to "Learning for All."

This book highlights the experience of Liberia in both assessing and improving reading in primary schools. As a result of an Early Grade Reading Assessment, the Ministry of Education and partners, including the United States Agency for International Development, came together to identify and develop strategies for improving reading in our schools. Over the course of a year, the partnership provided support and training to teachers, reading books for students, and collaborated with parents to instill a culture of reading in the community. These efforts paid off; the share of students in program-supported schools that are reading with understanding more than tripled, while the results in a comparison group remained nearly flat.

Critical to this process was the use of data to inform decision making. Without information about which areas need improvement, we cannot decide which course of action to take. Assessments such as those described in this book are especially important as they identify which skills need reinforcement—information that can directly inform teaching and learning. With training and support, teachers can then use this information to improve their practice in schools and monitor student progress toward achieving goals and standards. Information can also help parents and communities to pressure for and support improvement in schools.

Teachers and communities cannot fight these battles alone. National-level leadership and support are needed if countries are to ensure learning for all. As a demonstration of my commitment to education, in addition to the Education Reform Act, our investment in education now accounts for nearly 12 percent, the second largest item of our national budget. Resources alone will not guarantee that all children will learn. However, continuous assessment of progress helps to adjust the course we take on the path to "Learning for All."

The future of Liberia, and of our continent, depends on ensuring that all children learn. If we are to thrive as a nation, we cannot ignore this challenge.

Ellen Johnson Sirleaf
President of the Republic of Liberia

Acknowledgments

First and foremost, this book is rooted in the daily efforts of teachers in schools around the world to introduce their students to the fundamentals of reading. It is on these educators that we rely for the early literacy skills that lay the groundwork for successful later learning. We are likewise indebted to the many young learners who participated in the assessments and for whom learning to read well at an early age can mean a concrete difference in available opportunities later in life.

We also owe much to partners in governments, donor agencies, civil society organizations, and schools who were instrumental to the assessments described here. We are grateful to USAID for providing the funding for EGRA since its inception and to the staff of Ministries of Education, USAID Missions, and World Bank offices in Kenya, Liberia, Mali, Nicaragua, Peru, Senegal, South Africa, and Uganda for their support in the field. Other collaborators include, among many others, Penelope Bender, Vanessa Castro Cardenal, Paula Gains, Ward Heneveld, Liberian Education Trust (LET), the Liberian EGRA Plus staff, coaches and teachers, Sylvia Linan-Thompson, Lynn Murphy, Saeeda Prew, Carol da Silva, and the William & Flora Hewlett Foundation. RTI International has also contributed a substantial amount of its own research and development funding to advance and improve the technical rigor of the early grade reading assessments; we are grateful to RTI leadership for believing in the effort and its willingness to support our open-source approach to collaboration in the name of improving reading for all.

Like all edited volumes, the writing of the book has been a collaborative effort. We are grateful to Melinda Taylor for her ongoing support of the project and detailed review of each chapter. Kathleen Lohr took her role as RTI Press Editor seriously, turning her critical eye on all aspects of the book, which significantly improved it. Karen Lauterbach, Joanne Studders, Sonja Douglas, and Alisa Clifford were critical to producing the book, and went out of their way to help us meet our deadline.

Thanks also to the anonymous reviewers who took the time to carefully read the chapters and make suggestions that strengthened each one. We were impressed by the rigor of the RTI Press review process and with the thoughtful comments it produced.

Erin Newton edited multiple drafts of each chapter before submission and after revisions in response to reviewers' comments. She improved not only the style and flow of the writing, but also drew on her extensive experience with EGRA publications to align facts and contribute substantively. Without Erin, the volume would not have been completed.

Finally, we would like to thank the chapter authors for their commitment to improving early grade reading and to writing their chapters in spite of the challenging time pressures and environments many of them faced. We appreciate their patience with the numerous queries and rounds of comments to which we subjected them over the many months it took to put the book together.

CHAPTER 1

The Early Grade Reading Assessment: An Introduction

Amber Gove and Anna Wetterberg

During the 1990s, many low-income countries committed to the United Nations Education for All goals of ensuring universal access to primary education and students' completion of all primary grades. Since that time, with support from donors, some countries have made impressive strides toward expanded access to schooling. Much of the progress has stemmed from additional *inputs*—such as classrooms, teachers, and textbooks. The assumption was that, with enough inputs, learning would naturally follow.

Improvements in enrollment rates, however, have not always translated into high-quality education—or even basic learning. To illustrate, the United Nations Educational, Scientific, and Cultural Organization (UNESCO) tracks both enrollment and quality in its Education for All Development Index. These data show that Nicaragua, for instance, has a 97 percent enrollment rate but scores below 50 percent on the quality indicator. Similarly, Cambodia's enrollment rate is 89 percent, but quality lags considerably at 62 percent (UNESCO, 2010).

Teaching young children to read is the cornerstone of improving educational outcomes and has far-reaching implications. Unless they learn to read at an early age, children cannot absorb more advanced skills and content that rely on reading. Children who do not learn to read in the early grades risk falling further and further behind in later ones, as they cannot absorb printed information, follow written instructions, or communicate well in writing. These challenges, rooted in poor reading skills, lead to disappointing results and often early dropout from the education system. In the aggregate, reading and learning achievement are central to economic productivity and growth. Recent research reveals that it is *learning* rather than *years of schooling* that contributes to a country's economic growth: a 10 percent increase in the share of students reaching basic literacy translates into an annual growth rate that is 0.3 percentage points higher than it would otherwise be for that country (Hanushek & Woessman, 2009).

Assessment data of early grade literacy in low-income countries, although still limited, reveal that many students are not mastering the basic skills of reading. In some countries a majority of students at the end of grade 2 are unable to read *a single word* of a simple paragraph in the language in which they are being taught (Gove & Cvelich, 2011).

To shift the focus of education improvement from access to achievement, it is critical to determine how serious and widespread low learning levels are among a country's students. As a first step, measuring how well students read can make policy makers, educators, and donors more aware of how low reading levels are and what the implications are for future learning. Such awareness can lay the foundation for discussions of how to best address the problem.

The early grade reading assessment (EGRA)[1] is one tool used to measure students' progress toward learning to read. It is a test that is administered orally, one student at a time. In about 15 minutes, it examines a student's ability to perform fundamental prereading and reading skills. Since 2006, RTI International, with the support of a range of donors, has worked with education experts (see Appendix A) to develop, pilot, and implement EGRA in more than 50 countries and 70 languages. Although these assessments have shown very low levels of basic literacy skills in many countries, the results have prompted policy makers and educators to search for solutions to address the shortcomings, including developing teaching and learning strategies and materials. Many of these efforts have resulted in impressive advances in reading levels (see Chapters 3 and 4).

Because interest in EGRA has grown quickly in a short period, this book aims to take stock of the substantial amount of information and experience generated. Its purpose is twofold. First, it seeks to elucidate particular aspects of the EGRA approach, to describe and explain *how* teachers, communities, development practitioners, and policy makers have applied and adjusted different elements and approaches to conducting early reading assessments. Drawing from these descriptions, the authors point to challenges and advantages of these adaptations. Second, this book also analyzes *why* the EGRA

---

[1] Throughout this book, the acronym EGRA is used to refer to early grade reading assessments. The reader should note that EGRA is neither a copyrighted term nor a proprietary tool. The term instead refers to assessment tools that are informed by a common conceptual framework and research base and that use standardized administration and training procedures; the tools are adapted to the linguistic context in which the test is developed and administered.

approach has been effective (or not) in specific contexts. Most of the chapters in this book discuss implementation in multiple countries to point to the underlying characteristics and factors that influence outcomes.

This book is addressed to multiple audiences. We hope that practitioners working on improving reading skills in low-income countries will use it both to learn how EGRA has been applied in other contexts and to generate ideas for using reading assessments to address urgent problems in their own countries. Such readers are likely to find Chapter 2, on the national reading diagnostic, instructive and they may also learn from the experience with continuous assessment in the classroom (Chapter 4). The developments in information and communication technology that can enhance EGRA applications could also be useful to practitioners who will carry out and analyze assessments (Chapter 6).

Policy makers at both national and local levels may also value the insights gathered in this volume for identifying investment priorities as well as curriculum and professional development needs in their countries. Previous experiences with impact evaluation may be useful to these readers for thinking about how to identify and monitor the impact of particular interventions designed to improve fundamental reading skills (Chapter 3). Further, the chapter discussing language-of-instruction issues analyzes the effects on educational outcomes when learners are not taught or tested in their first language, which could have implications for curricula in many countries (Chapter 5).

International donors—including those that have supported the development and implementation of many of the assessments described in this book—may also find new knowledge in the chapters. The contrasts between country cases demonstrate the conditions under which different applications of EGRA can be most effective. In particular, the chapter on transforming early grade reading and instruction describes the contexts in which reading assessments are particularly likely to shift educational approaches toward focusing on outcomes (Chapter 7).

The book is divided into two substantive sections. After this introductory chapter—which describes the conceptual foundations of the EGRA instrument; summarizes its subtasks, purposes, and implementation; and closes with challenges and future directions—the next three chapters focus on particular applications of EGRA. By dedicating a chapter to different uses of EGRA, we identify specific benefits and challenges associated with particular applications. Chapter 2 details experiences with using EGRA instruments to identify regional variations and inform national policy and curriculum development. Such national or system-level diagnostics can deepen policy dialogue and identify particular instructional needs. EGRA has also been used to evaluate the impact of specific reading interventions, such as in South Africa and Mali (Chapter 3). Such evaluations can identify specific instructional approaches that, if more widely adopted, could dramatically improve learning outcomes. Then, to explain how assessment results can be used in the classroom, Chapter 4 outlines teachers' experiences in Liberia. In this application, EGRA has been used for mastery checks, which allow teachers to verify that students are learning to read, and for progress monitoring, to keep parents and the community aware of outcomes.

The second section of the book puts EGRA in the context of broader issues and developments in literacy and education. In many countries, the language of instruction is not the same as that spoken in students' homes. This situation presents particular hurdles for improving reading; EGRA has highlighted some of these issues in Kenya and Uganda (Chapter 5). Also, information and communication technologies are playing an increased role in literacy development and assessment. Chapter 6 points to the benefits, as well as limitations, of some of these technologies, with implications for the use of EGRA and other reading assessments. This chapter also describes potential approaches to data analysis and software use in administering and analyzing the results of EGRA. Finally, Chapter 7 describes the political, social, and economic factors that affect both applications of EGRA instruments and policy makers' willingness to make effective use of assessment findings. Experiences in Kenya, South Africa, and Liberia demonstrate how a match with the existing curriculum, sense of crisis, and predisposition to data use can facilitate early adoption of assessment methodology and results.

Developing the Early Grade Reading Assessment

As discussed above, countries around the world have boosted primary school enrollment to historically unprecedented rates. Seeking to honor the commitments of the United Nations' Education for All campaign and Millennium Development Goals, low-income countries had enrolled children in primary school at nearly the rates of high-income countries by 2008 (Figure 1.1). In some countries, enrollment grew by as much as 20 to 30 percentage points in less than a decade. (Note: This section of the chapter draws on the English version of the EGRA toolkit [RTI International, 2009a], as well as Gove & Cvelich [2010, 2011].)

In isolation, these considerable gains in enrollment appeared to signal sizable educational improvements in low-income countries. However, the share of children in low-income countries who complete primary school was still only about two-thirds that of high-income countries as of the late 2000s. Furthermore, progress has been slow; at this pace, it would take another three decades to reach completion rates similar to those in high-income countries (Figure 1.2).

Underlying these low completion rates is a combination of factors, including economic hardship and low school quality. Attrition begins early: In sub-Saharan Africa and in South and West Asia, 9 and 13 percent of students, respectively, will become dropouts before the end of their first year of school (UNESCO, 2010). In household surveys conducted around the world, financial difficulties top the reasons listed for children dropping out before completing primary school.

Figure 1.1 Gross primary school enrollment in high-income and low-income countries, 2000–2008

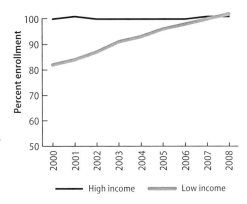

Source: The World Bank, *EdStats Query*, 2010.

Figure 1.2 Primary school completion in high-income and low-income countries, 2000–2008

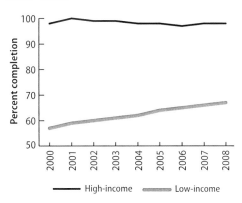

Source: The World Bank, *EdStats Query*, 2010.

Following closely on the list of challenges is low-quality schooling (Bedi & Marshall, 2002; Crouch, 2005; El-Zanaty and Gorin, 2007; Hanushek & Lavy, 1994; NPC Nigeria and ORC Macro, 2004; World Bank, 2007). Even with the promise of universal "free" primary education for all, millions of parents have to sacrifice to send their children to school. In addition to the opportunity costs of lost labor, sibling care, and household work, direct outlays even the poorest parents must absorb include those for school uniforms, materials, books, and in some cases transport. In exchange for their efforts parents expect the most basic of returns—a child who can read and write.

The available evidence indicates that average student learning in most low-income countries is quite low. Evaluation of World Bank education lending shows that improvements in student learning are lagging significantly behind improvements in access to schooling (World Bank: Independent Evaluation Group, 2006). The leading international assessments on literacy and numeracy (Progress in International Reading Literacy Study [PIRLS] and Trends in International Mathematics and Science Study [TIMSS]) show that the average student in low-income countries is at the bottom of the learning curve in high-income countries, only performing at the 5th percentile, worse than 95 percent of the students in Organisation for Economic Co-operation and Development (OECD) classrooms (Crouch & Gove, 2011).

From these results, we can tell what students from low-income countries did *not* know, but we cannot ascertain what they *did* know (often because they scored so poorly they were below the "floor" of the test). Furthermore, most national and international assessments are paper-and-pencil tests administered to students in grades 4 and above; thus, they assume students can read and write. Evaluators cannot always tell from the results of these tests whether students score poorly because they lack the knowledge tested by the assessments or because they lack basic reading and comprehension skills.

In the context of these questions about student learning and continued investment in Education for All, education officials and development professionals at the World Bank, the United States Agency for International Development (USAID), and other institutions called for the creation of simple, effective, and low-cost measures of student learning outcomes (Abadzi, 2006; Center for Global Development, 2006; Chabbott, 2006; Wagner, 2003, 2011; World Bank: Independent Evaluation Group, 2006). Some analysts advocated for the establishment of a global learning standard or goal, in addition to the existing Education for All and Millennium Development Goals (Filmer et al., 2006).

To respond to this demand, work began on the creation of a measure to assess reading skills in the early grades. What was needed was a simple instrument that could report on the foundations of student learning, including assessment of the first steps that students take in learning to read: recognizing letters of the alphabet, reading simple words, and understanding sentences and paragraphs. Development of EGRA began in October 2006, when USAID, through its Education Data for Decision Making (EdData II) project, contracted with RTI International to develop an instrument for assessing early grade reading. The objective was to help USAID partner countries begin the process of measuring, in a systematic way, how well children in the early grades of primary school are acquiring reading skills; ultimately the aim was to spur more effective efforts to improve performance in this core learning skill.

Based on a review of research and existing reading tools and assessments, RTI developed a protocol for what eventually became known as EGRA. Our process included an exhaustive review of the literature and existing assessment approaches in English and other languages, including such well-known tools as DIBELS (Dynamic Indicators of Basic Early Literacy Skills), CTOPP (Comprehensive Test of Phonological Processing), the Woodcock-Johnson Tests of Achievement, and the Peabody Picture Vocabulary Test. We also examined tools developed by nongovernmental organizations (NGOs), university researchers, and research institutions for various research and development projects. Drawing lessons from these tools and the available research evidence, RTI developed a flexible protocol that could be adapted to the particular linguistic requirements of each language but would maintain similar characteristics to facilitate reporting across countries and languages.

To obtain feedback on this protocol and to confirm the validity of the overall approach, RTI (with USAID and the World Bank) convened a meeting in November 2006 of cognitive scientists, experts in early grade reading instruction, research methodologists, and assessment experts to review the proposed key subtasks of the instrument. During this workshop, participants were charged with bridging the gap between research and practice—that is, merging advances in the reading and cognitive science research fields with assessment practices from around the world. Researchers and practitioners presented evidence on alternative ways to measure reading acquisition within the early primary grades. In addition, they were asked to identify the key issues to consider in designing a multicountry, multilanguage, early grade reading assessment protocol. Participants included more than a dozen experts from a diverse group of countries and some 15 observers from governments, donors, NGOs, and universities, such as the William and Flora Hewlett Foundation, George Washington University, the South Africa Ministry of Education, and Pratham, among others.

During 2007, the World Bank supported an application of the draft instrument in Senegal (for the French and Wolof languages) and The Gambia

(English), while USAID supported the application in Nicaragua (Spanish). In addition, national governments, USAID missions, and NGOs in South Africa, Kenya, Haiti, Afghanistan, Bangladesh, and other countries began to experiment with applying certain subtasks of the assessment (with and without the involvement of RTI).

In the interest of consolidating these experiences and developing a reasonably standardized approach to assessing children's early reading acquisition, the World Bank requested that RTI develop a "toolkit" that would guide countries beginning to work with EGRA in such areas as local adaptation of the instrument, fieldwork, and analysis of results. Toolkits are available in English, Spanish, and French (RTI International, 2009a, 2009b, 2009c) at the EdData II project website, www.eddataglobal.org. A Portuguese version will be completed by 2012. Because many of the stated objectives of this chapter overlap with the guidance provided in the toolkits, we struggled to strike a balance between referring readers to an external document and repeating what had been stated elsewhere. We hope that readers will refer to the toolkits whenever they seek additional, more detailed descriptions.

As noted earlier, as of January 2011, EGRA had been applied in nearly 50 countries and 70 languages. (RTI and USAID maintain a list of EGRA applications, including the intended purpose, sample size, and other key information, at www.eddataglobal.org.) The rapid expansion and deployment of the tool was made possible by a vibrant community of practice working together, with varying degrees of affiliation, toward the common goal of improved learning in the early grades in low-income countries (see Appendix A for members of the Early Grade Learning Community of Practice). This community of practice, consisting of staff from ministries of education, local and international NGOs, foundations, and donor agencies, has been instrumental in advancing the cause of early reading assessment and improvement; much of the work described in this book has benefited from the shared lessons of this dedicated group of practitioners.

Underlying Conceptual Framework of the Early Grade Reading Assessment

Drawing on an extensive body of research on early reading acquisition (such as the National Reading Panel [National Institute of Child Health and Human Development, 2000], the National Literacy Panel [2004], and the Committee on the Prevention of Reading Difficulties in Young Children [Snow et al.,

1998], among others), two main principles underpin EGRA. First, learners acquire early reading skills in (sometimes simultaneous) phases; the level of complexity of a language affects how long students need to acquire these skills. Second, reading assessment (and its complement, instruction) is complex, but sufficient research evidence supports the development of specific assessment tools to understand which critical skills require additional reinforcement, *regardless of the method by which students are being taught*. Each of these principles is explained in detail below.

Reading Is Acquired in Phases

Acquiring reading skills is a multiphased process. Reading acquisition takes longer in some languages than others, with the length of time determined by the level of correspondence between the written language, or orthography (represented by graphemes [letters and symbols]), and the spoken language (represented by phonemes [sounds]). In spite of differences in the amount of time it takes to acquire reading skills, EGRA is based on the premise that learners of all alphabet-based languages pass through the same phases. EGRA concentrates on the assessment of foundational skills, as shown in Figure 1.3.

According to Seymour et al. (2003), for alphabetic languages, learners acquire reading in three phases (Figure 1.3).[2] In the first phase, basic skills such as letter-sound knowledge (the ability to map each letter to its corresponding sound or sounds), word recognition (logographic process), and simple decoding of letters into sounds (alphabetic process) are established. The learner is acquiring a knowledge of the smallest building blocks of reading, by recognizing letter sounds (grapheme-phoneme correspondence) and their combination into simple words. Crucial to the development of the foundation laid in this first phase is identifying and storing familiar words by creating a bank of automatic or "sight" words—those that children can recognize on sight. Equally important is the establishment of fluent decoding, the ability to decipher new or unfamiliar words through an understanding of letter-sound correspondence.

In the second and third phases, children encounter printed text that reinforces and helps them internalize language complexities—including rules

---

[2]   Although the model is based on research on alphabetic languages (both Latin and non-Latin scripts), some similarities exist in reading acquisition for logographic languages (e.g., Chinese). Nonetheless, debate continues regarding the extent to which learning is parallel between these different forms of language (Chow et al., 2005).

Figure 1.3 Phases of reading skill development

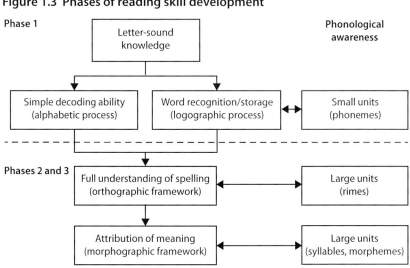

Source: Adapted from Seymour et al., 2003.

and language patterns that they may know from the oral form of the language. Learners build an orthographic framework as they acquire a full understanding of the spelling system and fluency with rimes (larger units of letter-sound correspondence). Subsequently, learners progress to fluency with morphemes (an association of phonemes with semantic meaning), building a framework that involves not only decoding letters into sounds but also, crucially, attributing meaning to written text. Regardless of the order of phasing, the model highlights the need for children to learn a large number of complex skills in order to become successful readers.

Research comparing reading acquisition in 13 European languages provides evidence in support of the assertion that the regularity or complexity of a language affects the speed of acquisition of foundation reading skills. All else equal, children learning to read in English required two to three times the amount of instruction as children learning to read in languages that are more regular in their construction. In linguistic terms, regular languages—such as Spanish—are those that have more transparent or shallow orthographies; they are sometimes also called phonetically spelled languages (see Seymour et al., 2003). Furthermore, the level of complexity of a language appears to affect reading acquisition from the very beginning of the learning process; acquisition of even the basic foundation skills (such as letter naming) occurs at a slower rate in languages with more complex constructions. Several reviews of cross-language differences in reading acquisition have confirmed this hypothesis (see Sprenger-Charolles et al., 2006; Zieger & Goswami, 2005). Results from dozens of applications of EGRA lend further support.

Of course, the level of complexity of a given language is but one (albeit critical) influence on the rate of reading acquisition. Use of instructional time, availability of materials, and whether students are being taught in their mother tongue are all important factors that determine how soon children learn to read. The important lesson, however, is that regardless of language, successful readers are likely to pass through each of the phases depicted in Figure 1.3. An additional implication of this principle is that comparison of results across languages that differ in their orthographic complexity is complicated by the differences in the rate at which children typically learn to read in those languages. The difficulty of comparing results across languages is discussed in more detail below.

To draw this discussion back to EGRA, the phased process of reading acquisition implies that, although differences in complexity may affect rates of acquisition, commonalities exist in the building blocks of early reading across languages. EGRA draws on this insight by breaking down each assessment into subtasks corresponding to the building blocks of reading acquisition. Rather than bluntly gauging whether a learner can read or not, EGRA enables a nuanced identification of the prereading and reading skills that a specific child has already acquired and those that the child still must master to become a competent reader in the language in which he or she is being taught to read.

Assessing Early Reading: Common Foundations, Flexible Design

With the knowledge that reading is acquired in phases and that the rate of acquisition is likely to vary by language and context, how is it possible to design an assessment approach that can capture the range of skills that are foundational to reading acquisition? Our response is codified in the second basic principle underlying EGRA: Learning to read in all alphabetic languages requires acquisition of similar foundation skills, but the importance of each of those skills may vary by language. As a result, EGRA has a reasonably common approach based on core foundation skills, but it is flexible in its design based on the linguistic context.

As an example, English is notorious for its association of multiple sounds with a single letter, described in linguistic terms as high orthographic complexity. There are 26 letters but approximately 44 phonemes in the English language (the number of phonemes varies depending on the source, country, and region, as different dialects have different pronunciations). Vowels in English are particularly complex: the letter "a" has approximately 11 different possible sounds. In comparison, the 27 letters of the Spanish alphabet have approximately 35 phonemes, and Spanish vowels have only one sound each (the letter "a" always sounds like the "a" in "father").

Regardless of these differences, in both Spanish and English learning to read requires the knowledge that each letter (or group of letters) in a word can be associated with a particular sound. This holds true whether the student is learning to read "cat" or "*gato*" (cat in Spanish). The implication of this fact for assessment is that whereas students learning English will require more instructional time than their Spanish-speaking peers to internalize these rules, knowledge of letter sounds is nonetheless a critical foundation skill in both languages, as is the case for any alphabetic language. This principle—that the critical foundation skills are important for all alphabetic languages, but that less instructional time may be needed in more regular languages—is true for all of the skills tested in EGRA; it has important implications for the interpretation of the results of each assessment.

Putting both the phased and common skill nature of reading acquisition together results in a model of reading assessment that responds to the linguistic characteristics of each language but contains common components to facilitate comparisons (and therefore lessons for policy makers and donors) across different languages and contexts. Table 1.1 provides rough guidance for when most children should acquire these skills and maps each phase to the specific EGRA subtasks, which are then explained in detail in the subsequent section.

Although a core set of subtasks is common across nearly all applications (see subtasks denoted with an asterisk in Table 1.1), not all subtasks are applied in every language and context. Oral vocabulary, for example, has been used primarily to understand the basic *receptive vocabulary* (those words the child hears and understands) and *productive vocabulary* (those words the child speaks and understands) of second-language learners, whereas letter sound (rather than letter naming) is preferred in many Francophone countries, as the letter name and sound of the letter are somewhat interchangeable.

Table 1.1. EGRA subtasks and skills

Skill and approximate timing	EGRA subtask	Skill demonstrated by students' ability to:
Emergent literacy: Birth to grade 1	Concepts about print	Indicate text direction, concept of word, or other basic knowledge of print
	Phonemic awareness: identification of onset/ rime sounds; phoneme segmentation	Identify initial or final sounds of words or segment words into phonemes (words are read aloud to student by assessor)
	Oral vocabulary	Point to parts of the body or objects in the room to indicate understanding of basic oral vocabulary
	Listening comprehension*	Respond correctly to questions about a passage read aloud to the student by the assessor
Decoding: Beginning grade 1	Letter identification: names and/or sounds*	Provide the name and/or sound of upper- and lowercase letters presented in random order
	Syllable naming	Identify legal syllables presented in random order
	Nonword reading*	Identify nonwords composed of legal syllables presented in random order
	Familiar word reading	Read a list of words drawn from a corpus of frequent words presented in random order
Confirmation and fluency: End of grade 1 to end of grade 3	Oral reading fluency (paragraph reading) with comprehension*	Read a narrative or informational text with accuracy, with little effort, and at a sufficient rate and respond to literal and inferential questions about the text they have read
	Dictation	Translate sound to print and spell correctly
	Maze or cloze	Silently read a passage and select an appropriate missing word (multiple choices are provided in the case of maze)

* Core EGRA subtasks included in nearly all assessments conducted by RTI International. Remaining subtasks vary depending on country and language.

Sources: Roskos et al., 2009; RTI International, 2009a.

EGRA Subtasks: Content, Purpose, and Implementation

This section describes each EGRA subtask and its assessment objectives. Examples of subtasks drawn from completed EGRAs are shown in Appendix B. More information is also available in the EGRA toolkits available on www.eddataglobal.org (RTI International, 2009a, 2009b, 2009c).

Concepts About Print

One subtask that EGRA developers initially tested was derived from Marie Clay's (1993) Concepts About Print assessment. In several countries, use of three of Clay's items (3 through 5, directional rules concerning where to begin reading, which direction to read, and where to read next) demonstrated ceiling effects (that is, nearly all children successfully completed the task). Print awareness, however, appears to have little ability to predict later reading skills; it mainly serves as a proxy measure for print exposure and literacy environments (Paris & Paris, 2006). In environments where print awareness is very low, this subtask (see Appendix B for an example) is useful for raising awareness and documenting access to printed materials. Students are presented with a short paragraph and are told not to read the text, but to point with a finger in response to three questions that the assessor asks orally, as follows:

1. Where would you begin reading?

2. In which direction would you read?

3. When you get to the end of the line, where would you read next?

Phonemic Awareness

Reading requires turning the letters we see into sounds, sounds into words, and words into meaning. Successfully managing this process requires the ability to work in reverse. That is, to understand the process of moving from letters to sounds to words, students should also grasp that words are composed of individual sounds and understand the process of separating (and manipulating) words into sounds. This ability to identify sounds in words, to separate words into sounds, and to manipulate those sounds is termed *phonemic awareness*; it is a subset of *phonological awareness*, a more general appreciation of the sounds of speech as distinct from their meaning (Snow et al., 1998).

EGRA has tested phonemic awareness in two ways: phoneme segmentation and identification of onset and rime sounds (first and last sounds, respectively). For evaluating phoneme segmentation, the assessor reads aloud a series of 10 words, asking students to divide each word into its component sounds ("cat," for example, would be divided into the sounds: /k/ /a/ /t/; see Appendix B for an example). For identifying onset and rime sounds, the assessor either reads aloud a single word, asking the student to identify either the first or last sound, or reads aloud three words, asking the student to identify the word that begins or ends with a different sound. For example: "What is the first sound in 'map'? and "Which word begins with a different sound: top, touch, stand?" The assessor times the student and records the number of correct sounds identified in 1 minute. Appendix B provides examples of both ways of identifying onset sounds.

Oral Vocabulary

Oral vocabulary tests are most frequently used in contexts in which the language of instruction is not the student's first language; this approach assesses the child's receptive oral vocabulary and helps the child to warm up to the assessment with a simple achievable task. Students are asked to carry out a series of 5 to 10 simple commands in the language of instruction, such as "point to your head" or "touch the table" (see Appendix B for an example). Poor performance on an oral vocabulary assessment indicates either that children simply do not have the basic vocabulary or that they have difficulty processing what they hear (or possibly both).

Listening Comprehension

The listening comprehension assessment involves passages that the assessor reads aloud. Students then respond to comprehension questions or statements that the assessor also reads aloud. Testing listening comprehension separately from reading comprehension is important because of the different ways in which learners approach, process, and respond to text. As in oral vocabulary testing, poor performance on a listening comprehension tool suggests that children simply do not have the vocabulary that the reading materials expect. Passages are about 30 words long and narrate an activity or event that is familiar to local children (see Appendix B for an example). Direct factual questions (answers are available directly in the passage) and inference questions (answers require additional information, insight, or knowledge not directly available from the text) are included.

Letter Identification

In this EGRA subtask, assessors present students with a sheet listing between 50 and 100 letters of the alphabet (in some languages, graphemes, or sets of letters and/or symbols representing a single sound, are presented—e.g., in French, "é" is presented separately from "e"). Students are asked to provide the names or the sounds (depending on the language in question) of all the letters that they can in 1 minute (see Appendix B for examples of both types of letter identification subtask). The full set of letters of the alphabet is listed in random order, 10 letters to a row, using a clear, large, and familiar font in horizontal rows with each letter presented multiple times. EGRA developers select letters for the instrument based on the frequency with which the letter occurs in the language in question. Adjustments are made to accommodate each letter at least once. Randomization is used to prevent students from reciting a memorized alphabet—that is, to test for actual *automaticity* (a level of fluency that no longer requires concentrating on the separate steps) of letter recognition and translation of print to sound.

Syllable Naming

Building on the letter identification exercise, some EGRA test developers have created syllable naming tasks for countries where syllables are the most common way to teach initial reading. In languages with limited legal syllable combinations, assessing nearly all of the more frequent syllable combinations can be done within a standard 50- or 100-item assessment (e.g., in Kiswahili, legal combinations containing the letter "k" would include "ka," "ke," "ki," "ko," and "ku"). Students are asked to name as many syllables as they can in 1 minute. The syllables are listed in random order, 10 syllables to a row. Syllables are selected for the instrument based on the frequency with which they occur in the language in question and are randomly ordered; legal syllable combinations that are actual words are avoided.

Nonword Reading

Nonword reading (sometimes also called invented words) is a measure of decoding ability and is designed to avoid the problem of sight recognition of words. Many children in the early grades learn to memorize or recognize a broad range of "sight" words (words that primary school children should recognize on sight, as many of these words are not easy to sound out and thus must be memorized). Exhaustion of this sight-word vocabulary at around age 10 has been associated with the "fourth-grade slump" in the United States (Hirsch, 2003). Considerable evidence suggests that memorization of text is a significant problem in many low-income countries as well.

To be successful readers, children must combine both decoding and sight-recognition skills; tests that do not include a decoding exercise can overestimate children's ability to read unfamiliar words (as the words tested may be part of the sight-recognition vocabulary). This portion of the assessment includes a list of 50 one- and two-syllable nonwords, five per row, with the following patterns of letters (C = consonant, V = vowel): CV, VC, CVC. (This may be adjusted by language.) Forms are legal for the language, using letters in legitimate positions (e.g., not "wuj" in English because "j" is not used as a final letter in English), they stick to combinations that are typical of the language, and they are not homophones of real words (not "kab," a homophone of "cab"). They are arranged in rows (five nonwords per row), using clear, well-spaced print. Examples in English include "fet," "ca," "ut," and "bleb." Students are asked to read as many of these nonwords as they can in 1 minute; the assessor times the student and records the number of correct (non)words read per minute (see Appendix B for an example).

Familiar Word Reading

Evaluators often assess children's decoding skills using reading lists of unrelated words. This allows for a purer measure of word recognition and decoding skills than does reading comprehension paragraphs, as children are unable to guess the next word from the context. For this assessment, "familiar words" are high-frequency words selected from early grade reading materials and storybooks for first, second, and third grade. Developers can find high-frequency word lists online for English, French, and Spanish or construct lists from existing materials. The latter requires typing or digitally converting materials, followed by analyzing word frequency and creating frequent-word or sight-word lists. High-frequency word lists usually include regular one- and two-syllable words (Moats, 2000). Words are arranged randomly and horizontally with good separation and clear, familiar print in 10 rows, five words per line (see Appendix B for an example). Students are instructed to read as many words as they can in one minute, while the assessor times them. The assessor then records the number of correct words per minute.

Oral Reading Fluency (Paragraph Reading) with Comprehension

Oral reading fluency is a measure of overall reading competence: the ability to translate letters into sounds, unify sounds into words, process connections, relate text to meaning, and make inferences to fill in missing information (Hasbrouck & Tindal, 2006). As skilled readers translate text into spoken language, they combine these tasks in a seemingly effortless manner (automaticity); because oral reading fluency captures this complex process, it can be used to characterize overall reading skill.

Tests of oral reading fluency, as measured by timed assessments of correct words per minute, have been shown to have a strong correlation with more complex assessments, for example a correlation of 0.91 with the Reading Comprehension subtest of the Stanford Achievement Test (Fuchs et al., 2001). Poor performance on a reading comprehension tool suggests that the student had trouble with decoding, with reading fluently enough to comprehend, or with vocabulary.

To develop the paragraph, examiners review one-paragraph stories from children's reading materials, avoiding copying directly from the school textbook. A narrative story has a beginning section that introduces characters, a middle section containing some dilemma, and an ending section with an action resolving the dilemma. It is not a list of loosely connected sentences. Typical character names from the school textbook are avoided as students may give automated responses based on the stories with which they are familiar. Names and places reflect the local culture. Texts contain some complex vocabulary (inflected forms, derivations, etc.) and sentence structures. Large, clear, familiar print and good spacing between lines are used to facilitate student reading. No pictures are included (see Appendix B for an example).

Assessors ask students to read the story, stopping them after 1 minute and recording the number of words read. Subsequently, students are asked comprehension questions that include direct fact-based questions as well as at least one question requiring inference from the text.

Dictation

Teachers frequently use dictation assessment to test both oral comprehension and writing skills. As discussed above, the reading process can also be tested in reverse: Students' ability to hear sounds correctly and then write the letters and words corresponding to the sounds they hear demonstrates their success with the alphabetic process. Several assessment packages offered by commercial test development specialists give teachers instructions on how to develop and score their own assessments. The EGRA dictation subtask is inspired by models promoted by the Educational Testing Service (2005) and Children's Literacy Initiative (2000) and supported by research by the International Reading Association (Denton et al., 2006). The dictation sentence is at most 10 words long and contains at least one difficult or irregular word (see Appendix B for an example).

Maze/Cloze

Teachers commonly use maze and cloze assessments in the classroom to assess comprehension. To develop a maze test, examiners create a 60- to 100-word paragraph. They leave the first and last sentences of the paragraph intact, but delete every fifth word of the sentences in between. Two alternative choices of legal replacement words, together with the correct word, appear in place of each deleted word. For example, if the correct word deleted from the story is "mice," the options presented could be "cat," "house," and "mice." Students are then asked to identify (usually by circling) the correct replacement word that goes in the blank. They have a limited time frame (usually 3 to 5 minutes, depending on the length of the passage) in which to complete the exercise.

For a cloze assessment, the examiners again leave the first and last sentences of the paragraph intact and delete every fifth word of the remaining sentences, but instead of replacing the deleted words with a choice of three words, they leave blanks in place of the missing words. The blanks are of equal length regardless of the word removed. The students are asked to read the passage orally and provide the word that would fit given the context of the story.

Fit for Purpose: Choosing the Right EGRA Application

Although from the outset RTI developed EGRA with a focus on the early grades and the foundation skills of reading, the appropriate uses of the results are open to debate. Interested donors push for cross-country comparability and system-level measures that can report on the effectiveness of their investments. Ministries request an instrument that can tell them how to support teachers through training and other means. Teachers require a tool that can help them identify individual children who need additional help while also assessing the effectiveness of their own instruction.

The EGRA instrument was first developed to be a sample-based "system diagnostic" measure. Its purpose was to document student performance on early grade reading skills to inform ministries and donors regarding system (including national, state, or district) needs for improving instruction (see Chapter 2). This system-level version of EGRA was not intended either for direct use by teachers or for screening of individual students. It was also not intended to be a high-stakes accountability measure for making funding decisions or determining student grade passing.

Table 1.2 Early grade reading assessment approaches

Type of Assessment	Purpose	Pros and Cons
Reading Snapshot (this chapter)	Quickly examine reading levels to raise awareness and spur policy makers, donors, and civil society into action.	**Pros:** minimum design and cost for maximum impact. **Cons:** low statistical significance, cannot make generalizable claims.
National or System-Level Diagnostic (Chapter 2)	Thoroughly examine gaps in reading competencies among students (and instructional approaches among teachers) to inform the improvement of teacher professional development and preservice programs.	**Pros:** statistical significance (accurate or narrow confidence intervals) ensured by adequate sample size; careful randomization assures representativeness. **Cons:** higher technical requirements and large sample sizes lead to higher costs.
Impact Evaluation (Chapter 3)	Conduct baseline—or "pretreatment"—assessment to gauge reading levels before intervention takes place. Monitor progress of programs that aim to improve reading instruction and outcomes. Compare to endline—or "post-treatment"—assessment to isolate change that may be attributable to a specific intervention used in treatment locations.	**Pros:** can detect change over time resulting from an intervention. **Cons:** higher technical requirements and more effort in creating equated or alternative forms; sample size needs to be larger.

Since the first EGRA application at the system level, however, the EGRA subtasks have been used to fulfill a diverse range of assessment needs, including screening, diagnostic, and progress-monitoring purposes (Table 1.2). The differences among these uses lie in the scope of the sample, frequency and comprehensiveness of use, and target audiences for the results.

Table 1.2 provides a brief overview of the structure and purpose of each of these approaches; system level, impact evaluation, and teacher level approaches are documented in depth in Chapters 2 through 4. In each of these cases, evaluators adapted the instrument (and sampling scheme) to reflect the purpose of the assessment (a critical aspect to consider in constructing and

Instrument Design	Sample Specifications	Results and Uses
Can include the full battery of skills testing. Limiting to two or three skills, such as letter identification and oral reading fluency with comprehension, may sufficiently raise awareness. Needs to be properly adapted to local context, which may not be cost saving.	Can be as few as 10 students in each of 20 schools (or even fewer if there is no need for system representativeness, e.g., if the oral assessment is being used only to examine nuances of results of an existing pencil-and-paper assessment), but should be representative of the decision-making unit or region the results seek to influence.	Results can be used to raise awareness, mobilize communities, alert ministry staff and teachers to early reading challenges. Can also be used to examine nuances or deepen understanding of results of other existing assessments.
Should include all subtasks that align with curriculum goals. Additional subtasks known to be predictive and to inform instruction (from local or international research) may be included even if they are not specified in the curriculum.	At least 500 students per cell or group of interest (e.g., grade, region). Standard is 10 students in 50 schools.	In addition to the above, can be used to deepen policy dialogue on how to use the results. Should be used to identify support needs and additional resources for teachers.
Should include all subtasks that align with curriculum goals and instructional approaches of the program under evaluation. Requires alternate and equated (equal difficulty) forms for the pretreatment and the post-treatment assessments. Should be complemented with degree of implementation measures (lesson achieved).	At least 500 students per cell or group of interest (e.g., grade, region). Standard is 10 students in 50 schools. Needs either to have a control group and treatment group or to have some other way of "identifying" the effect of the intervention, such as staggered introduction into the treatment group. Sample needs to be large enough to detect intervention effect.	Used to detect hypothesized effect of the intervention; requires that minimum detectable effect of intervention be specifically stated ahead of time. Results can be used to inform program improvements and evaluate program impact on reading outcomes.

(continued)

Table 1.2 Early grade reading assessment approaches *(continued)*

Type of Assessment	Purpose	Pros and Cons
Classroom Assessment: Mastery Checks (Chapter 4)	Teachers conduct regular (weekly or monthly) checks to verify that all students are learning skills that have been taught.	**Pros:** can be used to drive teaching improvement; low cash cost (although cost in use of teacher time). **Cons:** could be misused for excessive assessment; danger that aggregated results, reported up, could be inappropriately used for national reporting and averaging or for bureaucratic accountability pressure.
Classroom Assessment: Progress Monitoring (Chapter 4)	Teachers conduct regular progress monitoring assessment (every 2 to 3 months, including at beginning and end of school year) to compare student progress against norms and benchmarks for grade.	**Pros:** can be used to communicate to school director and parents on a regular basis about progress against benchmarks. **Cons:** could be misused for excessive assessment; danger that aggregated results, reported up, could be inappropriately used for national reporting and averaging or for bureaucratic accountability pressure.

Source: Adapted from Gove & Cvelich, 2011.

using any assessment tool; American Educational Research Association et al., 1999; Hasbrouck & Tindal, 2006; Kame'enui et al., 2006; Kaminski et al., 2006). In many of these applications, relevant EGRA subtasks are complemented by a short series of contextual questions that help analysts break down results by groups of interest, such as socioeconomic status, parents' education or reading ability, language used in the home, reading materials found in the home, or other factors.

1. **Reading Snapshot.** As the name implies, using EGRA in this way quickly gauges reading abilities but does not illuminate the whole picture, as the results cannot necessarily be generalized. This type of EGRA application can be used to demonstrate the need for reading interventions, often at relatively low cost and in a short time frame. For example, RTI used an early forerunner of EGRA in Peru to assess reading in a small sample of 150 students in 20 randomly selected schools. The results indicated very low reading levels; only 25 percent of grade 1 students could read at least one word. Even in grade 2, only 41 percent of tested students read one or

Instrument Design	Sample Specifications	Results and Uses
Informal mastery checks of student progress. Should reflect scope and sequence of instruction of each teacher and how the teacher intends to meet curriculum and standards.	Whole class.	Results used to inform instruction at the individual classroom level so teachers can modify their practice. Develop teacher capacity to use regular classroom-based assessment measures to identify student needs and to inform and modify reading instruction.
Should reflect scope and sequence of instruction of each teacher and how each teacher intends to meet curriculum and standards.	Subset of class; can target children experiencing difficulties on general outcome measure.	Results used to inform instruction at the individual classroom level and to communicate to school community about classroom progress.

more words (Abadzi et al., 2005). Although it was a small study that was not nationally representative, the poor reading results generated sufficient awareness to make reading a topic of a debate during presidential elections. A video (*Para mejorar la educación hay que comenzar por la lectura* [To improve education one must start with reading], available from the EdData II website) further provoked discussions about how to measure and improve reading among students in the early grades.

A reading snapshot often includes only a small number of subtasks, to focus attention and limit the cost of the assessment. In Peru, for example, students were asked only to read a paragraph aloud and answer questions about the passage (oral reading fluency with comprehension subtask).

The early example from Peru highlighted the potential strength of the now-mature EGRA to provide a reading snapshot. It has since proven appropriate for this use in several other countries, where the rigorously collected and easily communicable results have quickly drawn policy makers', researchers', and the public's attention to severe but often ignored problems with fundamental reading skills. This application of EGRA can be used to mobilize decision makers and resources to improve early reading instruction. Because of its limited scope, however, the snapshot cannot provide a reliable guide to priority areas for interventions that could be effective in the classroom. For these ends, we must turn to other EGRA approaches.

2. **National- or System-Level Diagnostic.** EGRA was originally designed to provide a representative picture of reading levels within a country to help identify priority areas for instructional improvement and teacher training. Researchers can use this application of EGRA to establish a national baseline for reading levels against which any future progress may be measured. A national- or system-level diagnostic application requires larger sample sizes and often includes more subtasks than an EGRA snapshot, and it brings accompanying increases in data reliability and nuance but also in cost. Chapter 2 contrasts the implementation of this type of EGRA in Nicaragua and Senegal.

3. **Impact Evaluation.** Over time, RTI and others have adopted EGRA as a means of gauging the effects of particular instructional interventions on reading skills (see Chapter 3). EGRA can capture more subtle impacts from specific teaching approaches than pencil-and-paper tests, as it incorporates subtasks that measure *pre*reading skills. Compared with other uses of EGRA, impact evaluations require relatively large sample sizes and are often costlier, as they need both pre- and post-intervention assessment.

4. **Classroom Assessment: Mastery Checks and Progress Monitoring.** The most recent use of EGRA is in the classroom; it helps educators, parents, and school administrators track progress and identify needs for additional instruction for specific classes and individual students. In contrast to other EGRA purposes, such as informing policy decisions, classroom uses are intended for teachers and can, in some cases, assess individual student progress. RTI used this approach in Liberia under the EGRA Plus project (Chapter 4).

Mastery checks assess whether instruction has resulted in the desired learning achievements, and they expose needs for additional teaching interventions. Investigators using EGRA instruments in this way should design them to reflect the specific skills targeted in instruction, introducing only the relevant subtasks. Mastery checks can help teachers identify specific areas of student knowledge and skills that require instructional improvement and alert them to areas that need further reinforcement before they proceed to more advanced instruction.

RTI has used EGRA in the classroom to monitor progress against established curricular benchmarks. In contrast to mastery checks, which teachers apply frequently to verify learning of specific skills, progress monitoring measures student achievements as compared with more general expectations for their grade at regular points throughout the school year. Evaluators can then aggregate the results to examine progress at the classroom or school level, or they can identify individual students who need assistance.

Cutting across these applications of EGRA is the use of assessment data for social mobilization at local and national levels. Concrete information on general reading levels, school performance, and individual student progress can spur officials, educators, activists, and parents to agitate for improvements. At the policy level, snapshot or national diagnostic uses of EGRA are particularly likely to spur change to existing curriculum or teaching practice, to the extent that stakeholders develop a sense of crisis based on the tangible quantitative data that EGRA produces (Chapter 7). At the community level, classroom use of EGRA can provide parents with data both to hold schools accountable and to mobilize additional support for teachers and students. Impact evaluation data can help educators and policy makers identify specific instructional interventions for which to mobilize financial and political support.

Although these groups may have had a vague sense of slow progress and dissatisfaction in the past, reliably demonstrating specific shortfalls and urgent needs for additional interventions can catalyze collective action. Clear data can also help disparate actors coalesce into a movement pushing for concrete changes. As in many other areas of development, however, this type of information is necessary but not always sufficient to instigate change.

Finally, another cross-cutting use of EGRA data is to illuminate the effects of particular policy decisions on learning outcomes. With appropriate attention to research design and consistent implementation, researchers can use EGRA data to inform policy makers about broad reforms that help students master reading more quickly. For instance, Chapter 5 sheds light on the debilitating effects that language-of-instruction policies can have when official languages do not correspond to those that students speak at home.

Implementation

Using the established EGRA subtask examples, stakeholders can adapt the instrument to suit specific linguistic and instructional contexts and needs. Although the purposes for using EGRA may differ, with implications for data analysis and presentation, the preparations for EGRA implementation share characteristics. Below we briefly describe these common implementation steps (more details may be found in the EGRA toolkits (RTI International, 2009a, 2009b, 2009c).

Translation and Adaptation

Assessor instructions for EGRA subtasks (that is, the oral guidance assessors give to students regarding the format of each particular subtask) remain essentially the same across assessments and languages. Thus, test developers can translate them directly for use in a new context. The subtasks themselves, however, require adaptation, rather than straight translation, for several reasons.

EGRA in any given application needs to reflect the specific rules of a language, correspond with local curricula, and assess students on locally and culturally appropriate words, texts, and concepts. The need for and focus of adaptation varies by subtask. For instance, the structure of stories for the oral reading fluency subtask is essentially the same across languages. Stories should, however, use names and subjects typical in the local context. For this subtask and the familiar word reading subtask, test developers must start by locating or constructing lists of words common in the local context to ensure that students' results reflect their reading abilities, rather than a lack of familiarity with words used in the assessment.

EGRA instruments that RTI and others have adapted to date, for a range of languages and countries, are freely available for download from the EdData II website (www.eddataglobal.org). RTI and the other contributors ask only that users acknowledge the source of their instruments and that they donate newly developed and adapted instruments to the EdData II website for reference and use by others. Guidelines for adapting specific subtasks appear in the EGRA toolkits.

Depending on the type of EGRA and specific information needs, adaptation may also involve adding a set of contextual questions. These questions—about family characteristics, reading habits and languages spoken at home, family assets, and similar variables—help analysts break down results by groups of interest.

In addition to instrument adaptation, users need to construct the sampling frame to fit the specific purpose, populations of interest, local conditions (such as distribution of students across schools and regions), and the desired level of confidence in estimates for a particular study. Sample sizes are likely to be constrained by limited funding and time. General sampling guidelines for specific EGRA purposes are in Table 1.2. An annex in each of the EGRA toolkits offers detailed instructions for identifying an appropriate sample size.

Training

Training staff who will be administering EGRA is critical to the reliability of EGRA data. Assessors need to become familiar with administration of an oral interview and with the specific implementation and coding practices associated with EGRA. For instance, assessors must be able to simultaneously listen to student responses, code them, and monitor elapsed time. Further, EGRA is individually administered by assessors who record student performance; it is not done in a group setting by having students complete a paper-and-pencil test. For that reason, interrater reliability (consistency of administration across assessors) is crucial. Thus, all assessors must code students' responses in the same way to ensure that data consistently reflect collective standards for reading abilities, rather than assessors' personal evaluations of skills.

Techniques for testing interrater reliability during training include (1) having two assessors simultaneously score the same student, (2) playing video or audio recordings of student assessments to multiple assessors, who simultaneously score the recorded student, and (3) arranging for adult trainers or assessors to play the role of student while two or more assessors score their reading performance. Subsequently, trainers collect scoring sheets and determine how closely the results match the standard set by an experienced assessor (interrater reliability). Assessors whose scoring deviates substantially from the mean require additional instruction to ensure that assessment results are reliable. Section V of the various language versions of the EGRA toolkit provides more information on these procedures.

Fieldwork

Before full data collection, users typically pilot EGRA instruments with at least 100 students to ensure that the instruments perform as expected. Pilot results require analysis by a psychometrician, or test specialist, to check for consistency and appropriateness of the constructed test. Pilot testing is also an opportunity for assessors to gain valuable hands-on experience with EGRA implementation and for trainers to identify gaps in assessor understanding and skills before scale-up to full implementation.

The amount of time for the actual fieldwork in the final sample of schools depends on the geographic coverage and on the numbers of assessors and supervisors deployed, schools sampled, and children tested. Other chapters in this book offer examples of team composition (number of teams, supervisors, assessors) and give additional information on fieldwork logistics (see especially Chapter 6), as do the EGRA toolkits.

Data Analysis and Reporting

The analysis and reporting of results from an EGRA depend largely on the purpose of the assessment (Table 1.2). For example, for a national-level diagnostic, analysts might focus on examining differences in regional or urban/rural outcomes; summarizing grade-level averages; and comparing reading levels by sex, ethnic group, socioeconomic class, or other large social categories. In contrast, for classroom mastery checks, teachers use EGRA results to gauge reading progress of individual students. Chapter 6 of this book provides more guidance on the use of information and communication technologies in EGRA applications and analyses.

Challenges and Constraints

EGRA has many strengths—such as its standardized but flexible design—but the approach also has some inherent challenges.

Uniform Methodology

One of the challenges of EGRA lies in striking a balance between flexibility and standardization. Although EGRA benefits from its construction around a uniform set of subtasks that assess a broad range of foundation reading skills, the flexibility across languages means that users can adapt these subtasks within a specific assessment and that not all subtasks are tested in all languages. This can sometimes lead to confusion about the purpose of EGRA; potential users may wonder whether it is meant to be comparable across languages and countries and how it fits into the spectrum of available assessment options.

Although EGRA is standardized in its research foundations and underlying principles, it is designed to respond to local conditions. The standardized nature of the subtasks (but not the overall test) allows for some comparability, but users should be cautious in how they compare results across countries and languages.

Comparability

As noted above, the uniform subtasks do not equate to comparability across assessments and countries. Differences in language structure and complexity introduce variation that precludes direct comparisons. In addition, as we have explained, students tend to learn to read at a faster rate in languages with shallow/transparent orthographies than those with deeper/opaque orthographies (Seymour et al., 2003). For these reasons, we discourage direct comparisons of EGRA subtask results (reported in correct letters or words per minute, for example) across countries and languages.

The exceptions to this rule are the reporting of zero scores (percentage of students who are unable to read a single word, letter, etc.) and within-country comparisons based on locally established benchmarks. Calculating zero scores, typically reported for oral reading fluency, is a simple way to report results across countries and languages as it does not require standardization or equating of test sections (as presumably the inability to read even a single word is relatively comparable across languages).

In terms of reporting against locally established benchmarks, researchers and educators often use results from an EGRA to inform the development of learning goals and targets. For example, stakeholders can analyze fluency and comprehension results to indicate the share of students reading with at least 80 percent comprehension (answering four of five reading comprehension questions correctly). As an illustration, results from national-level applications of EGRA indicated that nearly 24 percent of grade 2 students in The Gambia were reading with at least 80 percent comprehension. In both Mali and Senegal, EGRA results showed that only 1 percent of grade 2 students read with at least 80 percent comprehension. By setting locally relevant benchmarks, policy makers *within each country* can use these results to track and report on the share of children reading with understanding.

Use in Early Grades

Practitioners working with youth and young adults have shown considerable interest in a measure of early reading skills. Frequently these students are entering school for the first time at age 15 and above and are therefore learning basic reading skills, much like younger children do in the early grades. Although the skills tested are similar for these older students and the younger children for whom EGRA was designed, we discourage direct use of existing subtasks with older cohorts who are likely to have already acquired these basic skills.

Adaptation of the approach requires careful consideration of both the curriculum goals of the particular intervention and the skill level of a typical student in these remediation programs. Such adaptation is possible, however. In Liberia, EGRA has been successfully adapted for youth, in particular returning child soldiers and individuals who did not have the opportunity to attend school during the Liberian conflict.

Future Directions

As discussed at the outset of this chapter, RTI developed EGRA in response to the dearth of information on learning outcomes for early grade reading. One reason for the lack of information was the absence of a clear global mandate for the collection of data on learning outcomes. From the time of their creation in 1990, the Education for All goals were successful in drawing attention to the problems of access to education and, in particular, to enrollment and completion of primary schooling. Countries around the world collected and tracked information on student enrollment and dropout; over time, the quality and reliability of the data collected improved. Attention to these goals meant that many countries worked to improve their results, and those countries at risk of backtracking or not achieving the access goals received additional international support. What was absent from the Education for All and subsequent Millennium Development Goals, however, was a set of clear, measureable, and actionable *learning* goals that would draw similar attention to the improvement of learning outcomes.

In September 2009, recognizing the absence of learning in the global goals, the Education for All Fast Track Initiative (FTI) proposed the creation of two indicators that would allow countries and international agencies to track progress toward improved learning and, in particular, reading. In January 2011, a panel of experts in reading acquisition and assessment, psychometrics, and cognitive science met to review the proposed indicators and suggest approaches to their revision and measurement. The resulting indicators, pending formal adoption by the FTI board of directors, are as follows:

- proportion of students who read with understanding by the end of 2 years of primary schooling, and

- proportion of students who read with sufficient fluency and understanding to "read to learn" by the end of primary school (between years 4 and 6 of primary schooling).

Whether gauged by group-administered written measures or individual oral assessment like EGRA, the message is clear: decision makers are asked to report on reading outcomes in their country both at the end of grade 2 (while there is still time to intervene and improve before many children in low-income countries drop out) and at the end of the primary school cycle.

These indicators align quite well with the underlying framework of EGRA in that they reflect country-level goals and objectives for reading in the early grades, including the particular characteristics of each language. Thus, policy makers in each country can set their own benchmarks using the global indicators. For instance, if policy makers in The Gambia decide that "reading with understanding" implies at least 80 percent comprehension, then they can report on the nearly one-quarter of their students who meet that target. Obviously countries such as Mali and Senegal will have even farther to go, given that they are starting with fewer than 1 percent of students reading with at least 80 percent comprehension at the end of grade 2.

All involved in creating these indicators hope that their adoption will catalyze better learning outcomes around the world. Much as Education for All and Millennium Development Goals helped to revolutionize the expansion of access to primary education in poor countries, the FTI panelists anticipate that the indicators will spur dramatic improvements in early reading levels.

Given these developments, the widespread and rapid adoption of EGRA in its various forms is striking. Although we cannot attribute cause and effect, the parallel renewed attention to learning, rather than merely to access and enrollment, is encouraging. The same direction of change is reflected in the recently released education strategies of the leading multi- and bilateral donor agencies, including the World Bank (*Learning for All: Investing in People's Knowledge and Skills to Promote Development*; see World Bank, 2011), the United Kingdom's Department for International Development (*Learning for All: DFID's Education Strategy 2010–2015*; see DFID, 2010), and USAID (*Education: Opportunity Through Learning*; see USAID, 2011). The growing recognition among scholars and policy makers alike is that learning, rather than simply years of schooling completed, is the driver of economic and social development. This perception provides the framework for global investment in education in the coming years—a dramatic and welcome change from the focus of the past two decades.

References

Abadzi, H. (2006). *Efficient learning for the poor.* Washington, DC: The World Bank.

Abadzi, H., Crouch, L., Echegaray, M., Pasco, C., & Sampe, J. (2005). Monitoring basic skills acquisition through rapid learning assessments: A case study from Peru. *Prospects, 35*(2), 137–156.

American Educational Research Association (AERA), American Psychological Association (APA), & National Council on Measurement in Education (NCME). (1999). *Standards for educational and psychological testing.* Washington, DC: AERA.

Bedi, A. S., & Marshall, J. H. (2002). Primary school attendance in Honduras. *Journal of Development Economics, 69*(1): 129–153.

Center for Global Development, The Evaluation Gap Working Group. (2006). *When will we ever learn? Improving lives through impact evaluation.* Retrieved January 17, 2011, from http://www.cgdev.org/content/publications/detail/7973

Chabbott, C. (2006). *Accelerating early grades reading in high priority EFA countries: A desk review.* Retrieved January 17, 2011, from US Agency for International Development EQUIP website: http://www.equip123.net/docs/E1-EGRinEFACountriesDeskStudy.pdf

Children's Literacy Initiative. (2000). *Dictation task.* Retrieved March 2007 from http://www.cliontheweb.org/pd_asmntsamp2.html

Chow, B., McBride-Chang, C., & Burgess, S. (2005). Phonological processing skills and early reading abilities in Hong Kong Chinese kindergarteners learning to read English as a second language. *Journal of Educational Psychology, 97*(1), 81–87.

Clay, M. M. (1993). *An observation survey of early literacy achievement.* Ortonville, Michigan: Cornucopia Books.

Crouch, L. (2005). *Disappearing schoolchildren or data misunderstandings? Dropout phenomena in South Africa.* Prepared for South Africa's Department of Education and the US Agency for International Development under the Integrated Education Project, Contract No. 674-C-00-04-00032-00. Research Triangle Park, North Carolina: RTI International. Retrieved August 19, 2010, from RTI International website: http://www.rti. org/pubs/disappearing_schoolchildren.pdf

Crouch, L., & Gove, A. (2011). Leaps or one step at a time: Skirting or helping engage the debate? The case of reading. In J. N. Hawkins and W. James Jacob (Eds.), *Policy debates in comparative, international and development education.* Basingstoke, UK: Palgrave Macmillan.

Denton, C. A., Ciancio, D. J., & Fletcher, J. M. (2006). Validity, reliability, and utility of the observation survey of early literacy achievement. *Reading Research Quarterly, 41*(1), 8–34.

Department for International Development (DFID) [UK]. (2010). *Learning for all: DFID's education strategy 2010–2015.* London: DFID. Retrieved April 19, 2011, from: http://www.ungei.org/resources/files/educ-strat.pdf

Educational Testing Service. (2005). Dictation assessment. Retrieved March 2007 from http://www.pathwisestore.com/index.asp?PageAction=VIEWPR OD&ProdID=161

El-Zanaty, F., & Gorin, S. (2007). *Egypt Household Education Survey 2005–06.* Prepared by El Zanaty & Associates and Macro International for the Egyptian Ministry of Education and the US Agency for International Development under the Egypt Education Reform Program. Retrieved August 19, 2010, from USAID EQUIP website: http://www.equip123.net/ docs/e2-EgyptERPEducationReportEN.pdf

Filmer, D., Hasan, A., & Pritchett, L. (2006). *A millennium learning goal: Measuring real progress in education.* Washington, DC: World Bank.

Fuchs, L., Fuchs, D., Hosp, M. K., & Jenkins, J. (2001). Oral reading fluency as an indicator of reading competence: A theoretical, empirical, and historical analysis. *Scientific Studies of Reading, 5*(3), 239–256.

Gove, A., & Cvelich, P. (2010). *Early reading: Igniting education for all. A report by the Early Grade Learning Community of Practice.* Research Triangle Park, North Carolina: RTI International. Retrieved January 17, 2011, from RTI International website: http://www.rti.org/pubs/early-reading-report_gove_ cvelich.pdf

Gove, A., & Cvelich, P. (2011). *Early reading: Igniting education for all. A report by the Early Grade Learning Community of Practice* (Rev. ed.). Research Triangle Park, North Carolina: RTI International. Retrieved May 9, 2011, from RTI International website: http://www.rti.org/pubs/early-reading-report-revised.pdf

Hanushek, E. A. & Lavy, V. (1994). *School quality, achievement bias, and dropout behavior in Egypt.* Living Standards Measurement Study Working Paper No. 107. Prepared for the World Bank.

Hanushek, E. A., & Woessmann, L. (2009). *Do better schools lead to more growth? Cognitive skills, economic outcomes, and causation.* Working Paper 14633. Cambridge, Massachusetts: National Bureau of Economic Research.

Hasbrouck, J., & Tindal, G. A. (2006). Oral reading fluency norms: A valuable assessment tool for reading teachers. *The Reading Teacher, 59*(7), 636–644.

Hirsch, E. D., Jr. (2003). Reading comprehension requires knowledge—of words and the world. *American Educator* (Spring), 1–44.

Kame'enui, E. J., Fuchs, L., Francis, D. J., Good, R. H., III, O'Connor, R. E., Simmons, D. C., ... Torgesen, J. K. (2006). The adequacy of tools for assessing reading competence: A framework and review. *Educational Researcher, 35*(4), 3–11.

Kaminski, R. A., Good, R. H., III, Baker, D., Cummings, K., Dufour-Martel, C., Fleming, K., ... Wallin, J. (2006). *Position paper on use of DIBELS for system-wide accountability decisions.* Retrieved July 2011 from Colorado Basic Literacy Act website: http://www.cde.state.co.us/coloradoliteracy/cbla/download/Accountability_2006-11-16.pdf

Moats, L. (2000). *Speech to print: Language essentials for teachers.* Baltimore, Maryland: Paul H. Brookes.

National Institute of Child Health and Human Development [US]. (2000). *Report of the National Reading Panel. Teaching children to read: An evidence-based assessment of the scientific research literature on reading and its implications for reading instruction: Reports of the subgroups* (NIH Publication No. 00-4754). Retrieved August 2007 from http://www.nichd.nih.gov/publications/nrp/report.cfm

National Literacy Panel [US]. (2004). *National Literacy Panel on Language Minority Children and Youth: Progress report.* Retrieved August 2007 from the Center for Applied Linguistics website: http://www.cal.org/projects/ archive/nlpreports/progress.pdf

NPC Nigeria (National Population Commission, Nigeria) and ORC Macro. (2004). *Nigeria DHS EdData Survey 2004: Education Data for Decision-Making.* Prepared by NPC Nigeria and ORC Macro for Nigeria's Federal Ministry of Education and the US Agency for International Development. Retrieved August 19, 2010, from http://www.usaid.gov/ng/downloads/ eddatasurvey_dhs.pdf

Paris, S. G., & Paris, A. H. (2006). Chapter 2: Assessments of early reading. In W. Damon & R. M. Lerner (Eds.), *Handbook of child psychology: Theoretical models of human development, 6th Edition* (Vol. 4: Child Psychology in Practice [p. 48-74]). Hoboken, New Jersey: John Wiley and Sons.

Roskos, K., Strickland, D., Haase, J., & Malik, S. (2009). *First principles for early grades reading programs in developing countries.* Prepared by the International Reading Association for the US Agency for International Development under the Educational Quality Improvement Program (EQUIP1) Project. Washington, DC: American Institutes for Research. Retrieved August 20, 2010, from http://www.equip123.net/docs/e1-EarlyGradesToolkit.pdf

RTI International. (2009a). *Early Grade Reading Assessment toolkit.* Prepared for the World Bank, Office of Human Development, under Contract No. 7141961. Research Triangle Park, North Carolina: RTI International. Retrieved August 23, 2010, from https://www.eddataglobal.org/documents/ index.cfm?fuseaction=pubDetail&ID=149

RTI International. (2009b). *Manual para la evaluación inicial de la lectura en niños de educación primaria* [Early Grade Reading Assessment toolkit, Spanish adaptation]. Adaptation by J. E. Jimenez. Prepared for the US Agency for International Development under the EdData II project, Task Order 3, Contract No. EHC-E-01-03-00004-00. Research Triangle Park, North Carolina: RTI International. Retrieved April 19, 2011, from https://www.eddataglobal.org/documents/index. cfm?fuseaction=pubDetail&ID=187

RTI International. (2009c). *Manuel pour l'evaluation des competences fondamentales en lecture*. [Early Grade Reading Assessment toolkit, French adaptation]. Adaptation by L. Sprenger-Charolles. Prepared for the US Agency for International Development under the EdData II project, Task Order 3, Contract No. EHC-E-01-03-00004-00. Research Triangle Park, North Carolina: RTI International. Retrieved April 19, 2011, from https://www.eddataglobal.org/documents/index. cfm?fuseaction=pubDetail&ID=175

Seymour, P. H. K., Aro, M., & Erskine, J. M. (2003). Foundation literacy acquisition in European orthographies. *British Journal of Psychology, 94*, 143–174.

Snow, C. E., Burns, M. S., & Griffin, P. (Eds.). (1998). *Preventing reading difficulties in young children.* Washington, DC: Committee on the Prevention of Reading Difficulties in Young Children and National Academy Press.

Sprenger-Charolles, L., Colé, P., & Serniclaes, W. (2006). *Reading acquisition and developmental dyslexia.* New York: Psychology Press.

United Nations Educational, Scientific, and Cultural Organization (UNESCO). (2010). *Education for All global monitoring report: Reaching the marginalized.* Paris: UNESCO.

United States Agency for International Development (USAID). (2011). *Education: Opportunity through learning—USAID education strategy 2011–2015.* Washington, DC: USAID. Retrieved April 2011 from http://www.usaid.gov/our_work/education_and_universities/documents/USAID_ED_Strategy_feb2011.pdf

Wagner, D. A. (2003). Smaller, quicker, cheaper: Alternative strategies for literacy assessment in the UN Literacy Decade. *International Journal of Educational Research, 39*, 293–309.

Wagner, D. A. (2011). *Smaller, quicker, cheaper: Improving learning assessments in developing countries.* Washington/Paris: EFA Fast Track Initiative and UNESCO-IIEP.

World Bank. (2007). *Por una educación de calidad para el Perú: Estándares, rendición de cuentas, y fortalecimiento de capacidades* [Quality education for Peru: Standards, accountability, capacity building]. Washington, DC: World Bank.

World Bank. (2010). *EdStats Query* [data set]. Washington, DC: World Bank. Retrieved August 11, 2010, from http://go.worldbank.org/47P3PLE940

World Bank. (2011). *Learning for all: Investing in people's knowledge and skills to promote development; World Bank Group education strategy 2020.* Washington, DC: World Bank. Retrieved April 19, 2011, from http://siteresources.worldbank.org/EDUCATION/Resources/ESSU/Education_Strategy_4_12_2011.pdf

World Bank: Independent Evaluation Group. (2006). *From schooling access to learning outcomes—An unfinished agenda: An evaluation of World Bank support to primary education.* Washington, DC: World Bank.

Zieger, J., & Goswami, U. (2005). Reading acquisition, developmental dyslexia and skilled reading across languages: A psycholinguistic grain size theory. *Psychological Bulletin, 13*(1), 3–29.

CHAPTER 2

Using EGRA as a National Reading Diagnostic: Nicaragua and Senegal

Jessica Mejía and Sarah Pouezevara

Introduction

When conducting a national- or system-level diagnostic as defined in Chapter 1, a national-level stakeholder, such as a ministry of education (to use a generic term), may want to establish a nationwide baseline or to study the differences in reading ability among various groups—for example, second, fourth, and sixth grades—and determine average intergrade progression. Or, a national stakeholder might want to determine whether achievement differs between types of school systems (public vs. private) or curricular modalities (dual or monolingual programs).

In 2008 and 2009, Nicaragua and Senegal embarked on national-level diagnostic assessments of reading using the early grade reading assessment (EGRA) instrument. The purpose in both countries was to analyze—rigorously and in detail—the reading ability of children in the early grades and to examine the factors that may be responsible for those outcomes.

Although the two large-scale assessments discussed in this chapter had the same overall purpose, they differed not only by location but also by key parameters such as the implementation partnerships and language of testing. By comparing and contrasting them here, we aim to analyze what we know about the process of applying EGRA to the national reading diagnostic model. The main focus of the chapter is on comparing the *processes* of planning, implementation, and use of results; we examine specifically the *choices* that were made at each stage. In both countries, the choices were made based on experiences in other countries, national preferences and needs, and client priorities. These choices had significant implications for both short-term efficiency and long-term impact of the assessments.

For RTI International, providing technical assistance to a country or a client to investigate the state of early grade reading is usually a short-term activity; it is limited in time and has a specific scope that begins with planning and ends when we complete the data analysis and produce a final report. For the national stakeholders, however, the planning and implementation processes may actually be as important for education system reform as the results of the diagnostic, and attention to reading outcomes certainly does not end with the production of a final report.

In the cases of both Nicaragua and Senegal, RTI's role extended beyond implementation of the diagnostic testing to targeted dissemination and communication of results. However, the activities differed greatly in the degree to which RTI and its local subcontractors engaged national counterparts. The relative level of ownership may account for contrasts in subsequent use of the results, both by ministry staff and civil society partners (i.e., voluntary as opposed to government-affiliated organizations), as discussed below. For example, the national diagnostic in Nicaragua was conducted with the full support and involvement of the Ministerio de Educación (Ministry of Education), including ministry staff who participated in the adaptation and training processes. After the results were analyzed, the ministry took immediate, positive steps to address the quality of instruction. By contrast, in Senegal, the national diagnostic was funded and implemented mostly independently of the Ministère de l'Enseignement Préscolaire, de l'Elémentaire, du Moyen Secondaire et des Langues Nationales (Ministry of Education), and the dissemination of results led to little discernable action by the ministry. Instead, civil society became engaged in the follow-up processes.

The chapter is organized in the following manner: First we give some background on the country context and the characteristics of the two national diagnostics, including brief results for each country. The second section explains how each country applied the national diagnostic model and what activities took place after the data collection and analysis were complete. Next, we review the similarities and differences between the two cases, and finally, we provide several key lessons that can be taken away from a comparative analysis of the two EGRA implementations.

Although we present summary results from both countries, the intent is not to compare scores, or to analyze comparatively the factors leading to those scores. For more detailed analysis of each country's EGRA outcomes, please refer to the final technical reports for each country (CIASES & RTI International, 2009; Pouezevara et al., 2010).

Table 2.1 provides an overview of the key characteristics of each case, including the funding source, the driving policy question, and parameters of the assessment.

Table 2.1 Comparison of the two national EGRA diagnostics

Element	Nicaragua	Senegal
Funding source	• United States Agency for International Development (USAID)	• William and Flora Hewlett Foundation
Purpose	• To evaluate outcomes in schools that received USAID funding	• To examine the effect of the classroom environment (including language of instruction) on reading
Target group	• Grades 2–4 in public and private schools	• Grade 3 (cours élémentaires 1, or CE1) in French-language public schools only
EGRA subtasks[1]	• Concepts about print • Letter identification: names[2] • Phonemic awareness • Familiar word reading[2] • Nonword reading[2] • Oral reading fluency[2] with comprehension (subtask with two parts) • Listening comprehension • Dictation	• Letter identification: names and/or sounds[2] • Nonword reading[2] • Oral reading fluency[2] with reading comprehension
Other research instruments	• Teacher questionnaire • Director questionnaire	• Teacher questionnaire • Director questionnaire • Classroom observation tool
Sample size	• National-level sample of 6,649 students	• National-level sample of 687 students
Implementing agency	• RTI International/Centro de Investigación y Acción Educativa Social (CIASES) with Ministry of Education	• RTI International/FocusAfrica
Communication and dissemination activities	• Policy dialogue workshop • Teacher training workshops • Video production • National campaign	• Stakeholder workshop • Civil society communication training and workshop • Communication minigrants to civil society organizations • Mass media social-mobilization campaign

[1] As explained in Chapter 1, the subtasks chosen for inclusion in a particular version of the EGRA instrument, and the names of the subtasks, may vary somewhat from one application to another depending on the purpose, language, country, timeline, funding resources, and other contextual factors. In all cases, however, the subtasks represent similar, typical categories of skills or abilities that individuals have to master in order to learn to read. For examples of the subtasks, see Appendix B.

[2] This subtask is timed to 1 minute.

Context

Nicaragua

Country Context

Nicaragua is the poorest nation in Central America (second only to Haiti in the Americas), underemployment is widespread, and 48 percent of the population live below the national poverty line (2005 estimate; US Central Intelligence Agency [CIA], 2010). The 2005 national census results showed a total population of 5.1 million (Instituto Nacional de Estadísticas y Censos [INEC], Nicaragua, 2006). A country comparison compiled by the CIA using 2009 estimates ranked Nicaragua 169th of 227 countries, with a gross domestic product (GDP) per capita of US$2,800 (CIA, n.d.).

Education and Language of Instruction

In Nicaragua, the state has generally emphasized access to and reform of higher education to improve equity. In the early years of the first Sandinista government (1979–1990), for example, enrollment in higher education tripled from 11,000 in 1978 to 38,000 in 1984. The emphasis on higher education has also been evident in the current Sandinista administration (2006–). When RTI first began discussions in 2008 with Nicaraguan officials about the possibility of assessing early grade reading, the Minister of Education—who had been a high-ranking education official in the first Sandinista government—made clear that his focus was on higher education.

In the mid-2000s, however, the government started to emphasize the quality of early education as the Ministry of Education began dedicating considerable time and resources to improving instruction and outcomes in the primary grades. In July 2008, the Ministry of Education implemented a national-level campaign to improve primary education with the goal that all children will learn to read by the end of the first grade. Reminiscent of the first Sandinista government's National Literacy Crusade, this new campaign was dubbed the Batalla por el Primer Grado (Battle for the First Grade; see Ministry of Education, Nicaragua, 2008). Supported by the results of the 2008 EGRA national diagnostic assessment, the ministry has since collaborated with RTI on early literacy outcomes and implemented other projects designed to both improve teachers' knowledge of appropriate instructional methods and raise awareness of the importance of early grade reading.

Nicaragua's education system, like many in Latin America, generally has more resources than developing countries in other parts of the world. However, Nicaragua is still one of the poorest countries in the Western Hemisphere, such that resources and improvements remain necessary. Recognizing the shortcomings, Nicaragua has spent several years focusing on the Education for All goals and Millennium Development Goals.[1] Nicaragua's work toward these goals has increased net enrollment from 79 percent in 2000 to as high as 96 percent in 2007 and 92 percent in 2008, and the numbers of boys and girls in school reached parity in 2008. Its retention rate for primary school students has been relatively high among developing nations and is slowly increasing, as can be seen in the primary completion rate, which was 67 percent in 2000 and increased to 75 percent in 2008 (World Bank, 2010a). The adult literacy rate reached 78 percent in 2006, with females at 77.8 percent and males at 78.1 percent (Trading Economics, 2010).

As part of the national movement mentioned above to improve primary education, the Ministry of Education declared the following nationwide goals: that by 2011, all students will be staying in school until they complete sixth grade, and that by 2015, all students will complete all 12 grades.

By and large, the use of Spanish as the language of instruction at all education levels reflects the fact that Nicaragua, like many Latin American countries, has a fairly homogenous population linguistically; Spanish is the main language used throughout the country. However, the majority of Nicaragua's indigenous population resides along the Atlantic Coast (autonomous Regions VII and VIII in Figure 2.1). Languages spoken in this part of Nicaragua have a long oral history and have only recently been written down. Also in this region, English and Kriol are spoken, attributable in part to two centuries of British colonization.

---

[1] For more about the history and goals of Education for All, see the United Nations Educational, Scientific and Cultural Organization (UNESCO) website, http://www.unesco.org/education/efa/ed_for_all/. For the United Nations Millennium Development Goals, see http://www.un.org/millenniumgoals.

Figure 2.1 Regions of Nicaragua

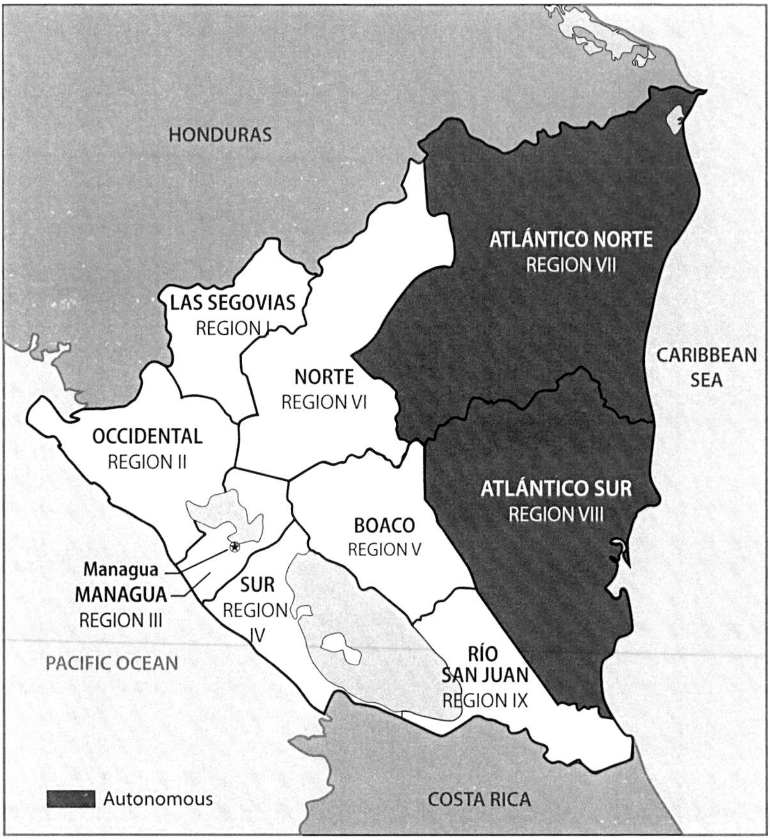

About the National Diagnostic

When the United States Agency for International Development (USAID) funded the (almost) country-wide EGRA diagnostic effort in Nicaragua in April–May 2008, it was the first effort to adapt and implement the full battery of EGRA into Spanish.[2] The effort resulted from ongoing discussions between the ministry and USAID/Nicaragua, as well as a long history of joint interventions and support in education. As part of the Education Data for Decision Making (EdData II) project, the Nicaragua activity originally included two EGRA implementations: a baseline administration and a follow-up application to estimate the growth in reading achievement.

---

[2] RTI and CIASES later carried out separate mother-tongue assessments in the Atlantic Coast region with World Bank funding in October–November 2009.

Upon receiving the results of the baseline, the details of which are described below, USAID/Nicaragua—at the request of the Ministry of Education—changed the scope of work to request that RTI help the ministry improve reading development immediately. Specifically, RTI was asked to focus on teacher training in early grade reading instruction, the use of EGRA in the classroom, and awareness raising through the development of videos, rather than on the follow-up assessment.

The work accomplished in Nicaragua can be attributed in large part to the selection of a key local nongovernmental organization (NGO) and partner, Centro de Investigación y Acción Educativa Social (CIASES). CIASES was founded by and is led by women dedicated to the improvement of education in Nicaragua. As is explained throughout this chapter, the collaboration between RTI and CIASES involved implementing EGRA in two phases. Phase 1 consisted of three main tasks: (1) editing the instrument into its final form based on the results of a small EGRA pilot study in 2007, (2) collecting national baseline data on reading outcomes using EGRA, and (3) leading a policy-dialogue workshop designed to disseminate the results and to advise and collaborate with the Ministry of Education regarding appropriate response activities.

Phase 2 focused on raising awareness, building capacity, and ensuring sustainability. Based on the EGRA baseline results, RTI and CIASES led teacher-training workshops four times (three in April and one in December 2009). In addition, the task team produced two videos. The first supported teacher training by demonstrating Nicaraguan teachers implementing best practices of reading instruction, and the second raised awareness of all children's ability (and the obligation of the system to encourage all children) to learn to read by the end of the second grade. These videos served as a catalyst for efforts by local partners to design and organize a social marketing campaign. Moreover, the campaign, which was funded by civil society organizations, NGOs, foundations, and the private sector, complemented the Ministry of Education's efforts in its Battle for the First Grade campaign.

Results

Although comparisons of results in reading performance across languages should always be done cautiously, results of the national diagnostic assessment in Spanish in Nicaragua demonstrated some of the highest performance scores of all the EGRAs that RTI had implemented in any language in developing countries to that point. However, the grade and age of students who were tested should be taken into account in any such comparison of scores. The assessments that we administered to students in grade 4 (ages 7–16) would not have been appropriate for fourth-grade students (ages 9–10) in the United States, for example, as US students would be expected to have mastered these skills by first or second grade.

Moreover, to ensure the validity of the statistical analysis, we limited the sample to readily accessible schools that had a minimum of 60 students enrolled in the first grade. Thus, the sample can be considered representative of the *larger schools in Nicaragua*, other than those along the Atlantic Coast, but not of the significant portion of students living in rural areas. Excluding students from relatively poor rural schools, where scores likely would have been lower, may further explain why EGRA scores were much higher in Nicaragua than in other countries.

RTI and its subcontractor CIASES sampled students in grades 2, 3, and 4 from 126 public and private schools around the country (minus those along the Atlantic Coast). The sample consisted of 6,649 students: 3,327 boys and 3,322 girls. To better understand the factors that affected literacy in Nicaragua, the assessment team also interviewed teachers and school directors using formal questionnaires; in total, we interviewed 467 teachers and 122 school directors.

Below we present a brief overview of the findings of the EGRA national diagnostic, including comparisons between the oral reading fluency and the responses from the supplemental questionnaires given to students, teachers, and head teachers. Table 2.2 shows means and standard deviations for each subtask. For the full report (in Spanish) of the results of this study, see CIASES and RTI (2009). For descriptions of the purpose and implementation of each subtask, see Chapter 1.

EGRA results in Nicaragua indicated that many students could read at rates comparable to international standards for Spanish speakers. However, large percentages of students (25 to 35 percent) did not meet the standard and were actually far below a rate that is considered optimal for full reading comprehension (for benchmarks, see University of Oregon Center on Teaching and Learning, 2008). Means for fourth-grade students in letter identification, nonword reading, and oral reading fluency were approximately what would be expected of second-graders, according to international standards. Students in private schools consistently performed slightly better than students in public schools.

Table 2.2 EGRA means and standard deviations by school type, grade, and subtask

| | EGRA Means (Standard Deviations) | | | | | |
| | Public school, by grade | | | Private school, by grade | | |
Subtask	2	3	4	2	3	4
Letter identification: names	37.3 (18.6)	51.1 (18.2)	60.9 (17.3)	41.4 (18.1)	53.7 (18.1)	64.0 (17.6)
Phonemic awareness: identification of onset/rime sounds	3.7 (3.2)	4.3 (3.1)	4.4 (3.0)	4.2 (3.2)	4.2 (3.1)	4.4 (3.0)
Phonemic awareness: phoneme segmentation	3.5 (2.1)	4.3 (2.5)	5.2 (2.7)	3.6 (2.4)	4.4 (2.8)	5.5 (2.9)
Familiar word reading	31.6 (19.7)	53.4 (20.8)	65.5 (21.1)	37.9 (20.9)	56.5 (21.5)	70.2 (20.7)
Nonword reading	21.0 (13.7)	34.3 (13.7)	40.3 (13.1)	24.8 (13.8)	35.8 (13.3)	43.3 (13.5)
Oral reading fluency	41.5 (28.7)	80.2 (33.6)	101.6 (33.1)	51.4 (32.4)	84.9 (34.1)	111.1 (33.0)
Reading comprehension (%)	51.6 (39.0)	80.4 (25.1)	85.3 (19.3)	61.8 (38.6)	83.1 (24.6)	88.4 (16.4)
Listening comprehension (%)	56.9 (30.5)	57.9 (31.4)	56.2 (30.4)	59.0 (30.4)	59.9 (31.1)	61.0 (30.2)
Dictation (%)	37.1 (22.8)	56.0 (19.9)	64.2 (18.6)	45.8 (24.3)	61.0 (20.4)	70.6 (19.0)

Note: Units for the first six subtasks listed are the numbers of correct letters, sounds, or words. For timed subtasks, scores are per minute (thus, for example, identifying all 100 letters in Nicaragua's instrument correctly in 50 seconds would have produced a score of 120). The comprehension and dictation subtasks are percentages of correct responses.

On the oral reading fluency subtask, the combined average of second-graders in public and private schools was 46.5 words read correctly per minute; in third grade, 82.7; and in fourth grade, 106.5. These reading fluency scores reflected second-grade students' understanding 56.8 percent of the passage read; the corresponding figures were 81.8 percent for third-graders, and 86.9 percent for fourth-graders. (Of course, because small, rural schools were excluded from the sample, these results could surpass the true country averages.)

As noted earlier, in order to more deeply understand the results obtained from the literacy measures, RTI and CIASES administered short questionnaires to students, teachers, and head teachers focused on contextual factors that might affect students' learning outcomes, such as literacy of other family members, socioeconomic status, teacher training, and experience. The following factors were found to have positive effects on student outcomes:

- parental support with homework,
- mother's educational level (completed secondary education or more),
- teacher experience of 4–8 years teaching at the same grade level,
- teacher assigning homework,
- educational activities that generate student motivation (the questionnaires asked whether teachers complimented or rewarded students),
- meetings between the teacher and the school principal to address educational issues at least once every 2 weeks,
- active participation of parents in school activities, and
- access to sewerage services within the school.

In contrast, a lack of reading material and textbooks in Spanish, a high student-to-teacher ratio (more than 30 students per grade), and teacher absenteeism had a negative influence on the results.

Results from the national diagnostic assessment, supplemented by the contextual data, yielded a concise picture of what early reading skills were being developed in Nicaragua and which ones still needed further intervention. From these results, the Ministry of Education had tangible evidence to help make decisions about where to focus its efforts.

Senegal

Country Context

Senegal's capital city, Dakar, lies on the Cap Vert peninsula—the westernmost point on the mainland continent of Africa (see Figure 2.2). Approximately 43 percent of the country's 12.6 million people are under the age of 14, and the estimated GDP per capita in 2010 was US$1,900, placing it 190th out of 227 countries (CIA, 2011, n.d.).

Senegal is considered politically and socially stable and economically successful. Between 1995 and 2005, its real GDP grew by about 5 percent annually—among the highest in sub-Saharan Africa. As part of the West African Economic and Monetary Union that shares the CFA franc (franc de la Communauté Financière d'Afrique) as a common currency, Senegal participates in many regional economic, environmental, and social initiatives. It also maintains close cooperation with France and participates

Figure 2.2 Regions of Senegal

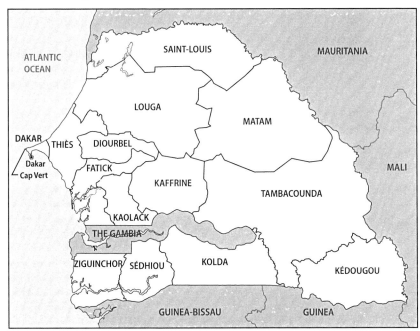

in many initiatives related to francophone language and culture, such as the Conférence des Ministres de l'Education des Pays ayant le Français en Partage (CONFEMEN) and its Programme d'Analyse des Systems d'Education (PASEC).[3]

According to government statistics reported by Diallo (2005, p. 9), in 1993 approximately 20 ethnic communities and 36 languages were present in Senegal. The Wolof community was dominant (42 percent), followed by Pulaar (24 percent), Seereer (15 percent), and Diola (5 percent).

Education and Language of Instruction

Senegal, like many other countries, has invested most of its basic education efforts and resources in increasing access to school. Net enrollment increased from 54 percent of eligible school-age children in 2000 to 73 percent in 2007 (World Bank, 2010b). Girls' enrollment has increased at an even greater rate;

---

[3] In English, PASEC is the Program to Analyze the Education Systems of the states and governments belonging to the Conference of Education Ministers of Francophone Countries. For more information in French about CONFEMEN and PASEC, see http://www.confemen.org/spip.php?rubrique3.

at the elementary level, girls' enrollment now surpasses that of boys. Although this demonstrates considerable progress in increasing the number of children enrolled in school, including access to preschools, improvements in the quality of education remain elusive.

Extremely low retention rates result in only about 5 percent of those who enter first grade actually completing the 10-year cycle of basic education to receive the middle-school leaving certificate (DeStefano et al., 2009). An international French-language reading assessment of second- and fifth-graders in 2006/2007 revealed increases in average scores but declines in the top percentiles (PASEC, 2008). The adult literacy rate improved slightly from 26.9 percent in 1988 to 41.9 percent in 2006 (Ministry of Education, Senegal, 2003), but for youth less than 15 years of age, the rate hovered around 50 percent between 2002 and 2006. Frequent school closures due to teacher and student strikes, actual start of the school year well past the scheduled opening, late entry into the school system (6 or 7 years old), and closures or teacher absences owing to administrative reasons all considerably reduce total teaching time and, hence, opportunity to learn.

Given the country's ethnic and linguistic diversity, French has been retained from the colonial period as a national, unifying language, and successive administrations have introduced laws and measures to maintain, defend, and promote French as the only way to ensure social cohesion and secure a place in the international economy (Fofana, 2003). In a recent study of the urban literacy environment in Senegal, Shiohata (2010) pointed out that the French language in its printed form is used far more frequently than are local languages, suggesting that local languages have not yet put down roots as written languages. The author further cited the trend noted by a sociolinguistic study in the 1990s that French words were predominantly used in the privileged areas of Dakar, whereas national languages were more frequently used in the deprived areas of the capital (Shiohata, 2010).

Thus, although the 2001 constitution stipulates that any officially codified language could be considered a "national" language (McLaughlin, 2008), French remains the most common language of instruction in schools as well as the officially preferred language of government and commerce. Despite French being designated as the "official" language, however, very few children grow up hearing this language in the home. Of the estimated 36 mother tongues (i.e., dominant language in the home) spoken in Senegal, most people speak one of the six most common languages—Wolof, Pulaar, Seereer, Diola, Malinké (Mandigué), or Soninké—as their mother tongue or as their second home/

community language. This means that it is not uncommon to have French as an even more remote third language.

Several important national initiatives have taken place in the past two decades to support the government's stated goals of reducing illiteracy, beginning with the Plan d'Action d'Eradication de l'Analphabétisme (Action Plan to Eradicate Illiteracy) in 1993. This action plan aimed to reduce the illiteracy rate by 5 percent per year, thereby bringing it from over 70 percent in 1988 to 30 percent by 2004 (Ministry of Education, Senegal, 2003). The plan used a combination of government funds and support from development partners (World Bank, Canadian International Development Agency, German Agency for International Technical Cooperation [GTZ]) to outsource literacy programs to NGOs and communities through an approach known as *faire-faire* (Diagne, 2007). However, these specific initiatives—as well as the larger government policy to reduce illiteracy—target adults and youths who are not attending school, and promote literacy in national languages. Specific strategies and programs for acquiring lifelong literacy in the early years—as distinct from learning French as a foreign language—are absent from the policy documents, apart from broad but relevant statements of textbook provision, teacher training, and curriculum reform that are included in the national development plans.

The government has been experimenting with various systems of dual-language instruction in schools since 1972, when the first decree related to national-language instruction was issued (Decree number 72-861 of July 13, 1972). It stipulated that "as long as we, the Senegalese, continue to teach our children a foreign language, whatever that language may be, without first teaching them their maternal language, our people will stay alienated." Yet lack of true political will and ownership, changes in leadership, failure to raise awareness among the population and subsequent lack of parental support, insufficient teacher training and lack of teaching materials, lack of monitoring and evaluation, and fiscal unsustainability have been cited as reasons that the most important efforts to create national-language classroom instruction have failed to take hold (Direction de la Promotion des Langues Nationales [DPLN], 2002; Fofana, 2003).

As of 2010, very few schools offered national-language instruction. These schools were either instances of the schools that remained from the World Bank–supported experimental schools project (2001–2009; see IDEA International, 2009) or community schools, often supported by local or international organizations, including SIL International, Tostan, and Associates in Research & Education for Development (ARED). Therefore, despite laws, decrees, and strategic plans in support of mother-tongue instruction as a basic right, the most common method of instruction—and the only one ostensibly supported by the current administration—remains French immersion from the first day, whether the children have any communicative competence (listening or speaking) in the language or not.

Consequently, the context of this study is one in which EGRA was assessing a nonnative language for the majority of the children, the teachers, and even the assessors.

About the National Diagnostic

In 2009, the William and Flora Hewlett Foundation issued a grant to RTI to carry out national EGRA diagnostics in four African countries: Senegal, Mali, Kenya, and Uganda. This grant was part of the Hewlett Foundation's overall strategy under its Quality Education in Developing Countries (QEDC) initiative. The purpose was to inform the Foundation's country profiles and to study the link between mother-tongue instruction and literacy (see Chapter 5 for more on language of instruction).

RTI consulted with Senegal's Ministry of Education before launching the assessment and formed a small technical committee, involving mainly staff from the Department of Elementary Education, which was kept abreast of progress. Additionally, one individual from the Ministry of Education's Institut National d'Etude et d'Action pour le Développement de l'Education (research and evaluation division, or INEADE) participated as a consultant in training and instrument adaptation and served to maintain the institutional link with the Ministry of Education.

After ensuring approval of the study by ministry officials, RTI selected a local research and consulting company (FocusAfrica) to handle logistics on the ground. These tasks included hiring assessors, organizing training, organizing transportation for fieldwork, handling data entry and participating in data analysis, writing reports, and disseminating the findings. Another local organization, ARED, was hired to support adaptation of the EGRA instrument from the version previously piloted in 2007.[4]

For the purposes of the 2009 national diagnostic, in acknowledgment of the widespread use of two particular mother-tongue languages, Wolof and Pulaar,

---

[4]   This was the second time that EGRA had been conducted in Senegal. The first time was in 2007, when RTI developed a French version with the support of the World Bank and piloted it among 502 children in grades 1 to 3 (Sprenger-Charolles, 2008).

RTI and ARED adapted and pilot tested the EGRA instrument in these two languages as well. We could not, however, complete a *full* national diagnostic because of the lack of classrooms functioning in any of the mother tongues at the time and the impossibility of ensuring an adequate sample size.

The Senegal instrument was limited to four subtasks: letter identification, nonword reading, and oral reading fluency with reading comprehension. These subtasks are the most predictive and measure the essential skills needed to be a successful reader.

Results

The fieldwork resulted in 687 evaluations of level CE1 (third year of primary school) students reading French; 183 language-of-instruction classroom observations, using a separate assessment tool; and data collected via formal interviews with 70 teachers and 56 directors. The complementary assessment instruments provided additional data for interpreting what turned out to be a wide range of differences in students' performance, both within and among classrooms.

Table 2.3 summarizes the results from this fieldwork. Again, these results for the French reading diagnostic need to be interpreted in the context of a country where most students were reading in a language they did not use regularly; only 2 percent of the sample (a total of 14 children) reported the use of French in the home.

Table 2.3 Summary EGRA results on four subtasks, Senegal

Subtask	N	Average	Standard deviation	Standard error	Confidence interval Upper bound	Confidence interval Lower bound
Letter identification: names (number of letters read correctly in 1 minute)	687	28.3	17.9	0.7	29.6	26.9
Nonword reading (number of invented words read correctly in 1 minute)	687	9.7	11.1	0.4	10.5	8.8
Oral reading fluency (number of words in a narrative passage read correctly in 1 minute)	687	18.4	20.6	0.8	20.2	17.1
Reading comprehension (percentage of correct answers in terms of total questions asked)	564	22.5%	28.2	1.2	24.9%	20.2%

The number of nonreaders, or those who were not able to read a single word of the first sentence of the reading passage, was very high—nearly one in five children (18 percent). Focusing only on the 586 students who could read at least one word of the sentence, the average fluency amounted to 22 words read correctly per minute, which is above the national average including the zero scores (18.4 correct words per minute, or cwpm), as indicated in Table 2.3. Moreover, the comprehension score for students who read at least one sentence of the paragraph was very low; in fact, only five students were able to answer at least five out of six questions correctly. Finally, performance among students in the sample, sometimes from the same school, differed markedly. The best reading score recorded from the sample was 134 words per minute, but only 9 percent of the sampled students read 50 words per minute or more.

Through questionnaires on students' learning environment, conditions in their classrooms and schools, and characteristics of their teachers and school principals, we sought factors related to student reading performance. The following factors seem to have been the most important predictors of reading skills. The numbers in parentheses indicate the correct-words-per-minute advantage for children who had this characteristic:

- The student had the textbook (+11 cwpm) and/or other French books at home (+7 cwpm).
- The student had attended kindergarten/preschool (+6 cwpm).
- A member of the student's household knew how to read (particularly the mother, +5 cwpm).
- The teacher reported spending more than 4 hours per week teaching French (+8 cwpm).
- The teacher possessed at least a high school diploma (+6 cwpm).
- The principal held a higher education diploma (up to +12 cwpm, depending on diploma).
- The school and/or the house had electricity (+5 or +9 cwpm, respectively).

Application of the EGRA Model

In this section we describe for each country how we carried out the EGRA work, highlighting key decisions at each stage. The stages included planning, implementation, and use of results, including communication and dissemination activities.

Nicaragua

Planning

Planning for the EGRA national diagnostic in Nicaragua began in 2007. At a week-long workshop held in Managua, language experts, Ministry of Education staff, and the local partner CIASES—which had an established track record of credibility with the Ministry of Education—came together with RTI staff to adapt EGRA for use in the country context. *Adapting* EGRA rather than *translating* it was key to its ability to assess students reliably in Nicaragua (Chapter 1 describes EGRA translation and adaptation). This meant that letters and words used as items were chosen based on Spanish-language rules and frequency of use specifically in Nicaragua. The stories that were used for oral reading fluency and listening comprehension were written to be relevant and appropriate for the children of Nicaragua.

The Ministry of Education's involvement in this process not only gave legitimacy to the assessment but also ensured that the government was a key part of the process of choosing appropriate items and writing the stories for the assessment. In all, two Spanish versions and two Miskitu versions were adapted in 2007, expecting that there would be two implementations—baseline and follow-up. Later, the contract was amended and the follow-up implementation was dropped, so only one of the Spanish versions was used for the national diagnostic in 2008. Following the adaptation workshop, we pilot tested all four versions of EGRA, used formal measures to ensure that the assessment had validity and reliability, and made adjustments based on the findings of the pilots and the validity/reliability tests.

RTI and CIASES presented the analysis of these initial pilot data to the Ministry of Education and workshop participants, who discussed the parameters for the national diagnostic. During this process, the Ministry of Education continued to collaborate and add input. This collaboration at the early stages of the EGRA planning and preparation allowed ministry staff to fully understand the process and utility of an EGRA application. Even at these early stages, the ministry staff and the director of primary education, in particular, expressed ownership and interest in EGRA.

Implementation

Because the purpose of the diagnostic was to understand early reading on a national level, the precision of the assessment administration was of paramount importance. In addition to using rigorous sampling methods, the RTI team ensured this precision by setting high standards for the assessors, with intense training, interrater reliability tests, and certification for individual assessors.

Assessor Selection and Training

Assessors have a substantial influence on the quality of any EGRA implementation, such that some additional detail about their selection and training in Nicaragua may be instructive. The local subcontractor CIASES recruited and chose the pool of assessors. Ministry of Education staff were included in this pool of assessors. The decision to include ministry staff in the assessor training at first seemed like a natural means of collaborating and building capacity. Doing so, however, led to some complications because several of the assessors who did not meet the minimum reliability standards were ministry staff and had to be asked not to continue with the work. The RTI implementing team made the decision to risk upsetting and complicating the relationship with the Ministry of Education in order to preserve the integrity of the assessment. Therefore, one lesson learned from this experience was that the process of building this type of capacity within the ministry could have consequences for the management of the project. As of early 2011, at least five EGRA-trained staff members remained in the ministry. Because of their technical skills, they are likely to remain even if the administration changes. If so, this outcome will ensure that key members of the ministry have experience with EGRA.

Data Entry and Analysis

Finally, RTI and CIASES planned a process for digitizing the assessor-collected data and analyzing it. CIASES had developed specific software to be used for data entry and assigned its statistical specialist to analyze and report on the findings. The analysis was the only significant portion of the EGRA process with which the ministry was not deeply involved, simply because of lack of technical capacity. RTI and CIASES completed the draft analytical report on the initial results of the national diagnostic in October 2008.

Use of Results

The completion of the EGRA baseline report was followed by dissemination to the ministry and USAID. The dissemination workshop served two purposes: (1) initiating a policy dialogue emphasizing the importance of early grade reading, while also reporting on the baseline results; and (2) opening a discussion among RTI, CIASES, and the Ministry of Education regarding implications for institutional improvements to the quality of instruction.

The ministry representatives noted that, based on the results, there was reason for concern about the quality of reading. This realization motivated them to consider ways to improve schools and teachers. They suggested conducting training for teachers to use EGRA in classrooms. The initial suggestion was to prepare eight workshops, one in each of the main *normales*, or teacher preparation centers. Another suggestion was that the monthly national professional development meetings could focus on EGRA and early grade reading. The Ministry of Education asked for further capacity building in the form of videos to support training and to promote awareness of early grade reading and, eventually, a national-level social marketing campaign.

The leaders and participants alike judged the dissemination and follow-up activities to have been very successful, an outcome that appeared to be related to the Ministry of Education staff's sense of ownership and involvement. Having been a part of the process from adaptation to implementation, Ministry of Education staff had experienced the utility of the assessment; in particular, they had learned by listening to distinguish between a child who could not read and one who could. This partnership allowed for deeper and more fruitful work with teachers and teacher trainers, and it eventually led the Ministry of Education to fully embrace the assessment, workshop, and videos as part of its Battle for the First Grade.

Teacher Training Workshops

Following the dissemination workshop, RTI and CIASES immediately went to work to design a professional development module that would address the instructional gaps identified through the results of the EGRA baseline. Once it had been designed—in the form of a 4-day workshop—RTI and CIASES implemented it at four separate locations and times, as noted earlier.[5] CIASES worked closely with the main office of the Ministry of Education to schedule the workshops, decide who should attend, and determine in what regions the workshops should take place to make the greatest impact. In the end it was decided that technical advisors, teacher trainers, and some teachers from four different regions would be trained.

RTI designed the workshops to train teachers on the proper use of EGRA as a means of informing instruction, to explain how to interpret the data, and to demonstrate ways to modify reading instruction based on best practices in reading instruction. The workshop included activities to reinforce early reading

---

[5]   Content of the workshops is available for download from the USAID EdData II project website, at www.eddataglobal.org.

skills, grouping, and differentiated instruction as well as progress monitoring and curriculum-based measures for teachers to use for this purpose. To maximize sustainability and replicability, RTI and CIASES compiled all workshop materials and gave them to the participants on a CD.

The Ministry of Education was very clear that it wanted teachers to use EGRA in their classrooms and that it was to become part of their national assessment system in order to inform curriculum and instruction on a continuous basis. The eagerness of the Ministry of Education to train teachers to use EGRA in the classrooms speaks to the importance to the ministry of improving early grade reading development. The director of primary education made it a point to speak at each of the four workshops to emphasize the seriousness with which the Ministry of Education was taking the baseline results and the content of the workshops.

By January 2010, the Ministry of Education officials had adapted the workshop material—sample lessons, EGRA instruments, and training materials—and made them into training guides for teachers. Furthermore, the Ministry of Education funded the duplication of the training guide materials entirely, as part of its Battle for the First Grade campaign, with the intent of replicating the training for primary teachers.

Video Production

In addition to the workshops, RTI made two videos to support the improvement of early grade reading in Nicaragua. The first was a best-practices video to support teacher trainings; it showcased Nicaraguan teachers demonstrating best practices in reading instruction. The second was a social marketing video that could be shown to parents, community members, government officials, and all other stakeholders. The video dealt with the importance of learning to read early and gave a standard or goal that parents and others could set to measure students' progress toward successful reading development.

Production of the videos was significant in giving the Ministry of Education tools with which to further the cause of improving early grade reading in Nicaragua. The unintended consequences of the video production are also noteworthy.

The production of the two videos required the use of local publicity firm Carlos Cuadra Cardenal Publicidad (CCCP). Through the filming of these videos, the firm became engaged in the importance of the subject matter. Its interest and commitment led to the creation of a social marketing campaign to create national-level awareness about the quality of early grade reading instruction as well as the importance of students learning to read by the end of second grade.

The campaign, called Todos a Leer (Everyone Reads), will focus on first-grade teachers and their classrooms. The objectives of the campaign are to increase the interest and participation of society to improve the reading skills of students in first grade, create awareness that all first-graders can learn to read well, and raise the professional dignity of teachers through national recognition of their work.

The campaign will be a public contest for first-grade teachers across the country to get their students reading and comprehending by the end of the academic year. Everyone Reads will focus on motivating teachers and their entire classrooms, as well as parents and the supporting community, to make special efforts directed at improving the reading skills of all first-graders.

To launch the social marketing video and CCCP's idea for the campaign, RTI helped organize a formal event that brought together local NGOs, donors, the private sector, the Minister of Education, and the local media with the purpose of raising awareness nationally that all students can and should learn to read by the end of second grade. The Minister of Education spoke of learning to read as the gateway to all parts of life. He emphasized that improving literacy in the primary grades had become a main focus of the ministry with its Battle for the First Grade campaign, which included plans to train teachers and support first-grade students in learning to read.

USAID staff members in Nicaragua said that the media coverage of this event was unprecedented in their experience. The conversation that took place at the end of the video launch event resulted in several offers of support for both logistics planning and funding from other local NGOs.

The social marketing campaign designed by CCCP—which has expanded beyond the original vision—will be a local and sustainable effort. It clearly promotes and extends the critical work being done in the country around early reading.

Senegal

Planning

The Senegal national diagnostic was officially launched in February 2009, with meetings in Dakar to consolidate agreement between RTI and the client (Hewlett Foundation) about the purpose, goals, and scope of the evaluation and to consult with local education stakeholders—particularly the Ministry of Education. RTI initially met formally with senior staff of the Ministry of Education's Department of Primary Education to introduce the study purpose and methodology, request their approval, and solicit their support. They agreed upon the importance of reading and mathematics as fundamental skills, and they asked to maintain an oversight role in the implementation of the study.

RTI then arranged a second meeting with key technical staff of the ministry to present in more detail the EGRA instruments, methodology, and plans for implementation. At this time RTI gave the Ministry of Education a draft of the instrument in French (the version that RTI was concurrently implementing in Mali) that would be adapted for the diagnostic in Senegal. Moreover, the ministry's technical staff were also involved in key decisions related to practical issues of doing fieldwork, such as timing (e.g., data collection had to begin before the end of May because some regions become inaccessible during the rainy season), the division of the country into regions and zones for sampling, and the appropriate grade level to assess. The Ministry of Education made the decision that the assessment would take place in the third year of primary, because this was the age (generally 8 years) when children were expected to be able to read fluently. Although they requested to be involved only in oversight, they encouraged RTI to involve the research and evaluation arm of the ministry (INEADE) in locating field researchers and other specialists.

The planning phase also involved consultation with various local and international partners active in Senegal to gather their input on the study aims and methodology and to learn from their previous experiences in assessing literacy. For example, the World Bank and PASEC had both recently conducted reading assessments in Senegalese schools. RTI held discussions with key project staff and reviewed the documents from these assessments to ensure that content and methodology were complementary (and comparable) but not duplicative and that RTI applied lessons learned relative to the construction of the instrument, training of assessors, and fieldwork.

As a result of the planning phase, RTI and the client defined additional key parameters for the national diagnostic. For example, the study would have to be limited to the schools that used French as the language of instruction, because fewer and fewer experimental mother-tongue instruction schools were functioning at this time. Reaching the required number of children (i.e., 500 per category of interest) for a reliable sample in those mother tongues would therefore have been impossible.

The original plan had been to implement the assessment as a capacity-building exercise involving ministry staff as assessors. However, legal complications arose with engaging ministry staff who were already paid civil servants, and those staff were not interested in taking on the assessment effort as part of their regular workload. In the end, RTI decided to outsource the logistics of the fieldwork to a local organization and to have that organization hire assessors from the private sector.

The company selected was a for-profit management consulting company rather than an education-sector NGO. Although the company had prior experience in education-sector research, it was not considered to be an education stakeholder in any conventional sense, making it a neutral partner in managing the logistics of the fieldwork and data analysis.

These decisions had important—positive and negative—consequences concerning the extent to which the Ministry of Education internalized the results of the study and subsequently acted on them.

Implementation

From the time the study was officially launched to the end of data collection in 2009, 15 weeks (approximately 3 months) elapsed. This is a remarkably short period of time for this type of fieldwork, demonstrating that although some planning is absolutely essential—particularly for developing and piloting instruments—a nationwide EGRA diagnostic effort can be completed within a very tight time frame. The key variable is availability of staff and assessors. Use of the private consulting company to carry out the work was likely the main factor in being able to complete the work quickly. Unfortunately, the limited time frame for the activity also introduced a trade-off between speed and deep ministry involvement in the implementation, as discussed in the conclusions at the end of this chapter.

The approximate distribution of time was as follows:

- 1 month for planning, recruitment, selection, and orientation of a local subcontractor for study implementation and instrument development,

- 1 month for recruiting and training assessors, preparing instruments, and pilot testing, and

- 1 month for data collection.

Data analysis and report writing extended approximately another 4 months after data collection ended.

Assessor Selection and Training

The local subcontractor, FocusAfrica, had primary responsibility for recruiting assessors. According to the sample size and time frame for data collection, there were seven data collection teams composed of one supervisor and two assessors. Qualifications and competencies of the 21 supervisors and assessors were discussed and curricula vitae were collected via local networks of education-sector associations, including the association of retired district education inspectors.

The choice to use retired inspectors as supervisors was appropriate because of their deep and historical knowledge of the Senegalese education system and their existing contacts with regional inspectors and school directors. These connections facilitated access to schools and ensured participation of selected schools in the study, even on short notice. Their participation was also expected to aid the dissemination of the results because all of these individuals were active in and passionate about education in Senegal and were, for example, continuing to provide consulting services to the ministry and other organizations.

Supervisors participated in 2 weeks of training. The first week was dedicated to introducing EGRA, refining and pilot testing the instruments, and discussing the role of the supervisor. The second week was a combined training for supervisors and assessors, during which the main focus was on repeated role play, drills, and practice testing (in schools, with local children) to ensure consistency and reliability in the testing procedures and scoring.

A critical aspect of assessor training was reviewing the instrument components letter by letter and word by word, to ensure that everyone agreed on the "correct" answer. This was particularly important in Senegal and for testing in French, because the assessment team had determined that either the letter name or the letter sound could be accepted, unlike in English or Spanish testing, for which typically only the letter name is requested (Sprenger-Charolles, 2008).

This process of reviewing the instrument components was repeated following the pilot testing in the schools to determine whether any examples arose of unusual or ambiguous responses from the students that had not previously been anticipated. RTI created a reference sheet that summarized acceptable pronunciations of certain more problematic letters in the assessment, as an effort to ensure interrater reliability. For these reasons, and according to standard practices for a rigorous assessment, the training team led several exercises to measure interrater reliability directly and indirectly and to reinforce the importance of consistent test marking within the team. An interesting innovation in Senegal was the use of a prerecorded videotaped EGRA administration with a child (see Chapter 6). Assessors watched the video and scored the student. Results were used to measure trainees' performance as if they were in a real field situation.

Fieldwork

We pilot tested the instruments during the 2-week training, thus creating an additional practice opportunity for the assessors and supervisors. After tabulating the results from the pilot, discussions with the field assessors, and a rapid psychometric analysis, the implementation team adjusted certain test items. In sum, the pilot testing helped to ensure validity of the tests and increased the competency of the field supervisors and their understanding of the methodology, thereby increasing reliability.

We collected the data over a 4-week period from May 4 to June 5, 2009. Two days were allocated for each school: the first day was dedicated to conducting the EGRA and the second day to observing classrooms. The assessment teams visited two schools each week (Monday/Tuesday and Thursday/Friday), with Wednesdays and weekends reserved for travel between schools. A key decision was to limit the number of students tested per school and increase the total number of schools visited in order to record more variance across schools rather than within them. Each team assessed 14 students per school and observed a minimum of three classroom lessons (for 3 observation hours total) at each school. Supervisors were responsible for filling out reports for each school visit detailing standard aspects of administration and any conditions that might have biased the results. For example, we had to replace 10 schools from the original random sample because they either were no longer open or did not have a CE1 classroom.

Use of Results

In periodic meetings throughout the planning and implementation phase, the Ministry of Education reiterated its hope that this effort would not be "just one more study." This was an encouraging statement for the implementation team, because the movement to introduce EGRA in national diagnostics worldwide grew out of the need for a new type of reading assessment that would be more directly and easily linked to actionable results.

Despite its advantages, the lack of familiarity with this type of criterion-referenced assessment[6] also presents one of the challenges to uptake of the assessment methodology and the results. That is, explaining the findings is not easy in contexts such as Senegal, where achievement tests are usually defined as percentage of correct responses and test content is usually linked directly to classroom content and teaching methods. Because EGRA is not linked to a specific curricular goal or teaching method (see Chapter 7 for further discussion of this point), many questions arose in Senegal about the validity of a test that, for example, presented children with a reading passage without pictures, titles, or prereading exercises to help with comprehension.

Perhaps for this reason, or perhaps because of testing fatigue, Ministry of Education officials reacted to the results of the study with obvious *déjà vu* when RTI and FocusAfrica presented them for the first time. Indeed, the bottom line of the EGRA results—that kids read poorly for their age—reflected and supported those of many other evaluations or assessments that are implemented either periodically (i.e., PASEC, World Bank) or regularly (i.e., SNERS, the BAC[7]). Most people, especially teachers, education inspectors, and other civil servants involved in the education sector, are aware that results are dismal, and they may have their own explanation for who or what is responsible, but these discussions remain at the level of debate without translating into concrete action, or are overshadowed by other priorities. In discussions surrounding the EGRA results, very different opinions arose about the age at which children should know how to read, the age at which they are capable of beginning to learn, and, naturally, the issue of language of instruction.

Therefore, the challenge was to bring the conversation to *accountability for quality* in the school system, and to provoke responsibility for using specific information from the EGRA diagnostic to identify concrete actions. For example, the results of the assessment clearly show the relationship between letter knowledge and reading: children who can identify letters by name or sound read more fluently than those who cannot. Therefore, a clear action would be to improve the teaching of the alphabet in the first year of school.

---

6   That is, a test in which the score clearly indicates what children can or cannot do relative to the subject matter tested (or whether they have mastered the subject according to desired standards). This is in contrast to a norm-referenced test, whose score indicates how a child performed relative to other children.

7   SNERS is the national school examination system: Système National d'Évaluation du Rendement Scolaires. BAC is an abbreviation for " Baccalauréat," or the national high school leaving examination.

This requires taking time to really understand the EGRA methodology and the information that it provides. With that in mind, a second dissemination meeting extended the results of the diagnostic to civil society partners and donors. This activity, in April 2010, involved local and international NGO representatives, the media, and Ministry of Education representatives. The aims of the meeting were to talk about the results of the assessment, to learn how to interpret and communicate the results to different stakeholders, and to develop some suggested dissemination activities. The morning portion of the meeting concentrated on the presentation of EGRA results couched in a discussion of education (and literacy) indicators in general, a comparative analysis of EGRA indicators with other norm-referenced tests used in Senegal to date, and a discussion of benchmarking (determining an "acceptable" level for the grade tested).

The afternoon session consisted of training in a methodology of communication and social mobilization known as the Smart Chart.[8] This methodology is a step-by-step framework for defining a problem, setting communication objectives, defining target audiences, and creating messages designed to motivate people to change their behavior, practices, or policies in support of the stated objective. This approach allowed participants to practice translating the EGRA results into clear messages for different target audiences, then focus on solutions and determine who was responsible for change. It also allowed RTI to understand more about how different stakeholders perceived the results.

Finally, the Smart Chart methodology also served as a call for proposals. That is, workshop participants were invited to submit proposals for activities (to be funded by minigrants) that could disseminate the results of the EGRA study. The proposed activities were to be linked to messages that children *can* learn to read early, that children *should* learn to read early, and that currently children are *not* learning to read early or well enough in Senegal. From June through October 2010, we gave six local nonprofit organizations grants of approximately US$2,000 each to conduct a range of exploratory activities to promote reading, including producing radio programs and television documentaries, publishing newspaper and online articles, holding community meetings, designing and distributing posters, painting murals in strategic locations, and leading community music and theater programs.

---

[8] Smart Chart, a communications strategic planning tool designed for nonprofit organizations, was originally created by Spitfire Strategies for the Communications Leadership Institute. See http://www.smartchart.org for more information about the tool and free downloads.

These efforts targeting parents and communities prompted RTI to involve a private-sector social marketing firm to launch additional, high-profile communications activities to coincide with events such as International Literacy Day (September 8) and the start of the new school year. One activity was a reading tour that involved 20 well-known Senegalese celebrities and opinion leaders, such as musicians, television journalists, and community leaders, who made school visits in five major cities and talked about the importance of literacy. This drew the attention of the media and community members, who wanted to know why these celebrities were visiting their school. In response, the organizers gave them information about the EGRA results and the campaign to improve reading.

Choosing a multidimensional communications approach involving various implementing partners, media types, and target audiences allowed us to learn more about what works and what does not in this context; to test communication strategies, modes of delivery, and messages; and to identify key allies among local institutions, while at the same time getting the message out before too much time had passed. This has paved the way for a more specific national reading campaign, should there be interest in developing one. International research shows that knowledge of the target audiences, including their beliefs and attitudes, is critical to the success of any communications campaign (Russell & Hirschhorn, 1987; Wasek, 1987) and the minigrant activities led by local organizations were designed to gather this type of feedback during implementation. In this manner, RTI was able to maintain some momentum from the analysis and dissemination of results, while collecting critical information to use to inform future efforts.

We chose to focus communications activities on communities and parents, asking them to get more involved in their children's education, in the hopes that these local efforts would create pressure on government institutions to initiate change at the systemic level. If this does not happen, we can hope that the communications activities have at least had some impact on the children of the families who were reached by the information. However, the actual effects of the communications activities will not likely be discernable immediately, if at all, without subsequent evaluation activities.

An alternative approach would have been to focus communication directly on government institutions, but our experience with initial dissemination of results indicated that effective advocacy at this level would require a much more sustained presence on the ground and a more influential mandate. In this case, conducting a detailed power analysis (see Hinans & Healy, 2007) to understand who really makes decisions and who influences those decision-makers would have been critical.

Comparison of Implementation Choices

The above discussion of the stages of implementation in these two cases allows us to see that EGRA is flexible enough to allow variations in national-level diagnostics, and teams can adapt planning, implementation, and follow-up activities based on country context. However, certain decisions have consequences, and a few aspects, such as assessor training and instrument reliability/validity, must adhere to research standards. This section reviews some of the similarities and differences in the way EGRA was used for national diagnostic testing in the two countries; the final section then discusses some of those consequences and lessons learned.

Country Context and Study Design

The contexts of the two diagnostics—country characteristics, origin and goals, client, etc.—were naturally very different, which led to differences in how EGRA was implemented. Both countries showed a commitment to literacy in policy statements and actions, but the interest in using diagnostic testing to support educational improvement was much stronger in Nicaragua than in Senegal, as evidenced by the Nicaraguan government's support of and participation in all stages of the EGRA diagnostic. This commitment was also related to the important difference in initiators of the studies and whether the education ministries were involved or not in requesting technical assistance to carry out the assessments.

In Nicaragua, the ministry requested the evaluation, whereas in Senegal the ministry agreed to allow RTI to conduct the study with ministry oversight. The timing and duration of the studies was also different. In Nicaragua, the adaptation and piloting of the instrument took place in 2007, and the national baseline study took place in 2008 as a larger project with several activities, whereas in Senegal, the study was launched in February 2009 with the requirement of completing it by June of the same year. Thus, what was completed over the course of 2 years in Nicaragua was accelerated into less than 1 year in Senegal.

On a methodological level, the sample sizes were very different, but both are still adequate for national diagnostics. This is because in Nicaragua, researchers and policy makers were interested in *both* overall national results *and* accurate estimates for certain subsamples (e.g., grade, type of school). To ensure that we had acceptable confidence levels for the estimates made for all variables of interest, we had to expand sample sizes for subpopulations substantially. By contrast, the concern in Senegal was only an overall national baseline; for that reason, even though Senegal has a population much larger than that of Nicaragua, we were able to use a smaller total sample but have an equivalent level of confidence in generalizing the results.

Finally, the language-of-instruction issue also differed in the two countries: children in Nicaragua were tested in their mother tongue, which was also the country's most common language and the one in which they were taught, whereas children in Senegal were assessed in a language that few of them used at home *or* at school. This is also a reflection of the larger country context. The prevalence of Spanish in Nicaragua stands in contrast to Senegal, where an estimated 36 languages are present, and where up to five different languages might be represented in a given classroom, according to data from the EGRA diagnostic.

Flexibility in Implementation

Likewise, the ways in which EGRA was carried out in each country had both similarities and differences; some steps were more open to adaptation, whereas others adhered to standard practice for generating reliable national results. For example, both countries adopted the standard instrument format—Nicaragua from the English model and Senegal from a preexisting version in French—but adapted it to the country based on careful analysis of the language, the target grade level, and the context. Both countries involved linguists and the Ministry of Education in this process. In neither case were instruments simply adopted or translated without attention to localization. However, the lesser involvement of the Ministry of Education in Senegal did result in some contesting of the validity of the methodology, because the subtask items did not reflect standard test items or methods that are common in Senegal. They did not have time to understand fully and accept the process and utility of the EGRA model as in Nicaragua.

Another less flexible step in the process, which was therefore similar in both countries, was ensuring reliability of the instrument through rigorous sampling, internal validity checks, intense assessor training with interrater reliability testing, and built-in quality control checks during field data collection. A notable difference, however, is in the conflict that arose in

Nicaragua by including ministry staff as potential assessors. Having to turn away a certain number of individuals who did not meet minimum criteria for assessor reliability meant risking good will and potentially causing larger complications with the client. This was not an issue in Senegal, as all of the assessors were independent consultants hired only for this short task and they were informed of the selection procedures when they applied.

Clearly, where flexibility was most acceptable was in dissemination of results. Both countries started with dissemination workshops to present the results to the relevant ministry staff. In Nicaragua, this approach led to concrete action by the ministry, activities that led to proactive uptake of the results by civil society. For example, at the end of the dissemination workshop in Nicaragua, the head of primary education in the ministry announced that the results would be used to design and implement several teacher-training workshops. Also, the videos the ministry requested led to the publicity company's idea and implementation of the social mobilization campaign, with only minimal RTI funding for design. The same type of results briefing to the Ministry of Education in Senegal, however, led to little uptake by the ministry; hence, the focus shifted to dissemination by civil society, but only after RTI offered to fund proposed dissemination plans. Though no less important, the results of civil society efforts in Senegal are likely to take longer and be more difficult to discern than the concrete steps taken by the Ministry of Education in Nicaragua.

Conclusions and Lessons Learned

This section summarizes some of the key conclusions and lessons learned that stand out from comparative analysis of the two different country cases. We also speculate about how the differences in implementation may have influenced the actions and activities that followed each assessment.

The Degree to Which the Ministry Is Involved and "Owns" the Results

As reiterated throughout the chapter, the Ministry of Education in Nicaragua was much more involved in the EGRA national diagnostic than was the ministry in Senegal, in terms of both implementation of EGRA and action based on the findings. After the assessment results were released, Nicaragua's ministry reinvigorated its focus and efforts on quality improvements at the elementary, instead of tertiary, school level. We cannot claim that the EGRA efforts led by RTI were the cause of the shifting priority, but the assessments clearly facilitated some of the subsequent actions. The collaborative dialogue among stakeholders, which allowed for mutual exchange and engagement of the ministry and the donor, was likely also related, as was having a Nicaraguan subcontractor (CIASES) with excellent relations with the high levels of the ministry. We believe that because the Ministry of Education in Nicaragua was involved from inception, it also had a greater stake in using the results, disseminating them, and planning follow-on activities.

In the case of Senegal, although the ministry gave prior approval for the EGRA implementation, officials did not seek assistance or commission the diagnostic in the first place. Instead, RTI and its subcontractor carried out the assessment at the initiative of a private foundation as part of its grant-making strategy. This did not in itself preclude us from involving ministry staff in implementation, but another key factor affected our ability to do so—the timing of the study. In Senegal, barely 4 months were available for fully implementing the assessment before the school year ended. Thus, it was implemented rapidly (albeit with appropriate rigor) with a research consultancy to handle logistics. This timing did not allow for the negotiation, planning, training, and capacity building necessary for ministry officials to take an active role in EGRA implementation. Looking at it another way, conducting EGRA through the ministry would have been better for government ownership, but also would have required a much longer time frame. Again, we can conclude that as a result of these two major factors, the national government of Senegal felt little ownership of the results and, not surprisingly, sensed less urgency concerning either the uptake of the results or follow-up for changing policy and practice.

In Nicaragua, as mentioned earlier, the choice to involve ministry staff as assessors created some risk to the relationship between RTI and the ministry. In Senegal, the alternative—using short-term labor—may have undermined the sustainability and longer-term impact of the investment in the diagnostic assessment because no one in the ministry will have in-depth knowledge of the methodology so that they might use it again. Arguably, the Ministry of Education staff in Nicaragua may also have been more convinced of the utility of the study and of the need for action because they participated in data collection and saw firsthand the difference between students who could read and those who could not. For many assessors in Senegal, participation in the fieldwork completely changed their perception of the quality of education;

unfortunately, they were not necessarily the people best positioned to provoke change as a consequence.

The Degree to Which Civil Society and Private Stakeholders "Own" the Results

In Nicaragua, uptake by civil society was supported but not formally managed by RTI. As a result of their work with RTI, CCCP and CIASES formed committees for planning the national social marketing campaign, gathering together several other local NGOs and advocacy groups. These groups formed a consensus to work toward the improvement of early grade reading in Nicaragua.

The local counterpart, CIASES, managed a significant part of both the EGRA implementation and RTI's work in Nicaragua after the national diagnostic was completed. Over time, its commitment has fostered relationships across the Ministry of Education as well as with several donors, including USAID. CIASES had several qualities that made it invaluable as a partner in this work, such as its staff members' technical knowledge of theories of evaluation and education, their relationships with personnel at the highest levels of the ministry, and their commitment and dedication to seeing the project to a successful end.

Ideally, RTI would have implemented EGRA in Senegal as had been done in Nicaragua—by using a local contractor to manage logistics while also involving the ministry in implementation and fieldwork. Once we recognized the coinciding factors that would preclude substantial ministry involvement in implementation, however, we then had to choose between either a for-profit management/research consulting firm or a nonprofit, education-sector NGO similar to CIASES in Nicaragua. We had considered the relative benefits of investing in an existing education-sector NGO in the interest of building capacity—based on the assumption that they would have a longer-term interest in the results and therefore increase the overall long-term impact of the study. However, we were concerned about the capacity of the local NGOs to manage considerable logistics and to absorb a significant amount of resources required for this intense, national research, since very few of them had this prior experience. We opted for the management consulting company because of its experience with large-scale research and its ability to accurately estimate costs of different inputs and get the work done under a short deadline.

An unexpected outcome of our final choice was that we ended up creating a new education-sector interest group in the private sector. The subcontractor selected to help manage the study locally, FocusAfrica, is now much more of an advocate for children's literacy; it has committed time and resources outside the project's scope of work to continue working on education sector issues, and it has gotten other private sector companies involved. The EGRA national diagnostic was just one of several Hewlett Foundation studies taking place in the country at the time. All these partners, linked by their common relationship to the Hewlett Foundation, began sharing information and agreeing upon strategies for communication and social mobilization moving forward. Together, they consist of a local NGO, an international NGO, a civil society education platform group, a university, and a private sector institution. FocusAfrica helped to facilitate this collaboration, which was not expected as part of the original scope of work.

Although they were not directly involved with EGRA implementation, the Senegalese civil society organizations became engaged in education advocacy and support for early learning through the minigrants process that followed the EGRA diagnostic. It is difficult to say whether they have fully internalized the EGRA methodology or indicators, but they have been persuaded that current outcomes are unacceptable, that children are capable of more and at an earlier age, and that everyone needs to begin living up to their responsibilities to help change the situation.

Effect of National Language of Instruction on Implementation and Results

A key lesson demonstrated by the EGRA national diagnostic in Senegal is that testing reading competency in a second language (i.e., not the mother tongue) introduces a range of complications that need to be carefully addressed. For example, it requires a great deal of discussion during the training period to ensure that all assessors have the same understanding of what constitutes a "correct" response for each item. Different assessors come with different tolerance for perfection in pronunciation and different physiological capacities for distinguishing subtle differences in sounds. The assessor preparation process must, therefore, make a convincing and clear-cut distinction between accents caused by mother-tongue influence and actual inability to decode the written words. This is no simple task. The implication for a national diagnostic is that results can underestimate reading capacity if the assessors insist on a textbook pronunciation without taking into consideration mother-tongue influence.

Those overseeing the adaptation of the EGRA instruments can try to minimize the inclusion of items that are deemed likely to cause coding discrepancies and thereby skew the results. However, stricter assessors might feel that eliminating such items would not accurately test the range of competencies that individuals are expected to acquire. Sprenger-Charolles and Messaoud-Galusi (2009) reviewed reading assessment approaches and recommended that "it is thus necessary to adapt the assessment's material in a given LOI [language of instruction] according to possible interferences between languages coexisting in a given context which are likely to lead to reading difficulties" (p. 26).

In Nicaragua, because students were tested only in Spanish, and because Spanish was the native language of almost all of the students, these second-language issues did not arise in training for data collection. Nevertheless, the issue of "teaching the correct sounds" did arise during the preparations for every teacher-training workshop. The technical advisors and trainers leading the workshops were always concerned about knowing the proper pronunciation of each sound so that they would train the teachers correctly. They tended to assume that the teachers would not know the proper pronunciation.

Additionally, including the listening comprehension subtask in EGRA is especially important when testing is done in a second language. In Senegal, the client opted to limit the assessment to letter identification, nonword reading, and oral reading fluency with comprehension, because these would cover the key competencies of automaticity,[9] vocabulary, and comprehension. However, we discovered that children were indeed learning to decode syllables and words but without registering the meaning of those words—either because of lack of fluency (they were reading too slowly) or because they had not yet acquired the basic French-language competency that would allow them to apply preexisting knowledge of vocabulary and sentence structure to new situations. Without having tested listening comprehension or familiar word reading—measures of oral language knowledge as well as reading ability—we cannot be certain which factor is more influential. However, it was clear through the difficulties that children had with the test administration that basic French skills were limited; in several cases, the assessors had to have translators explain the test

---

[9] "Automaticity" means fluency in word recognition so that the reader is no longer aware of or needs to concentrate on the mental effort of translating letters to sounds and forming sounds into words.

instructions to the children, since the children could not understand them in French and the assessors were not always fluent in the local language.

In terms of the reaction to the results, the language of instruction was also one of the key rationales given for the poor results in Senegal. Indeed, it is intuitive that most children exposed to reading instruction only in a second language that they do not use, hear, or see outside of school will reach reading fluency later than children who learn to read first in their native language, in which they are immersed. However, as these and other results referenced in this chapter (i.e., PASEC and World Bank studies) show, other teacher and school-level factors also affect reading acquisition. All methods—immersion, dual-language instruction, or mother-tongue instruction with transition to a second language—require targeted strategies, trained teachers, and school and home environments conducive to literacy. Nevertheless, the EGRA results were easily contested or dismissed as a consequence of the language issue, at which point the policy dialogue reached an impasse.

Language of instruction may also explain why uptake and action based on the EGRA results was more significant in Nicaragua than in Senegal; in Nicaragua, policy dialogue could focus on more concrete, actionable strategies for change without the distraction of the language-of-instruction debate.

Effect of the Studies and Communication Activities on the Education Sector

The themes of the communication and dissemination activities were similar across the two countries. For example, in Nicaragua the social mobilization video was aimed at educating parents and community members about what expectations they should have of children's reading progress and how to hold teachers and schools accountable. Similarly, the majority of messages and themes chosen by the communication grantees in Senegal focused on the role of the family and the community in supporting education, particularly in the preschool years.

However, Senegal's targeted social marketing activities led to more specialized and varied communications follow-up through multiple channels—community meetings, radio programs, video, flyers, contests, murals, etc.—whereas in Nicaragua, communications activities were mostly limited to social marketing videos (funded by USAID) and the locally organized and funded contest for first-grade teachers. It is too early to know whether these efforts will have an effect on attitudes and behaviors, and further research would need to be done to confirm; however, there was some indication that the campaign in Senegal helped to reignite the language-of-instruction debate, to increase awareness of the need for parents and schools to share responsibility for quality, and to reconsider attitudes concerning the age at which children should begin learning.

One lesson that can be drawn from these two cases is that advocacy and communication targeted directly at government decision makers need to happen at some point when the objective is to change system-level factors, but doing so requires a long-term and influential presence. The effect of this type of influential local champion—CIASES—was evident in the case of Nicaragua. In Senegal, where this long-term presence was not established yet, RTI hoped to identify and encourage the establishment of such a champion as well as to initiate some small wins in the sector by first targeting parents and communities with simple messages and realistic, easily implemented solutions.

If EGRA results are expected to influence the education sector in any significant way, communication with government officials must touch upon the value of the criterion-referenced evidence that EGRA provides. The results of the EGRA assessment could be used to establish benchmarks and to articulate more explicitly incremental expectations for student performance. At present, for example, the national curriculum in Senegal for CE1 is based on the expectation that students should be able to understand everything they read and that the goal is lively, natural, and rapid reading.[10] The policy goes on to suggest that the methods for obtaining this goal are to select texts that are easy to comprehend and that refer to situations to which children can relate, and to give children time for silent prereading to prepare for comprehension assessments. For the first two grades, however, the national curriculum does not specify when foundational skills such as letter knowledge, reciting the alphabet, word decoding, or even writing one's name should be acquired. Consequently, when teachers are questioned concerning the age at which children should know fundamental skills, the answers vary considerably. Neither Nicaragua nor Senegal arrived at a point at which discussions of this depth could take place.

The Senegal EGRA results clearly showed a positive correlation between (1) the competencies of letter-sound knowledge and the ability to decode nonwords and (2) the ability to read fluently (Pouezevara et al., 2010). Recognizing this association should be a first step in ensuring that these

---

[10] For information in French on Senegal's approach to education and curricula, see the government web pages on the education program, http://www.gouv.sn/spip.php?article809.

skills are promoted intensively in the early grades. Using mother-tongue instruction can be an effective way for children to build these basic skills before transferring them to the French language (see Chapter 5 on language of instruction), but establishing and articulating clear, incremental expectations is also a way to reach the goal of fluent reading, regardless of language of instruction. If the national diagnostic program in Senegal helps achieve some constructive action around language-of-instruction policy, then it will make a significant contribution to education quality improvement in Senegal, but these advances will require time and concentrated efforts involving a variety of stakeholders beyond those who sponsored or implemented the assessment.

In Nicaragua, ministry involvement—and the flexibility and willingness of USAID to adapt the activities in the project—allowed the post-diagnostic work to have some impact on teachers and instructional improvement. As evidence, in April 2010 the Ministry of Education took part in a high-level international meeting organized in Washington, DC, by RTI, the Education for All Fast Track Initiative,[11] and the READ Trust. The purpose of the meeting was to bring together reading experts, donors, and representatives from eight countries to work on the beginnings of a plan to scale up efforts in these countries to have all second-grade students reading by 2015. At the end of the workshop, each country's representatives presented an outline of the plan they had constructed based on the meeting. Nicaragua's outline was the most complete and well thought out of the plans put forth by the eight countries in attendance, in part because the Ministry of Education had already put so much effort into thinking through this goal before the meeting.

Summary and Conclusions

In these two distinctly different countries, unique choices were made about how to carry out the national diagnostic using EGRA; not surprisingly, then, the effect of the results (their uptake) diverged. Moreover, these examples show how such choices can have an impact on sustainability. For example, up-front work establishing a relationship with the Ministry of Education and involving it in planning and implementation can pay dividends in the long run, as the ministry will likely be more convinced of the results and motivated to act.

Senegal's approach was independent of the government and driven instead by civil society, whereas Nicaragua's approach was centralized through the

---

[11] For more information about the Education for All Fast Track Initiative, see the initiative's website, http://www.educationfasttrack.org/.

ministry and linked to existing education reforms. Consequently, Senegal's results were taken up by civil society without demonstrably affecting national education policy or programs, but Nicaragua's were immediately acted upon with serious policy input and direction. In both countries, however, the EGRA implementation process—regardless of the specific aspects of implementation such as local partners or selection of assessors—yielded rich and representative data that are available for any number of purposes in the future.

This comparison does not allow us to say which approach is better than the other, but it does offer several lessons and areas for further exploration. One lesson from the comparison is that considering the purpose of the diagnostic program before work begins is essential. If the purpose is simply to have a nationally representative study of early grade reading, then the approach taken by Senegal seems sufficient. If, however, the intent is to use this diagnostic as the beginning of deeper reform and long-term engagement, then ministry buy-in and involvement seem to be the solution, as in Nicaragua.

Another closely related lesson is that information on its own is not enough to change attitudes or policies. In other words, sharing results—even if they cause sudden shock and outrage—may not necessarily lead directly to changes in behavior. In between these stages are the critical prerequisites of convincing people that the results are reliable; that the results are indeed "bad" or of concern (often a question of relative expectations and values); that they should care about reading results at all; that changing behaviors or policies to improve reading will have an impact on their lives; that there are, in fact, things that can be done; and that it is not "someone else's business" to do them. The extent to which these elements can be successfully communicated requires sustained effort. The presence of strong local champions with charisma and a great degree of political and social capital is critical as well.

A great deal of change in education systems and approaches to reading will happen organically, despite the most well-intentioned of projects or programs. Factors that remain hidden or unknown, but that could have a significant effect on the extent to which information leads to action, might be the prevailing political climate, curricular issues, generational gaps in education and attitudes, and even social and cultural trends. Any of these may prevent a country from reaching a tipping point toward early grade literacy that an external observer might assume is inevitable. That said, collecting rigorous, reliable, and objective data remains the best first step.

References

Centro de Investigación y Acción Educativa Social (CIASES) & RTI International. (2009). *Informe de resultados: EGRA 2008* [Report on the results of the EGRA 2008 pilot assessment]. Prepared for the US Agency for International Development (USAID) under the EdData II project, Task 5, Contract No. EHC-05-04-00004-00. Research Triangle Park, North Carolina: CIASES and RTI. Retrieved September 17, 2010, from: https://www.eddataglobal.org/documents/index.cfm?fuseaction=pubDetail&ID=198

DeStefano, J., Lynd, M. R., & Thornton, B. (2009). *The quality of basic education in Senegal: A review*. Final report. Prepared for USAID/Senegal. Independence, Ohio: The Center for Collaboration and the Future of Schooling. Retrieved September 17, 2010, from: http://pdf.usaid.gov/pdf_docs/PNADP648.pdf

Diallo, I. (2005). *Language planning, language-in-education policy, and attitudes towards languages in Senegal*. PhD thesis. Queensland: School of Languages and Linguistics, Griffith University, Australia. Retrieved September 17, 2010, from http://www4.gu.edu.au:8080/adt-root/uploads/approved/adt-QGU20070105.113405/public/02Whole.pdf

Diagne, A. (2007). *Case study: The costs and financing for reducing illiteracy in Senegal*. Hamburg, Germany: UNESCO Institute for Lifelong Learning. Retrieved March 23, 2011, from: http://uil.unesco.org/fileadmin/bamako_conf_2007/CostFinanceLiteracy_Diagne_EN(2).pdf

Direction de la Promotion des Langues Nationales (DPLN) [Office for the promotion of national languages], Senegal. (2002). *État des lieux de la recherche en/sur les langues nationales (synthese)* [The current state of research on national languages (synthesis)]. Dakar: DPLN, Ministère de l'Enseignement Préscolaire, de l'Elémentaire, du Moyen Secondaire et des Langues Nationales [Ministry of Preschool, Elementary and Middle School Education and National Languages].

Fofana, R. (2003). *L'Édition au Sénégal: Bilan et perspectives de développement* [Publishing in Senegal: The state of affairs and perspectives for development of the sector]. Graduate thesis. Villeurbanne, France: École Nationale

Supérieure des Sciences de l'Information et des Bibliothèques [National School for Information and Library Sciences]. Retrieved September 17, 2010, from: http://www.enssib.fr/bibliotheque-numerique/document-727

Hinons, S., & Healy, R. (January 2007). *Theories of power for activists.* Cambridge, Massachusetts: Grassroots Policy Project. Retrieved April 8, 2011, from: http://www.grassrootspolicy.org/system/files/theories_power_ for_activists_0.pdf

IDEA International. (2009). *Enseignement bilingue : Etude des résultats et recherche action. Rapport pays : Sénégal* [Bilingual education: Survey results and applications. Country report: Senegal]. Summative evaluation report for a World Bank pilot bilingual education project implemented in three West African Counties (Niger, Mali and Senegal). Dakar, Senegal: IDEA Dakar.

Instituto Nacional de Estadísticas y Censos (INEC) [National Institute for Statistics and the Census], Nicaragua. (2006). *VIII Censo de Población y IV de Vivienda: Censo 2005* [Eighth population census and fourth housing census: Census 2005]. Managua, Nicaragua: INEC. Retrieved December 2, 2010, from http://www.cies.edu.ni/documentos/censo2005/Informe%20 Resumen%20del%20VIII%20Censo%20de%20Poblacion.pdf

McLaughlin, F. (2008). Senegal: The emergence of a national lingua franca. In A. Simpson (Ed.), *Language and national identity in Africa* (pp. 79–97). Oxford, England: Oxford University Press.

Ministère de l'Education [Ministry of Education], Senegal. (March 2003). *Programme de Développement de l'Education et de la Formation/Education Pour Tous* (PDEF/EPT) [Program for Development and Training in Education/Education for All]. Retrieved September 14, 2010, from http:// www.ipar.sn/IMG/pdf/03_pdef.pdf

Ministerio de Educación [Ministry of Education], Nicaragua. (2008). La educación es responsabilidad del estado y tarea de todos: *La Batalla por el Primer Grado* [Education is the responsibility of the state and the task of all: The battle for the first grade]. Managua: Dirección de Educación Primaria [Office of Primary Education], Ministerio de Educación. Draft. Retrieved April 18, 2011, from http://www.nicaraguaeduca.edu.ni/uploads/BatallaPG. pdf

Pouezevara, S., Sock, M., & Ndiaye, A. (2010). *Evaluation des compétences fondamentales en lecture au Sénégal* [Early grade reading assessment for Senegal]. Report prepared for the William and Flora Hewlett Foundation. Research Triangle Park, North Carolina: RTI International and Focus Africa. Retrieved September 17, 2010, from USAID website : https://www. eddataglobal.org/documents/index.cfm?fuseaction=pubDetail&ID=250

Programme d'Analyse des Systèmes Educatifs de la CONFEMEN [Conférence des ministres de l'Education des pays ayant le français en partage] (PASEC). (October 2008). *Resultats provisoires de l'évaluation diagnostique PASEC 2006/2007* [Preliminary results of the PASEC diagnostic evaluation]. Working paper. Dakar, Senegal: PASEC.

Russell, J. M., & Hirschhorn, N. (1987). For want of a nail: The problems of implementation—A national oral rehydration program. in R. Cash, G. Keusch, & J. Lamstein (Eds.), Child health and survival: *the UNICEF GOBI-FFF program* (pp. 233–239). Beckenham, Kent: Croom Helm Ltd.

Shiohata, M. (2010). Exploring the literacy environment: A case study from urban Senegal. *Comparative Education Review, 54*(2), 243–269. Retrieved July 13, 2011, from http://www.jstor.org/stable/10.1086/651451

Sprenger-Charolles, L. (2008). Senegal Early Grade Reading Assessment: *Résultats d'élèves sénégalais des trois premiers grades ayant appris à lire en français et en wolof* [Results from Senegalese primary school students learning to read in French and in Wolof]. Washington, DC: World Bank. Retrieved September 17, 2010, from USAID website: https://www. eddataglobal.org/documents/index.cfm?fuseaction=pubDetail&ID=118 (French) or https://www.eddataglobal.org/documents/index.cfm?fuseaction =pubDetail&ID=117 (English)

Sprenger-Charolles, L., & Messaoud-Galusi, S. (2009). *Review of research on reading acquisition and analyses of the main international reading assessment tools.* Paris, France: International Institute for Education Planning, United Nations Educational, Scientific, and Cultural Organization (IIEP– UNESCO). Retrieved July 13, 2011, from http://lpp.psycho.univ-paris5.fr/ pdf/2673.pdf

Trading Economics. (2010). *Literacy rate; adult male (% of males ages 15 and above) in Nicaragua* [database]. Retrieved April 14, 2011, from: http://www. tradingeconomics.com/nicaragua/literacy-rate-adult-male-percent-of-males-ages-15-and-above-wb-data.html

US Central Intelligence Agency (CIA). (n.d.). *The world factbook: Country comparison, GDP per capita*. Retrieved September 20, 2010, from https://www.cia.gov/library/publications/the-world-factbook/rankorder/2004rank.html

US Central Intelligence Agency. (2010, November). *The world factbook: Central America and Caribbean—Nicaragua*. Retrieved December 1, 2010, from https://www.cia.gov/library/publications/the-world-factbook/geos/nu.html

US Central Intelligence Agency. (2011, April). *The world factbook: Africa—Senegal*. Retrieved April 14, 2011, from https://www.cia.gov/library/publications/the-world-factbook/geos/sg.html

University of Oregon Center on Teaching and Learning. (2008). I*DEL benchmark goals*. Retrieved April 14, 2011, from https://dibels.uoregon.edu/idel_benchmark.php

Wasek, G. K. (1987). The social marketing approach: Concepts and implications for international public health. In R. Cash, G. Keusch, & J. Lamstein (Eds.), Child health and survival: *The UNICEF GOBI-FFF program* (pp. 75–98). London, England: Croom Helm.

World Bank. (2010a). *EdStats—Education statistics: Country profiles* [database]. Enrollment data from the UNESCO Institute for Statistics. Retrieved April 14, 2011, from: http://web.worldbank.org/WBSITE/EXTERNAL/TOPICS/EXTEDUCATION/EXTDATASTATISTICS/EXTEDSTATS/0,,contentMDK:22614780~menuPK:7196605~pagePK:64168445~piPK:64168309~theSitePK:3232764,00.html

World Bank. (2010b). *World development indicators (WDI) 2010* [database]. Retrieved September 17, 2010, from: http://data.worldbank.org/data-catalog/world-development-indicators

Gauging Program Effectiveness with EGRA: Impact Evaluations in South Africa and Mali

Wendi Ralaingita and Anna Wetterberg

In recent years, developing-country governments, donors, and practitioners have sounded increasingly urgent calls for better identification of effective interventions in all sectors (see, for example, Duflo & Kremer, 2003; Maredia, 2009; Savedoff et al., 2006). In particular, the lack of rigorous studies of social sector programs leaves "decision-makers with good intentions and ideas, but little real evidence of how to effectively spend resources to reach worthy goals" (Savedoff et al., 2006, p. 1). In response to this gap, the interest in impact evaluations has increased substantially, in education as well as in other sectors (Banerjee, 2007).

In this chapter, we present two experiences with RTI's early grade reading assessment (EGRA) as an evaluation instrument to assess whether instructional interventions have improved reading performance in the early grades. In Mali and South Africa, EGRA was extensively adapted into students' mother tongues (i.e., dominant languages in the home) and then used in evaluations designed to measure the impact of specific interventions on core reading competencies.[1] Although the specific contexts, the program and evaluation designs, and the EGRA tools themselves were different in each country, these two experiences demonstrate EGRA's potential as an impact assessment instrument.

The chapter proceeds as follows. After providing some background on the use of impact evaluation in education in developing countries, and particularly for examining reading interventions, we summarize the evaluation studies conducted in South Africa and Mali. We present the outcomes of each and describe how these results were, or will be, used. Drawing on these experiences,

---

[1] Impact evaluations using EGRA also have been carried out in Liberia and Kenya. The experience in Liberia is described in Chapter 4, in the context of EGRA for continuous assessment.

we identify some of the advantages and trade-offs of using EGRA as an impact evaluation tool, along with some more general reflections on impact evaluation of reading interventions.[2] We conclude with recommendations for future applications of EGRA to evaluate instructional interventions.

Impact Evaluation in Education

The impact of a program or intervention can be most rigorously demonstrated through randomized designs that can isolate the set of variables responsible for change (see Kremer, 2006, pp. 73–77). Under such designs, researchers identify a target population and gather existing information on the relevant units of analysis (schools, teachers, classes, students, etc.). Based on this population, evaluators draw a sample and assign members (e.g., individuals, schools) randomly to either a treatment group or a control group (or, in some cases, to more than one experimental group). After baseline data are collected on both types of groups, the treatment group participates in the intervention of interest while the control group does not. Post-intervention, evaluators collect "endline" data from treatment and control groups to identify any group-specific changes in outcome measures over time and to assess differences between groups. The theory behind randomized assignment is that if selection into the two groups is indeed random, and if the samples are large enough, then the treatment and control groups will have pretreatment characteristics that are similar (or exactly the same, except for the fact of the treatment), and differences between the treatment and control groups after treatment can therefore be attributed to the program intervention.

Where randomized designs are not feasible, for practical or ethical reasons, nonexperimental or observational designs can be used. In these cases, statistical techniques such as propensity score matching[3] may be used to approximate the rigor of experimental designs (see, for example, Rodríguez

---

[2] We do not focus on impact evaluation as a methodology in this chapter; instead, we contrast EGRA with other means of measuring outcomes. Using EGRA to assess impact does not alleviate the need for design considerations important to all evaluations, such as randomization, comparable treatment and control groups, and measurement of explanatory variables. For discussions of evaluation methodology for education and development interventions, see, for example, Duflo and Kremer (2003), Kremer (2006), Savedoff et al. (2006), and Shi and Tsang (2008).

[3] Propensity score matching uses regression analysis to predict the likelihood that a given individual, based on all observable characteristics, is in the comparison or treatment group. Researchers can then use these probabilities to recreate a comparison group of individuals that has the same probability of being treated as those who were in the actual treatment group (Kremer, 2006, p. 75).

et al., 2010; Shapiro & Trevino, 2004). It is also worth noting that a randomized design is only one option in the arsenal of tools to assess what works in development and what does not (for a discussion, see Ravallion, 2009).

In both developed and developing countries, easily measurable inputs—such as the use of teaching aids, class size, teacher training, new instructional materials, etc.—are often used to characterize the content of an intervention (Wagner, 2003). The impacts of changes in such inputs have, in the past, often been assessed in terms of attendance, enrollment, or dropout rates. Rather than focusing on access, however, policy makers and practitioners now increasingly recognize that it is imperative to measure education quality by rigorously evaluating the impact of interventions on learning achievements.

Tools for Measuring Intervention Impact on Learning Achievements

Paper-and-Pencil Tests

At a general level, educational outcomes in primary school may be measured using existing assessment instruments that are already a regular part of a country's educational program. Standard achievement tests often measure multiple competencies. They can be used to assess impact, as long as they are given before and after the intervention of interest, and they capture relevant outcome variables.

For example, Rodríguez and her collaborators (2010) used the Colombian standard tests of mathematics, sciences, and language to assess the impact of flexible educational models, provision of specialized materials, and teacher trainings in rural schools. Standard tests may also be given at nonstandard times to capture baseline or endline data; an evaluation of a food-for-education program in Bangladesh used this technique to assess changes in academic achievement in four subject areas (Ahmed & Arends-Kuenning, 2006).

Using standard tests, however, can be challenging when the program of interest targets early reading competencies. Many standard achievement tests are administered in higher grades, such as grade 4 or 6. With these students in mind, they are typically paper-and-pencil tests and are aimed at higher-level skills. Such assessments often aim strictly at measuring comprehension, or they are constructed in ways that inherently assume that students are proficient readers. If they are used too early, students will score at or near the bottom of the assessment scale (this result is called a floor effect). Thus, in this scenario, the majority of students will not be able to demonstrate any of the assessed skills and will score very poorly. For that reason, little insight can be gleaned on the distribution of emergent reading skills.[4]

Further, researchers need to be careful to specify the aim of the test. Beyond the "competency assessment" aim, many standardized tests are intended to survey curricular goals at a particular level (such as at the end of a cycle), and so they may not include items to assess basic competencies.[5] They are not likely to capture the specific fundamental competencies that students need to gain to become fluent readers. Most end-of-cycle assessments, or even midcycle but later-grade assessments, do not (re)test the curricular goals of the earlier grades; instead, they simply test for the goals of the given grade. This assumption of proficiency at goals taught in earlier grades makes it difficult for both teachers and policy makers to pinpoint reasons why performance is so low in the grade assessed.

In addition to standardized achievement tests used in individual countries, various international reading assessments have been undertaken on a large scale across countries (for a discussion of these assessments, see Greaney and Kellaghan, 2008). These include the Progress in International Reading Literacy Study (PIRLS), which is administered to grade 4 learners and evaluates reading comprehension through a paper-and-pencil test; and prePIRLS, which was developed in 2010 to assess reading comprehension through the use of shorter, easier texts for fourth-grade students who "are still developing fundamental reading skills" (International Association for the Evaluation of Educational Achievement, 2011). In addition, regional tests of both reading and mathematics include the Programme d'Analyse des Systemes Educatifs de la CONFEMEN, or PASEC[6] (administered at grades 2 and 5), the Southern and Eastern Africa Consortium for Monitoring Educational Quality (SACMEQ, given during grade 6), and the Latin American Laboratory for Assessment of the Quality of Education (LLECE, targeting grades 3 and 4).

---

[4] Emergent reading skills are "the skills, knowledge, and attitudes that are developmental precursors to conventional forms of reading and writing. These skills are the basic building blocks for how students learn to read and write" (Connor et al., 2006, p. 665).

[5] For a discussion of the advantages of correspondence between EGRA and a country's national curriculum for motivating instructional improvements, see Chapter 7.

[6] As noted in Chapter 2, PASEC in English is the Program to Analyze the Education Systems of the states and governments belonging to the Conference of Education Ministers of Francophone Countries (Conférence des Ministres de l'Éducation Nationale des Pays ayant le Français en Partage, CONFEMEN). For more information in French about CONFEMEN and PASEC, see http://www.confemen.org/spip.php?rubrique3.

These assessments were designed for large-scale, comparative studies, and the tests themselves generally are not available to the public. Therefore, they are not accessible for outside evaluations, except for selected released items from the tests. In addition, because most of them are pencil-and-paper tests, they run into the same problem of floor effects mentioned above, as they miss the basic competencies that an early grade reading program would target.

Oral Tests

In developed countries, a wide range of research and evaluation tools is available, including paper-and-pencil tests, but also oral tests similar to the EGRA subtasks. In the United States, oral tests such as the Dynamic Indicators of Basic Early Literacy Skills (DIBELS) allow ongoing assessment in the classroom. DIBELS has been shown to correlate with future reading ability (see, for example, Burke et al., 2009; Good et al., 2001; Roehrig et al., 2008), and it has been used to evaluate the impact of specific reading interventions (Hartry et al., 2008; Wang & Algozzine, 2008; see also tables in Slavin et al., 2009, for impact evaluations using DIBELS). These oral tests, in fact, provided a starting point for the development of EGRA, which was adapted for use in varying linguistic contexts (as described in Chapter 1).

To evaluate the impact of a specific intervention on educational outcomes, researchers should review the range of available tools to identify instruments that will produce relevant data on indicators of interest. For interventions that aim to improve emergent reading skills, an oral test, such as EGRA, can provide detailed information on changes in these capacities.

Background of Cases

South Africa

EGRA was introduced to South Africa through the Integrated Education Program, which was funded by the United States Agency for International Development (USAID) and managed by RTI International, in close collaboration with the South African Department of Education (DOE) and several South African nongovernmental organizations (NGOs). In early 2007, the DOE adapted EGRA for the South African context and carried out a limited field test of instruments. Later that year, the DOE piloted EGRA on a larger scale as a means of providing specificity to and measuring progress toward standards outlined in the South African National Reading Strategy and the national curriculum. The pilot tested about 400 learners in 18 schools in four provinces (Eastern Cape, Gauteng, Limpopo, and Mpumalanga) using instruments in six languages (English, isiXhosa, isiZulu, Sepedi, Tshivenda, and Xitsonga). Because of the small sample, especially given the number of languages, the pilot results were not intended to be used as a population baseline. Rather, the focus was on testing the reliability of the South African EGRA instruments as a diagnostic tool for monitoring learners' reading competencies.

In 2009, the DOE and RTI worked with the Molteno Institute for Language and Literacy (MILL), a South African NGO with expertise in literacy development and support, to develop revised versions of the piloted instruments for the pre- and post-intervention assessments described below. These instruments included the following four subtasks (described in Chapter 1):

1. Letter identification: names

2. Familiar word reading

3. Oral reading fluency

4. Reading comprehension

The DOE was interested in using EGRA to evaluate whether (1) a particular early literacy methodology (the Systematic Method for Reading Success, or SMRS, described below) could be adapted for use in South African schools and (2) students in schools using SMRS would perform better than those taught using standard methods (Hollingsworth & Gains, 2009). In each of the three provinces in which the evaluation took place (North West, Limpopo, and Mpumalanga), the evaluation team stratified sampling at the district level by the subset of schools that were receiving priority support from the DOE, based on poverty and need. The sample included 10 treatment and 5 control schools in each province (budget limitations precluded the inclusion of an equal number of control schools). Depending on the size of the school, the evaluators then selected between 10 and 20 grade 1 learners at random. In total, the baseline sample included 650 students (450 treatment, 200 control), with 546 assessed again at end of the project (383 treatment, 163 control). The attrition rates were similar across treatment (14.9 percent) and control (18.5 percent) schools. Given these comparable attrition rates, the research design enabled evaluators to estimate the average impact of the SMRS methodology on learner achievement by comparison of scores on baseline and post-intervention assessments (Piper, 2009, p. 3).[7]

Before data collection, assessors underwent a week of training conducted by RTI to ensure familiarity with the evaluation design and instruments and consistent implementation. MILL collected the assessment data, in collaboration with the DOE and RTI. The DOE, along with MILL, had piloted the South African instruments in 2007 and thus had prior experience with EGRA implementation. The assessment was carried out in three languages: Setswana (North West), Sepedi (Limpopo), and isiZulu (Mpumalanga). The team collected baseline data from first-grade students very early in the school year (late January 2009), and endline data slightly before the halfway point of grade 1 (early June 2009). The short timeframe was driven by the scheduled closeout of the Integrated Education Program and was unrelated to pedagogical issues.

In the intervening period, teachers in treatment schools used a set of early grade reading practices, the Systematic Method for Reading Success. The SMRS had been adapted by Dr. Sandra Hollingsworth from the Systematic Instruction on Phonemes, Phonics, and Sight Word model (Shefelbine et al., 2001) and Plan International had used it successfully in pilot projects in Mali and Niger (Mitton, 2008). In control schools, teachers received no support or extra materials, and instead usually relied on established methods of recitation, memorization, and rote learning.

The SMRS program is intensive and provides scripted routines to be adapted and used for daily 30- to 45-minute lessons to explicitly teach reading. It also, crucially, relies on mother-tongue instruction. SMRS operates on the premise that reading stems from teachers' systematically introducing students to learning letter sounds, blending sounds into words, recognizing sight words, learning vocabulary and comprehension skills through reading aloud, and reading words in decodable and predictable stories. Once learners master reading in the mother tongue, they will be able to transfer these skills to other languages. Key instructional materials include culturally appropriate, progressively leveled storybooks, and teacher read-aloud stories with comprehension and vocabulary questions. For more details on the SMRS intervention used in South Africa, see Hollingsworth and Gains (2009).

---

[7] For an introduction to sampling, see the appropriate annex of the EGRA toolkit. English version, RTI International (2009a); Spanish, RTI International (2009b); French, RTI International (2009c).

Dr. Hollingsworth and MILL adapted the SMRS to the three South African provinces where it was implemented. The linguistic structures of Setswana, Sepedi, and isiZulu required 45 lessons to complete the program. During the intervention period, on average, teachers finished 21 of the 45 lessons. Because not all of their learners were progressing at the prescribed pace, or because new students had joined their classes, many teachers chose to drop back to repeat less advanced readings. For those reasons, they finished only about half of the lessons by the time of the post-intervention assessment (Hollingsworth & Gains, 2009, section VI).

In addition to the EGRA data collected at the beginning and end of the evaluation period, the SMRS methodology included two other levels of assessment. Teachers and supervising facilitators used Teacher Performance Checklists after every 10th lesson to assess whether the program had been implemented correctly. Further, teachers and facilitators gave Mastery Tests to students after every 20th lesson to assess whether they had mastered the materials taught thus far (Hollingsworth & Gains, 2009, p. 4).

Mali

In 2007, a Malian NGO, l'Institut pour l'Education Populaire (IEP, Institute for Popular Education), worked with Dr. Hollingsworth and Plan International to develop a reading intervention based on SMRS in the Bamanankan language. IEP named the instructional approach "Ciwaras READ" and piloted it in 22 villages. Beginning in 2008, the William and Flora Hewlett Foundation awarded IEP a grant to expand its program that encompassed Ciwaras READ—titled Read-Learn-Lead (RLL)—to 20 districts and three additional Malian languages (Bomu, Fulfulde, and Songhoy), in a total of 210 schools. Concomitant with this expansion grant, the Hewlett Foundation awarded RTI a grant to undertake an impact evaluation of the reading intervention.

At the time the impact evaluation began, EGRA had recently been introduced to Mali under the auspices of the Programme Harmonisé d'Appui au Renforcement de l'Education (PHARE), a USAID-funded project.[8] Under the Hewlett Foundation grant, RTI adapted EGRA to be used in the four target languages included in IEP's RLL program. The core competencies

---

[8] Under PHARE (in English, Unified Program for Strengthening Support to Education), the EGRA instrument was adapted for Mali in French for three grades (2, 4, and 6) and in Arabic for two grades (2 and 4). More information about these instruments and results can be found in the project baseline report: Centre National de l'Education (CNE), PHARE, and RTI International (2009).

targeted in the EGRA instrument were closely aligned with the ministry's new *Référentiel de compétences en lecture-ecriture* (Ministère de l'Education, de l'Alphabetisation et des Langues Nationales, 2009), or learning standards in reading and writing—as well as with the skills targeted by the RLL intervention. We used EGRA for the baseline measurements in April/May 2009 (the end of the Malian school year) and for midterm measurements in April/May 2010, and we will use it for endline measurements in 2012.

Students were asked to complete the following eight subtasks (described in Chapter 1):

1. Concepts about print

2. Phonemic awareness: identification of onset sounds

3. Listening comprehension

4. Letter identification: sounds[9]

5. Nonword reading

6. Familiar word reading

7. Oral reading fluency

8. Reading comprehension

We selected these components because they cover the range of reading skills among students in grades 1–3: from children who have only prereading skills (as tested through concepts of print, phonemic awareness, and listening comprehension), to emergent readers (who may have some sight words and a beginning ability to decode, but are not yet fluent), to fluent readers. Piloting of the instrument illustrated that we needed to be able to target this full range, even in grade 3. The results for grade 1 students showed large floor effects on the higher-level skills, such as oral reading fluency, but even many grade 3 students were still nonreaders or only emergent readers.

Local partners, including ministry and university researchers, were involved throughout the process of EGRA development, training, and data collection. A consulting linguistics and reading specialist worked with local linguists to adapt the EGRA instrument into the four target languages (Bamanankan, Bomu, Fulfulde, and Songhoy), including the three parallel versions of each language test to be used for baseline, midterm, and endline testing. Researchers

---

9   In Mali, in all four target languages, the subtask included graphemes as well as individual letters. For simplicity, in this chapter we refer only to letter sounds.

who had been involved with the French-language EGRA instrument development and piloting (under PHARE) received training in the new instruments and piloted them in the respective language regions, including piloting the three parallel versions.

To ensure a sufficient sample size for the impact evaluation design for Mali, we identified 100 eligible schools[10] and randomly assigned them into treatment and control groups (IEP identified 110 additional schools to participate in order to reach their program goal of 210 schools). The 100 schools in the evaluation sample included 50 Bamanankan-language schools (25 treatment and 25 control schools) and 50 "other language" schools[11] (25 treatment and 25 control schools).

Because it quickly became apparent that the data available through the ministry were not sufficiently reliable to be sure of the eligibility characteristics of schools, IEP worked with us to seek out the advice of local district officials or, in some cases, to travel to schools to make sure they did indeed exist and met the eligibility criteria. Where they did not, the identified schools were replaced with ones that did exist and met the criteria. Only after the list of 100 eligible schools was established and verified were they randomly assigned into the treatment and control groups. This turned what is a rather short process in many impact evaluations into a major and time-consuming problem, somewhat reflective of the overall administrative challenges that bedevil Malian education.

Another complication was that, as is shown by the EGRA studies that have focused on language of instruction (see Chapter 5), the notion that a school has *a* language of instruction (or even a given set of languages) is a great oversimplification. Much more complex language usage is actually more common; schools in many developing countries frequently have only an approximate "language of instruction." The schools in question are often only very loosely coupled with national policy—in other words, schools may not follow certain policies in the way the central government mandates, and the central level has insufficient capacity to either observe that fact or to enforce its

---

[10] Eligibility requirements included instruction in the early grades in one of the target Malian languages, location in one of the targeted regions, and reasonable accessibility. Schools in Mali fall into three main categories: those that begin instruction with French only, those that begin in the local language, and *medersa* schools (madrasahs), which instruct in Arabic. The RLL program works only in schools that begin in the local language.

[11] Because each of the other three Malian languages is a minority language, we could not examine them individually, because the sample sizes would have been too small. As a result, we combined them into a single category.

will. Thus, teachers in multilingual societies use a variety of languages in ways that policy has a very hard time predicting or enforcing.

Within each of the 50 treatment and 50 control schools, we randomly selected students from grades 1–3 (17 per grade, for a total of 1,700 students tested per grade) to be assessed at the end of the school year, before the beginning of the program. Because of the difficulty of tracking individual students in the Malian context, where school data are fairly unreliable and many students are highly transient, assessments at the end of the first and final years of the program (2010 and 2012) will involve new randomized student selection in the same schools.

The evaluation is therefore tracking changes in achievement at the school or group level. Effectively, it is assessing teachers' changing ability to impart instruction, using the children's learning as a gauge of that ability, rather than tracking individual students. The fundamental hypothesis of this approach is that, if the intervention is successful, the average reading competency of students in treatment schools will increase to a greater degree than that of students in control schools, with both statistical and substantive significance.

Therefore, we are using the EGRA instrument to measure changes in reading skills to assess the overall impact of the intervention program on reading competence in Mali. The Ciwaras READ approach, which is at the center of the RLL program, is based on SMRS; the program includes teacher training, provision of reading and teaching materials, and monitoring and feedback. The program also has components targeting community involvement and leadership activities for older students, although these aspects are not specifically examined in RTI's evaluation. EGRA companion instruments, such as teacher and school director questionnaires and classroom observations, will allow us to describe various program components and possibly posit hypotheses as to the variable contributions these components make to the intervention's impact.

However, the evaluation will be able to test rigorously only whether the overall *package* has had an impact. The components of the package are not randomly varied so as to allow for independent identification of the effect of each component—nor would the sample size be large enough to do so. In the context of developed-country studies, which often test the effect of very specific components, this may seem odd. However, in developing countries there is an extreme dearth of proof that any systematic approach can improve quality fairly quickly. Thus, conventional wisdom holds that improving learning outcomes is an extraordinarily difficult and time-consuming process. The research in Mali aims to test that implicit hypothesis and to see whether any reasonable *package* of interventions can improve learning outcomes fairly quickly. (The "Overall Impact" section near the end of this chapter further explains this concept, including drawing on the 2008–2010 reading intervention in Liberia as an example.)

Results

South Africa

The baseline assessment indicated very low reading skills, which was expected given that initial measurements were taken at the start of grade 1. The average child identified fewer than 2 letters per minute (mean=1.8, standard deviation=4.3), and the mean score for familiar word reading was 0.2 (standard deviation=0.8). Only two learners attempted to read the presented passage, and one of these identified no words correctly (Piper, 2009). In both treatment and control schools, reading skills were equal before the intervention. Comparisons of age, sex, and kindergarten enrollment between learners in treatment and control schools revealed no sources of bias that would overestimate the effects of the SMRS intervention (Piper, 2009).

Post-intervention, learners in control and treatment schools differed significantly on all four EGRA subtasks (Table 3.1). The average gains in treatment schools were greater than those in control schools for letter identification, familiar word reading, oral reading fluency, and reading comprehension. Effect sizes were large, ranging from 0.6 to 0.8 standard deviations for different test components, indicating that learners in treatment schools made substantial gains compared to students in control schools.

Further statistical analysis confirmed the reliability of the sections of the South African EGRA tool, as simple bivariate Pearson correlation statistics showed high levels of correlation between the scores on the various subtasks (each significant at the $p < 0.001$ level). For a discussion of the statistical analysis, see Piper (2009, section VI).

The EGRA impact assessment data also allowed us to analyze the number of learners unable to finish each task and to identify the magnitude of gains for the least skilled learners. Table 3.2 shows that, before the intervention, 68.5 percent of control group students and 63.8 percent of students in the treatment schools were unable to complete the letter identification subtask. Similarly, 84.5 percent of students in control schools and 66.9 percent of those in the treatment group discontinued the familiar word reading subtask. Effectively all learners left the oral reading fluency and reading comprehension subtasks incomplete. After the SMRS program, however, far fewer learners in treatment schools discontinued the first three subtasks than did learners in the control schools.

Table 3.1 Average gains on EGRA sections, for control and treatment groups, South Africa

| | Average gains | | | | |
Subtask	Control	Treatment	T	p	Effect size
Letter identification (correct letters/minute)	8.8 (1.0)	22.9 (1.0)	−8.96	<0.001	0.8
Familiar word reading (correct words/minute)	2.5 (0.3)	7.1 (0.4)	-6.69	<0.001	0.6
Oral reading fluency (correct words/minute)	3.9 (0.5)	11.2 (0.8)	-6.16	<0.001	0.6
Reading comprehension (% correct)	0.0 (0.0)	0.1 (0.0)	-4.77	<0.001	0.6

Notes: Standard errors are in parentheses. Average gains are average score on post-assessment less average score on baseline. Effect size is difference in gains between treatment and control groups, divided by pooled standard deviations of the treatment group gain and control group gain.

Source: Piper, 2009, Tables 8–10.

Table 3.2 Number (and percentage) of children who discontinued an EGRA subtask, for control and treatment groups, South Africa

Subtask	Measurement timepoint	Control	Treatment
Letter identification	Baseline	137 (68.5%)	287 (63.8%)
	Post-intervention	38 (23.3%)	16 (4.2%)
Familiar word reading	Baseline	169 (84.5%)	301 (66.9%)
	Post-intervention	68 (41.7%)	88 (23.0%)
Oral reading fluency	Baseline	200 (100.0%)	449 (99.8%)
	Post-intervention	81 (49.7%)	108 (28.2%)
Reading comprehension	Baseline	200 (100.0%)	450 (100%)
	Post-intervention	163 (100.0%)	367 (95.8%)

Note: At baseline the number of learners in the control group was 200, with 450 in the treatment group. Post-intervention, 163 learners were assessed from the control group and 383 from the treatment group.

Source: Piper, 2009, Table 7.

For example, following the intervention, 4 percent of learners in the treatment schools and 23 percent of those in control schools discontinued the letter identification subtask. The 19 percentage point difference in completion of the letter identification subtask between control and treatment schools represents learners who would have made little progress on this preliteracy skill without the SMRS intervention. The EGRA impact assessment was thus able not only to measure overall improvement, but also to identify gains for a highly vulnerable group of learners who would have made few improvements toward reading under standard South African instructional techniques.

These results provide encouraging evidence that the SMRS intervention contributed to improving early reading skills for grade 1 learners. The SMRS pilot was short, very intensive, and only partially completed before the endline EGRA. It could therefore not be expected to bring the early learners in treatment schools all the way to a level of proficiency needed for reading fluency with comprehension. However, in at least one of the provinces in which the program was implemented, teachers in treatment schools demonstrated their appreciation of SMRS techniques by continuing to use it after the end of the pilot. In February 2010, although the DOE had not provided further resources to treatment schools, site visits in Limpopo showed teachers still implementing SMRS. Notable student improvements in reading appear to have motivated teachers and principals to extend the program, while the DOE deliberated over how the pilot evaluation would affect national programs and resource allocations.

Mali

As of April 2011, the EGRA baseline and midterm data for the Mali evaluation had been collected and analyzed. Results from the baseline indicated that the treatment and control groups were well matched on their reading performance and generally across environmental variables. We observed some very limited performance differences in phonemic awareness and identification of letters, to the advantage of the control group before the intervention. The number and magnitude of such differences, across all possible pairs of performance differences, however, were close to those expected in a random sample,[12] and the actual values were so low that we can conclude the treatment and control

---

[12] The only EGRA subtasks that showed any statistical differences at baseline were phonemic awareness and letter sound identification, and these differences appeared only in Bamanankan schools in first grade. These differences favored the control schools and were small in magnitude. For example, Bamanankan first graders in treatment schools correctly identified less than one initial sound on average in the phonemic awareness section, while Bamanankan first-graders in control schools correctly identified just over one initial sound on average.

sample school populations were sufficiently matched. Because of the sensitivity of the EGRA instrument, we were able to use multiple competencies (subtasks) to assess equivalence at the baseline.

Overall, the EGRA baseline results showed very low scores in reading for students in each of the three grades tested. For example, at the end of grade 1, between 50 percent (in Bamanankan schools) and 70 percent (in other languages) of students were not able to identify a single letter sound from their alphabet. Similarly, between 50 percent (Bamanankan) and 60 percent (other languages) of students at the end of grade 3 were not able to read a single word on a list of frequently used words in their language. We reiterate that each of the skills addressed in the EGRA instrument is fundamental to reading and necessary for students to acquire sufficient mastery of reading to be able to "read to learn." The students tested at baseline did not have the basic building blocks of reading and were nowhere close to being able to read to learn, even in grade 3 (Friedman et al., 2010).

The EGRA outcomes from the midterm evaluation of a limited sample of schools[13] showed that scores on every subtask outcome in both grades were higher in treatment schools. Detailed analysis indicated that this difference was robust, consistent across genders, and statistically significant. In grade 1, the estimate of the treatment effect overall was 0.81 standard deviations, which is quite a large effect. In grade 2, the treatment effects were more modest with an overall impact of 0.27. Still, an improvement of one fifth of a standard deviation is often used as a benchmark of success in an education intervention, so this is still an important magnitude.

Table 3.3 shows the outcomes at baseline and midterm for the primary subtasks for grades 1 and 2. While the scores at both baseline and midterm were low by international standards, treatment schools were able to make significantly greater gains than control schools. On some subtasks, in fact, control schools saw a decline in basic competencies (such as familiar word and nonword reading in grade 1, and oral reading fluency in both grades 1 and 2), while treatment schools progressed. At midterm, grade 1 students in treatment schools were able to identify an average of 9.6 letter sounds per minute, while the average in control schools was 4.8 words per minute, just slightly above where they had been at baseline. For a discussion of the statistical analysis, see Friedman et al. (2010).

---

[13] For the midterm evaluation, 80 schools (40 treatment and 40 control) were sampled from among the 100 schools included in the baseline evaluation. The evaluation team made the decision to limit the midterm sample for budgetary reasons.

Table 3.3 Grade 1 and 2 midterm outcomes, by control and treatment groups, Mali

Subtask	Grade	Control			Treatment			Treatment effect
		Baseline	Follow-up	Gain	Baseline	Follow-up	Gain	
Phonemic awareness: identification of onset sounds (% correct)	1	1.3 (2.6)	1.8 (3.2)	0.5	1.2 (2.5)	2.6 (3.5)	1.4	0.26*** [0.09]
	2	2.7 (3.5)	4.2 (4.1)	1.5	2.9 (3.6)	4.9 (4.0)	2.0	0.21* [0.12]
Letter identification: sounds (correct sounds per minute)	1	4.3 (7.5)	4.8 (7.5)	0.5	2.9 (6.3)	9.6 (11.1)	6.6	0.65*** [0.13]
	2	10.6 (12.7)	12.8 (13.5)	2.2	9.9 (12.1)	18.4 (16.6)	8.4	0.30* [0.17]
Familiar word reading (correct words per minute)	1	0.3 (1.5)	0.2 (1.1)	-0.1	0.2 (1.6)	1.5 (3.1)	1.2	1.25*** [0.21]
	2	1.9 (5.0)	2.2 (5.5)	0.3	1.8 (4.9)	4.7 (7.2)	2.9	0.33*** [0.14]
Nonword reading (correct words per minute)	1	0.2 (0.8)	0.1 (0.7)	-0.1	0.3 (2.1)	0.6 (1.9)	0.3	0.78*** [0.14]
	2	1.2 (3.5)	1.4 (4.2)	0.2	1.5 (5.0)	2.7 (5.3)	1.2	0.21* [0.12]
Oral reading fluency (correct words per minute)	1	0.4 (3.6)	0.1 (0.9)	-0.3	0.3 (2.3)	0.8 (4.0)	0.5	0.92*** [0.25]
	2	1.9 (7.2)	1.8 (6.7)	-0.1	2.0 (7.5)	3.2 (7.4)	1.2	0.12 [0.09]

* = $p < .1$; *** = $p < .01$.

Notes: The midterm evaluation sample included 80 of the 100 schools from the baseline evaluation. Standard deviations of mean outcomes are presented in parentheses. Standard errors of treatment effects are presented in square brackets. All estimates of the treatment effect were generated from regressions including controls for age and sex of pupils, class size at baseline, baseline test scores within group in school, language-group fixed effects, age and experience of teachers, the month of the EGRA administration, and whether it was administered in the morning or afternoon.

In sum, the EGRA baseline results for the Mali case demonstrated that the random sampling methodology used was successful in creating treatment and control groups that were effectively equivalent at baseline. The midterm EGRA results showed that students in the treatment schools had made significantly greater gains in reading performance than their counterparts in control schools. The final (endline) evaluation of the full sample of schools will be carried out in 2012 to determine whether these preliminary gains persist and/ or increase.

Discussion—EGRA for Impact Evaluation

The impact evaluations in South Africa and Mali demonstrate EGRA's potential to assess changes in student achievement after reading interventions. These experiences underscore several issues that are important to consider when using EGRA for impact evaluation.

Impact Evaluation as Distinct from Other Uses of EGRA

Although similar EGRA instruments may be used for impact assessment and for other aims (such as national testing or classroom diagnostics), impact assessment demands distinct methodological considerations and particular caution in the interpretation of results. For example, during the development and piloting of instruments, parallel (and statistically equated) versions must be developed to ensure that baseline and endline tests are equivalent. Also, impact evaluations require careful attention to sampling methodologies to ensure that comparisons between control and treatment groups and between pre- and post-intervention assessments are reliable. Other EGRA uses—for example, taking a national snapshot that compares socioeconomic subgroups and regions—also apply sophisticated sampling frameworks. To be confident that changes in reading skills can be attributed to an intervention, however, evaluators using EGRA must also ensure that the sampling for the endline data collection precisely matches the sampling used for the baseline.

Proper randomization can be a challenge for all impact evaluations, but can be particularly complex in a developing-country context. Randomization into equivalent comparison groups depends on maximizing the completeness of information. The implementers of an impact evaluation need a list of all the schools (or children, or teachers who make up the population of interest) to assign them randomly into treatment and control groups. With near-complete information, in fact, random selection will capture most of the representative characteristics of the target population and the sample can be stratified and/or clustered to ensure that particularly important features are equally represented across treatment and control groups (and to reduce data collection costs).

However, reliable information is not always readily available. This was the case in Mali, where the research design called for identifying a pool of schools that fit certain eligibility criteria (such as language of instruction and accessibility) and then randomly assigning those schools into treatment and control groups. The ministry did not have a data set that would enable the researchers to be sufficiently confident in the representativeness of such a pool—in other words, we did not have information that was adequate and valid for randomized selection. In this situation, we needed to take compensatory (and very expensive) steps to overcome the gaps in data, such as undertaking fieldwork to collect such information and identifying alternative data sources.

When EGRA is used as a snapshot or in national approaches (see Chapters 1 and 2), results may point to elements of fundamental reading skills that are not addressed in the current education system; alternatively, they may point simply and dramatically to extremely low levels of reading overall. Responding to EGRA findings, policy makers and educators can revise policy, curricula, and/or lesson plans to strengthen identified weaknesses. They can sometimes get to the core of the problem by claiming curricular or scheduling space for teaching reading and providing appropriate reading materials.

In contrast, when EGRA is used for impact evaluation, the focus is typically on determining whether a specific program or intervention improves performance in a particular context. Although the links between specific techniques and outcomes may seem apparent and likely, they cannot be established without a more complex research design than those described for South Africa and Mali. For example, a notable improvement in comprehension skills in South African treatment schools cannot be assumed to be a result of the progressively leveled stories developed for the SMRS intervention because we made no effort in the evaluation design to measure this *specific* effect.

Overall impacts should still alert policy makers and educators to areas for improvement, but to isolate the impacts of components of an intervention, evaluators must specifically structure the research design for this purpose. They must then randomize each component of the approach—an expensive proposition. Unless an impact evaluation's research design is structured to isolate and test different parts of an intervention, any changes in outcome between the baseline and endline assessments are attributable to the intervention as a whole (assuming, of course, that control and treatment groups were also subject to the same exogenous changes). For an example of a research design that isolated particular techniques, see the "Overall Impact" section below.

Such information on the whole intervention's impact is needed, however, in contexts where improving learning outcomes is perceived as a challenging, long-term objective. Identifying interventions that can show significant improvements in a short period can thus provide valuable input to policy makers, even without more complex analyses of individual intervention components.

This aspect of impact evaluation can be misunderstood in any context, but it may risk increased confusion where such research is relatively new. In addition, it demands close collaboration between evaluators and the intervention/ program implementers, where the latter are willing to follow the research design required for rigorous evaluation. This may be difficult for implementers who do not fully accept these research demands and who are reluctant to allow schools to be randomly selected into treatment or control groups, or even to have control groups at all, which would deny elements of the intervention at particular sites in order to test their effect. In such situations, the impact evaluation involves not only a strong research design and skillful conduct of the research, but also a carefully balanced relationship between the evaluators and the implementers.

EGRA Compared with Other Impact-Evaluation Tools

Language and Cultural Adaptations

In contrast to impact evaluation that measures outcomes with existing assessments, such as annual pre- and post-assessment tests in each grade, any new EGRA instrument will require a rather extensive adaptation process to ensure that the instrument is sufficiently aligned with the local context to ensure instrument reliability and validity.

One dimension of adaptation is ensuring appropriate conversions of evaluation tools to, in some cases, several mother tongues; another is adequate piloting of adapted instruments. In the case of EGRA, this effort can be reduced if the assessment tools have already been adapted to the local context for purposes other than impact evaluation. In the South African case, for example, the DOE had already taken the initiative to develop locally appropriate versions of EGRA in six mother tongues, which saved evaluators the effort of further adaptation and piloting. For countries where an EGRA has not been implemented previously, evaluators may be able to start with one of the existing EGRA instruments, which can be downloaded in numerous languages[14]—but the instrument will still need to be adapted to the local context.

---

[14] See the USAID EdData II project website, https://www.eddataglobal.org/. EGRA has been tested in numerous developing countries, where it has been crafted to include the core reading competencies, and guides and tools have been prepared. Prior studies can also provide models for researchers wishing to implement similar designs in other countries.

Compared with many written reading tests that require only translation and distribution to selected schools for use as impact-evaluation instruments, EGRA requires a more thorough process. Adaptation may be as simple as ensuring that word lists and passages are appropriate to the local context, if an EGRA instrument already exists in the appropriate language. "Simple" in this sense, however, is a relative concept. Many mother tongues lack preexisting lists of common words usable for instruction and assessment, and these must be compiled.

Adapting EGRA into new languages, however, involves linguistic analysis for each target language. In any case, adaptation, piloting, and finalization are necessary steps in the process of preparing the assessment. For example, crafting appropriate passages for the oral reading fluency assessment in several languages can be a laborious process requiring considerable tact as, often, even trained educators may produce passages that are mere recitations of unconnected descriptive facts without a narrative or instructional structure of any kind, or are written at levels of difficulty not suitable for the students to be tested.

Training Requirements

The training for using EGRA in impact evaluation is a rigorous process. Because we analyze results to detect even small differences in performance between groups, testing all students in exactly the same way is essential. Thus, we have to train assessors to be systematic and consistent in test administration.

We also need to take steps to ensure that administration and scoring do not vary too much among assessors; we meet this requirement by measuring interrater reliability (IRR) in several different ways. Some of the approaches that we use during training to ensure a high level of reliability across assessors include intensive review of administration procedures; simulation with critique; a significant amount of guided practice, including practice in local schools; and testing of assessors specifically to determine IRR.

Although numerous methods exist for measuring IRR, they generally involve having all trainees administer the assessment to the same "student" (a trainer often plays this role) who makes prearranged errors, to determine whether the assessors score that student's performance correctly. To be retained for data collection, assessors must pass the IRR test (for example, correctly scoring at least 90 percent of the "student's" assessment).

Resources

Implementing EGRA is also more resource-intensive than administering a pencil-and-paper test. Pencil-and-paper tests can be given simultaneously to a group of students by a single teacher or assessor. Compared with written assessments, EGRA requires more time and/or personnel to assess an equal number of learners.

Richness of Data

The additional training and implementation requirements of EGRA, relative to other assessment tools, pay dividends in the depth of data on early reading skills, as well as the capacity to detect subtle changes or distinctions. Paper-and-pencil tests will capture important skills in later grades that are not assessed with EGRA. For example, PIRLS measures different aspects of reading comprehension (Wagner, 2010). PIRLS cannot, however, assess the fundamental reading skills that are targeted for development in early grades and that build the basis for more advanced reading and learning. As demonstrated by the Mali and South Africa evaluations, EGRA can identify changes in specific elements of early grade reading skills that are not captured in written tests (such as fluency, letter sounds, etc.). This is a particular advantage in the quest to identify interventions that can successfully build these foundational skills and do so before many students drop out of the school system.

Further, EGRA can also distinguish impacts between more subgroups of learners than written texts can. Pencil-and-paper tests effectively lump nonreaders and emergent readers together, as both types of learner will have similarly low scores on such assessments. In contrast, the breakdown of reading elements in EGRA can capture small changes in progress toward literacy, even if fluency is not yet reached. In the SMRS evaluation in South Africa, the post-intervention data showed considerable impact on learners who were nonreaders at baseline but achieved some ability to read, decode, or identify letters by the end of the pilot program (Piper, 2009). EGRA's ability to track progress in these groups of non- or near-readers is critical for identifying interventions that can reach this segment of learners; EGRA thus offers a clear advantage over using written tests for impact evaluation of early reading programs.

This breakdown of subgroups also allows for greater confidence in the comparability of control and treatment groups. The small differences in skill sets between non-, near-, and more fluent readers should be clear at EGRA baselines. For example, the Mali baseline data indicated that, in both the control and treatment groups, approximately 78 percent of grade 2 Bamanankan students were nonreaders. Such a figure demonstrated that, in both groups, a large majority of students could not read even a single word. It did not, however, show what they *could* do. Further, the letter sound identification subtask allowed us to compare these same groups at an even more fundamental level: We found no significant differences between control and treatment schools at baseline, with about 25 percent of students unable to identify any letters or sounds. Thus, EGRA allowed us to undertake a more fine-grained analysis at baseline as well as at post-intervention.

A *Reading* Assessment

The richness of data on elements of reading and the distinctions among various learners underscore that EGRA is a *reading* assessment. As an impact evaluation tool, it is therefore appropriate for measuring the effects of interventions that target fundamental reading skills. Because of this clear focus, however, EGRA is not a good choice of instrument for assessing interventions aimed at other language skills (such as grammar) or particular subjects. If an evaluation's objective is to assess an intervention's effect on curricular goals, other assessment instruments will be more appropriate. EGRA may, however, be used in combination with other outcome measures designed for these purposes, if an intervention targets a combination of educational outcomes.

Overall Impact

In this section we elaborate on an important point alluded to several times in this chapter: EGRA, like other evaluation tools, measures the *overall* impact of an intervention. General impact data cannot be assumed to link directly back to specific elements of an intervention unless the research design isolates each component, such as materials, training, or instructional approach.

This concern plagues many evaluators of instructional interventions. Compared with more clearly defined interventions in other fields (such as, for example, immunizations, or access to clean water), evaluation of instruction is generally less concrete and less discrete. Two important questions arise:

1. How can one ensure that all the teachers are really following the model?

2. Where does the "model" start and end? That is, if the instructional model actually includes materials, training, and support, as most good ones do, how can the implementers differentiate the instruction in the classroom itself from these other factors?

The answer to the first question is, "one cannot"—at least not without enormously increased budgets and time spent convincing counterparts of the benefits of obtaining more detailed information. Instead, additional data on inputs can be collected *during* the intervention, to observe and track the teachers and assess the degree to which they are following the model. This approach contrasts with use of the EGRA instrument alone to collect outcome data before and after the intervention. For example, the Mastery Checks and Teacher Performance Checklists used during the implementation of the SMRS intervention in South Africa were drawn upon to further probe the EGRA results in Mpumalanga province (Hollingsworth & Gains, 2009, section V). Observations made during an intervention can offer information as to (1) whether the intervention was implemented as intended and (2) what aspects of the implemented intervention might explain results. That is, such data on inputs can inform analysis and interpretation of the outcome data collected with the EGRA instrument.

Such an approach takes advantage of natural variation (and the intensity of that natural variation). Such information cannot be compared, however, in the same way as EGRA data from a random sample of students in control and treatment schools. For data on inputs collected during the intervention, the "selection" of schools into the various intensities of application of the models component is nonrandom and therefore may hide systematic predisposing differences between schools. But a randomized study design accounting for all variation would be immensely complex and costly; use of observations gathered during the intervention may be the only practical alternative, unless enormous budgets become available.

For the second question—regarding the boundaries of the model—only evaluation of the intervention as a whole is possible, unless elements of the interventions are differentiated across the population. In South Africa, the package was relatively discrete, because it examined a fully established, short-term, and very directed reading intervention. However, it still included materials and a defined level of training and support. So, evaluation cannot make strong claims about the in-class instruction in absence of materials or training and support (although it can make hypotheses about the effect of any of these). In Mali, the intervention program in progress through 2012 is much more complex than that in South Africa. In addition to materials and significant training, ongoing support, and internal monitoring, the Mali effort also involves components beyond training in reading instruction, which are intended to involve parents and community. Thus, similarly, the impact evaluation will allow us to make scientifically reliable statements about the "full package" and whether it affects student learning, but we will gather only somewhat indirect evidence as to which elements of this package might be most essential, presenting hypotheses about these at best.

To examine the impact of individual elements of an intervention, a more complicated design is necessary; any one component of the "package" needs to be purposely altered in order to examine its impact separately.[15] For example, in Liberia, an impact evaluation using EGRA isolated feedback to parents on their children's learning results from other aspects of the intervention to measure the impact of this component (see Chapter 4). The study compared the role of (1) implementing a full package of intervention, which in that case included providing schools and families with feedback on student performance, or (2) just providing the feedback itself without an intervention, versus (3) tracking the control group, which experienced no intervention or feedback whatsoever (Piper & Korda, 2009).

This research design allowed evaluators to isolate the accountability effect of the feedback on reading scores from the rest of the intervention and to draw conclusions about this intervention element. Note, however, that this capability was a result of the research design, rather than a change in the EGRA instrument itself (which continued to gather data on outcomes, not on the intervention per se). The cases discussed in this chapter, in South Africa and Mali, did not undertake such purposeful altering of internal intervention elements, but the potential is there to do this in future studies if the desired identification warrants the high cost. The design of such studies can be informed by the results of these initial ones.

Conclusion

This chapter has drawn on experiences in South Africa and Mali to demonstrate the use of EGRA in impact evaluation. To conclude, we point to considerations for using EGRA to assess effects of reading interventions. First, like all evaluations, the reliability with which EGRA can be used in this context depends on the rigor of the research design. Critical to this goal is that the sample be randomized and clustered from dependable population data and

---

[15] With a larger number of considered interventions and/or groups of interest, the sample sizes required also increase, as—inevitably—do costs.

that control and treatment groups not be significantly different at baseline data collection.

Second, evaluators must ensure that EGRA is an appropriate (valid) instrument for the intervention in question. EGRA is well suited to assess fundamental reading skills and therefore is appropriate to evaluate interventions designed to address these particular abilities, but it is less suitable for other types of interventions (e.g., those that teach grammar).

Third, researchers must allow sufficient time and resources for assessor training and EGRA implementation, which can be more intensive than for other evaluation instruments. Given that EGRA is administered orally, interrater reliability must be emphasized in training and tested before data collection.

Finally, like other evaluation instruments, EGRA measures only pre- and post-intervention outcomes; it does not capture characteristics of the intervention itself. Unless EGRA data are complemented by information from other instruments that track how an intervention was implemented, or the research design isolates particular intervention techniques, an evaluation using EGRA itself can assess only the impact of interventions as a whole. As we strive to identify specific instructional techniques and approaches that improve reading skills, evaluators should focus on clear and discrete interventions or consider research designs that discern the impacts of the individual components of more complex interventions. With these points in mind, EGRA can contribute reliable and valuable information to identify interventions that can help children learn to read—and read to learn.

References

Ahmed, A., & Arends-Kuenning, M. (2006). Do crowded classrooms crowd out learning? Evidence from the Food for Education Program in Bangladesh. *World Development, 34*(4), 665–684.

Banerjee, A. V. (2007). *Making aid work.* Cambridge, Massachusetts: MIT Press.

Burke, M. D., Hagan-Burke, S., Kwok, O., & Parker, R. (2009). Predictive validity of early literacy indicators from the middle of kindergarten to second grade. *The Journal of Special Education, 42*(4), 209–226. doi:10.1177/0022466907313347

Centre National de l'Education (CNE [National Education Center]), Programme Harmonisé d'Appui au Renforcement de l'Education (PHARE [Unified Program for Strengthening Support to Education]), and RTI International. (2009). *Evaluation initiale des compétences fondamentales en lecture écriture basée sur l'utilisation de l'outil 'EGRA' adapté et complété en français et en arabe au Mali* [Preliminary evaluation of early grade reading skills using EGRA adapted into French and Arabic in Mali]. Bamako, Mali: Ministère de l'Education, de l'Alphabetisation et des Langues Nationales (MEALN) [Ministry of Education, Literacy, and National Languages].

Connor, C. M. D., Morrison, F. J., & Slominski, L. (2006). Preschool instruction and children's emergent literacy growth. *Journal of Educational Psychology, 98*(4), 665–689.

Duflo, E., & Kremer, M. (2003, July). *Use of randomization in the evaluation of development effectiveness.* Presented at the World Bank Operations Evaluation Department (OED) Conference on Evaluation and Development Effectiveness, Washington, DC. Retrieved September 3, 2010, from http://people.bu.edu/jgerring/Conference/MethodsGovernance/documents/DufloKremerprogrameval.pdf

Friedman, S., Gerard, F., & Ralaingita, W. (2010). *International independent evaluation of the effectiveness of Institut pour l'Education Populaire's "Read-Learn-Lead" (RLL) program in Mali: Mid-term report.* Prepared for the William and Flora Hewlett Foundation under Grant No. 2008-3229. Research Triangle Park, North Carolina: RTI International.

Good, R. H., Simmons, D. C., & Kame'enui, E. J. (2001). The importance and decision-making utility of a continuum of fluency-based indicators of foundational reading skills for third-grade high-stakes outcomes. *Scientific Studies of Reading, 5*(3), 257–288. doi:10.1207/S1532799XSSR0503_4

Greaney, V., & Kellaghan, T. (2008). *Assessing national achievement levels in education.* Vol. 1 of V. Greaney & T. Kellaghan (Series Eds.), National Assessments of Educational Achievement. Washington, DC: International Bank for Reconstruction and Development/The World Bank. Retrieved April 22, 2011, from http://siteresources.worldbank.org/EDUCATION/Resources/278200-1099079877269/547664-1099079993288/assessing_national_achievement_level_Edu.pdf

Hartry, A., Fitzgerald, R., & Porter, K. (2008). Implementing a structured reading program in an afterschool setting: Problems and potential solutions. *Harvard Educational Review, 78*(1), 181–210.

Hollingsworth, S., & Gains, P. (2009). *Integrated Education Program: The Systematic Method for Reading Success (SMRS) in South Africa: A literacy intervention between EGRA pre- and post-assessments.* Prepared for USAID/Southern Africa under Contract No. 674-C-00-04-00032-00. Research Triangle Park, North Carolina: RTI International.

International Association for the Evaluation of Educational Achievement (IEA). (2010). *Progress in International Reading Literacy Study 2011 (PIRLS 2011).* Retrieved April 19, 2011, from http://www.iea.nl/pirls2011.html

Kremer, M. (2006). Expanding educational opportunity on a budget: Lessons from randomized evaluations. In H. Braun, A. Kanjee, E. Bettinger, & M. Kremer (Eds.), *Improving education through assessment, innovation, and evaluation* (pp. 73–97). Cambridge, Massachusetts: American Academy of Arts and Sciences.

Maredia, M. K. (2009). Improving the proof: *Evolution of and emerging trends in impact assessment methods and approaches in agricultural development.* Washington, DC: International Food Policy Research Institute. Retrieved April 22, 2011, from http://www.ifpri.org/publication/improving-proof

Mitton, G. (2008). *Success in early reading. Pilot project in Mali and Niger—Implementation report* (GAD ML10080 and NER064). Washington, DC: Plan International. Retrieved September 24, 2010, from https://www.eddataglobal.org/documents/index.cfm?fuseaction=pubDetail&ID=173

Ministère de l'Éducation, de l'Alphabétisation et des Langues Nationales (MEALN) [Ministry of Education, Literacy, and National Languages], Mali. (2009). *Référentiel de compétences en lecture-ecriture.* Bamako, Mali: MEALN.

Piper, B. (2009). *Integrated Education Program: Impact study of SMRS using Early Grade Reading Assessment in three provinces in South Africa.* Prepared for USAID/Southern Africa under Contract No. 674-C-00-04-00032-00. Research Triangle Park, North Carolina: RTI International.

Piper, B., & Korda, M. (2009). *EGRA Plus: Liberia data analytic report baseline assessment.* Prepared for USAID under the EdData II project, Task Order 6, Contract No. EHC-E-06-04-00004-00. Research Triangle Park, North Carolina: RTI International. Retrieved September 17, 2010, from https://www.eddataglobal.org/documents/index.cfm?fuseaction=pubDetail&ID=200

Ravallion, M. (2009). Should the randomistas rule? *The Economists' Voice, 6*(2), Article 6. Berkeley, California: The Berkeley Electronic Press. Retrieved April 27, 2011, from http://www.bepress.com/ev/vol6/iss2/art6

Rodríguez, C., Sánchez, F., & Armenta, A. (2010). Do interventions at school level improve educational outcomes? Evidence from a rural program in Colombia. *World Development, 38*(3), 415–428. doi:10.1016/j.worlddev.2009.10.002

Roehrig, A. D., Petscher, Y., Nettles, S. M., Hudson, R. F., & Torgesen, J. K. (2008). Accuracy of the DIBELS oral reading fluency measure for predicting third grade reading comprehension outcomes. *Journal of School Psychology, 46*(3), 343–366. doi:10.1016/j.jsp.2007.06.006

RTI International. (2009a). *Early Grade Reading Assessment toolkit.* Prepared for the World Bank, Office of Human Development, Contract No. 7141961. Research Triangle Park, North Carolina: RTI International. Retrieved April 19, 2011, from https://www.eddataglobal.org/documents/index.cfm?fuseaction=pubDetail&ID=149

RTI International. (2009b). *Manual para la evaluación inicial de la lectura en niños de educación primaria* [Early Grade Reading Assessment toolkit, Spanish adaptation]. Adaptation by J. E. Jimenez. Prepared for USAID under the EdData II project, Task Order 3, Contract No. EHC-E-01-03-00004-00. Research Triangle Park, North Carolina: RTI International. Retrieved April 19, 2011, from https://www.eddataglobal.org/documents/index.cfm?fuseaction=pubDetail&ID=187

RTI International. (2009c). *Manuel pour l'evaluation des competences fondamentales en lecture.* [Early Grade Reading Assessment toolkit, French adaptation]. Adaptation by L. Sprenger-Charolles. Prepared for USAID under the EdData II project, Task Order 3, Contract No. EHC-E-01-03-00004-00. Research Triangle Park, North Carolina: RTI International. Retrieved April 19, 2009, from https://www.eddataglobal.org/documents/index.cfm?fuseaction=pubDetail&ID=175

Savedoff, W. D., Levine, R., & Birdsall, N. (2006). *When will we ever learn? Improving lives through impact evaluation.* Washington, DC: Center for Global Development.

Shapiro, J., & Trevino, J. (2004). *Compensatory education for disadvantaged Mexican students: An impact evaluation using propensity score matching.* Washington, DC: World Bank.

Shefelbine, J. L., Newman, K. K., Center, D. S., & Inc, S. (2001). SIPPS: *Systematic Instruction in Phoneme Awareness, Phonics, and Sight Words.* Oakland, California: Developmental Studies Center.

Shi, Y., & Tsang, M. C. (2008). Evaluation of adult literacy education in the United States: A review of methodological issues. *Educational Research Review, 3*(2), 187–217.

Slavin, R., Lake, C., Chambers, B., Cheung, A., & Davis, S. (2009). Effective reading programs for the elementary grades: A best-evidence synthesis. *Review of Educational Research, 79*(4), 1391–1466.

Wagner, D. A. (2003). Smaller, quicker, cheaper: Alternative strategies for literacy assessment in the UN Literacy Decade. I*nternational Journal of Educational Research, 39*(3), 293–309. doi:10.1016/j.ijer.2004.04.009

Wagner, D. A. (2010). *Smaller, quicker, cheaper—revisited. A review of learning indicators in developing countries, with a focus on reading assessments.* Draft report. Washington, DC: Fast Track Initiative Secretariat, World Bank.

Wang, C., & Algozzine, B. (2008). Effects of targeted intervention on early literacy skills of at-risk students. *Journal of Research in Childhood Education, 22*(4), 425–439.

CHAPTER 4

Teachers' Use of EGRA for Continuous Assessment: The Case of EGRA Plus: Liberia

Marcia Davidson, Medina Korda, and Ollie White Collins

My real commitment is to get them [children of Liberia] decent food, decent housing, decent education.... Our democracy simply cannot be advanced when the majority of our citizenry is functionally illiterate and lacks the knowledge and skills required to lead our national efforts and to compete in a global community.... If you ask a former child soldier—and there are thousands and thousands in our country—'What do you want?' the answer in every single case is 'I want to go to school.'
— Ellen Johnson Sirleaf, President of the Republic of Liberia (2009, pp. 291–292)

In this chapter, we address the importance and use of continuous assessment in the primary grades at the classroom level, using reading instruction as our curriculum example. Our context is the EGRA Plus: Liberia project, a randomized controlled trial that was conducted in 180 schools in grades 2 and 3 between 2008 and 2010.[1] We provide examples of continuous assessment and highlight links to student learning, accountability, and parent and community involvement.

Note that this chapter focuses on use of the early grade reading assessment (EGRA) as a classroom tool rather than on the design and outcomes of the randomized controlled trial. To provide sufficiently detailed explanations for readers interested in using EGRA for continuous assessment, who are the main audience for this chapter, we limit our discussion of the evaluation of EGRA Plus to a brief summary. Readers interested in the full details and results are referred to Piper and Korda (2009, 2011), supplemented by Piper (2011).

---

[1] RTI International led the project implementation, with assistance from Liberian Education Trust. EGRA Plus: Liberia was funded under the United States Agency for International Development's (USAID's) Education Data for Decision Making (EdData II) project.

The chapter is organized as follows. First, we give a brief overview of current research on continuous assessment in the primary grades. Next, we describe the EGRA Plus: Liberia project, including how continuous assessment was conducted and how the assessment data were used to inform instruction and to motivate improved student achievement. Finally, we consider some of the advantages and the challenges in implementing continuous assessment in EGRA Plus: Liberia.

Current Research on Continuous Assessment

We use the term *continuous assessment* with the understanding that it is synonymous with *formative assessment*, meaning assessments conducted by teachers in a classroom instructional context with the goal of monitoring learning and improving instruction. Below, we define the term in more detail and then review research that examines the relationships between continuous assessment and student learning.

Continuous Assessment and Curriculum-Based Measures

According to Scriven (1967; cited in Wiliam, 2006), being "formative" is a property that cannot simply be assigned to an assessment. There are different types of continuous assessments, but their critical distinguishing feature is that teachers can use the information obtained from the assessment to make instructional changes. That is, the only context in which one can describe an evaluation as formative is one in which the information generated from the assessment results in instructional changes that would not have occurred without the information from the assessment (Wiliam, 2006). Or, stated from the teachers' perspective: if teachers make the effort to administer continuous assessments, the time they spend administering and scoring them should yield information that will improve instruction, student learning, and student motivation.

In this chapter, we focus on a particular type of continuous assessment that is included in the class of measures referred to as *reading curriculum-based measures*, or "reading CBMs" (e.g., Deno, 1985; Deno et al., 2001; Deno et al., 1982; Fuchs & Deno, 1991; Fuchs & Fuchs, 1992, 1999). The specific CBM that has the strongest data linking the measure to student reading skill is oral reading fluency (defined as accuracy plus speed [Binder, 1996]; in other words, the ability to read effortlessly, accurately, and with appropriate expression that reflects understanding of the content). An oral reading fluency assessment requires a student to read a passage at a predetermined, standard level of difficulty for 1 minute. The score is the number of correct words read accurately in a minute.

Considerable research has been conducted with oral reading fluency measures (e.g., Fuchs & Fuchs, 1992; Hosp & Hosp, 2003; Marston, 1988). A number of studies have produced strong evidence that measures of oral reading fluency can be used as a proxy for reading proficiency in elementary-grade classrooms. Studies have repeatedly shown that performance on oral reading fluency measures is strongly related to reading comprehension skill (Deno, 1985; Fuchs et al., 2001; Jenkins & Jewell, 1993).

CBMs in reading have several advantageous characteristics. Perhaps most important, they have been described as curriculum neutral because they yield highly reliable and valid information related to predicting student performance on a variety of high-stakes tests regardless of the curriculum being implemented (Fuchs et al., 2001; Hosp & Fuchs, 2005). Thus, CBMs are well-suited for measuring progress toward more general goals, such as national standards for reading performance. The fact that they can be administered and scored very quickly means that teachers and administrators can obtain immediate feedback on student, classroom, and school performance without the long wait that occurs when high-stakes tests are remotely scored, often taking months for the results to arrive. Teachers can quickly respond to CBM scores by modifying instruction for those students who performed poorly on the measure, followed by frequent progress monitoring to determine if the instructional changes are working (Fuchs et al., 1989; Santi & Vaughn, 2007).

One key advantage of a CBM is that the content is always designed to reveal whether students have met a learning goal (usually defined as a correct-words-per-minute score and indexed as growth in skills over time), and not whether they have reached a certain instructional level (often referred to by grade level, or by percentage correct). This characteristic means that rather than being a mastery measure (a system for tracking whether students are incrementally mastering a hierarchy of objectives), it is a general outcome measure.

Another important feature of CBMs is efficiency and ease of administration and scoring. They are referred to as rate and accuracy measures because they are timed, and scores reflect correct responses provided within the time limit. The measures are quite simple to administer, scoring is straightforward, and an entire measure with five to six sections typically requires only about 15 minutes to administer to an individual student. No holistic scoring or rubrics are employed. Norms exist for students in the United States (Hasbrouck & Tindal, 2006), but have not been established in many other countries. In 2009, RTI

International introduced a toolkit (RTI International, 2009), based on various field experiences, to provide practical guidance for designing reading CBMs in countries that are beginning to develop assessment tools for awareness and policy dialogue. The *tool* in "toolkit" refers to the Early Grade Reading Assessment. The EGRA toolkit guides countries in the adaptation of the instrument, the fieldwork, and the analysis of the assessment results.

The EGRA Plus: Liberia project adapted two versions of EGRA specifically for Liberia, each for a different purpose. The first version of the instrument was used in *all* project classrooms (i.e., both control and treatment; see brief description of project design below) as the project evaluation tool. It was administered by trained assessors at baseline, at midterm, and at the end of the project. The second version was for continuous assessment. For this purpose, the project team modified the EGRA instrument for teachers to administer and use.

Continuous Assessment Standards and Accountability

While CBMs are quick, efficient, and valid screening measures to identify students who may be at risk for reading difficulties, they can also be used as a low-stakes accountability tool. For example, the data from CBMs are sometimes used to determine a school's adequate yearly progress requirements and can be used to monitor individual students' progress toward a school's or district's targeted improvement goal (Deno, 1985). In terms of general accountability and continuous assessment, Quenemoen et al. (2004) described the importance of aligning continuous assessment goals with national or local standards so that individual student progress is always linked to a national goal:

> Progress monitoring can exist outside of standards-based curriculum, instruction, and assessment, but it will be limited in its effectiveness. As the National Research Council (1999) suggests, alignment between tests and standards is a necessary condition of the theory of action of standards-based reform, and that includes alignment of assessments used for the purpose of monitoring progress. Any state or district that hopes to use progress monitoring as a tool to ensure the highest possible outcomes for every student needs to ensure that the educational system itself— including curriculum, instruction, formative and summative assessments, professional development and school improvement processes—is aligned, coherent, and focused on ensuring that every child is being taught and is learning the grade-level content. (Quenemoen et al., 2004, p. 4)

The importance of standards' alignment with continuous assessment is clear. If teachers are conducting assessments to determine whether children are making adequate progress in reading, they must have a goal against which they are evaluating student performance and judging whether the students' rate of growth is sufficient. Ideally, an accountability system includes transparent goals that educators, families, and community members know and understand.

In the case of EGRA Plus: Liberia, the goals were quite simple: students were to read a specified number of words correctly per minute for grades 2 and 3, and to answer a predetermined percentage of comprehension questions correctly. The treatment schools included these goals in every report card, and districts explained them through social marketing efforts such as radio shows and local reading competitions.

Project Context and Description

Liberia is often defined by the devastating 14-year civil conflict that ended in 2003. At the end of that conflict, most public schools had been destroyed and many teachers had left the country. To rebuild the public education infrastructure has been an enormous and daunting task, and some evidence suggests that student learning has not been progressing at an acceptable rate. The Ministry of Education requested assistance from the World Bank for a 2008 pilot study on reading levels and factors affecting them (see Crouch & Korda, 2008), and from USAID for implementing (1) a national study (2008–2010) that would provide baseline data on reading achievement in grades 2 and 3; (2) an intervention in reading at those grade levels; and (3) follow-up through coaching, continuous assessment, and midterm and final formal assessments.

As part of the design of the initial pilot study, RTI reviewed the proposed instrument and the individual subtasks with Liberian reading and education experts at an EGRA workshop in Monrovia in June 2008. Planning activities started in September 2008, and the assessment team administered the pilot instrument in a small sample of Liberian schools in November 2008; results and a reliability analysis are reported in Crouch & Korda (2008). The pilot instrument then served as the core for the student instruments in the EGRA Plus: Liberia intervention. With EGRA Plus, RTI and local subcontractor Liberian Education Trust field tested and then piloted all tasks in the measure. We established baseline data and applied local goals of 60 correct words per minute at the end of grade 3. During the instrument development, the project team used Stata data analysis software[2] to verify that the EGRA instrument developed for Liberia was reliable, based on an overall Cronbach's alpha (reliability coefficient) of at least 0.85 across the EGRA subtasks.

The objective of EGRA Plus: Liberia was to support the efforts of the Liberian Ministry of Education to improve the quality of primary education and the teaching of reading in Liberia. The project included 60 "full treatment" schools (teaching improvement, materials, community activity, and reporting-based accountability), 60 "light treatment" schools (reporting-based accountability and support), and 60 control schools. RTI randomly selected and assigned schools and matched groups of four schools with another nearby school that was randomly selected to be the cluster center. School-level work started in late January 2009.

As mentioned, social marketing efforts were an integral component of the EGRA Plus: Liberia project. These efforts included activities to increase community awareness of the importance of learning to read, and to show parents, teachers, and other community members how they could support their children's reading. In addition to organizing the aforementioned reading competitions and radio shows specifically for EGRA Plus, the project team also produced a video and presentation (separately funded activities that were not part of the EGRA Plus design). The EGRA Plus coordinator in Monrovia and the project director (a coauthor of this chapter) arranged for one of the reading competitions to be video-recorded to share with the ministry and other stakeholders. They also developed a slide presentation focusing on one of the local reading competition winners, and they created a video of a local teacher teaching a lesson from EGRA Plus for use during future trainings and to share with families, parent-teacher associations (PTAs), and other community stakeholders.

In June 2010, the final assessment indicated that full intervention schools made significant increases over control schools in all three EGRA subtasks employed in the continuous assessment activities[3]:

- letter identification (effect size [ES] = 0.63 standard deviations [SD]),

- oral reading fluency (ES = 0.73 SD), and

- reading comprehension (ES = 0.84 SD).

---

[2]   Stata is proprietary software of StataCorp LP; see http://www.stata.com.

[3]   See Chapter 1 for a discussion of the EGRA instrument and subtasks.

Light-treatment schools also made gains in comparison to control schools, but these gains were not large enough to argue that continuous assessment without an accompanying intervention can significantly improve student learning. In this chapter, we focus on the continuous assessment activities in the full-treatment classrooms, although the supplementary and classroom report card assessments also occurred in light-treatment classrooms.

The reading intervention implemented under EGRA Plus: Liberia focused on daily lessons (each 45 minutes long) in reading instruction, with the goal of teaching students to decode unfamiliar words and to build vocabulary, background knowledge, fluency, listening skills, and reading-comprehension skills. Each daily lesson included a standard explicit instructional routine and followed a fairly consistent format. In addition, the project included student and community literacy resources such as providing decodable books[4] to each child, improving existing libraries or creating new libraries, and encouraging parental and community involvement. The project required both informal continuous assessments and formal periodic assessments during implementation, and results from these assessments guided professional development activities and teaching at the classroom level in the full-treatment classrooms.

Next, we describe how teachers and "coaches" (master trainers) in EGRA Plus: Liberia employed continuous assessment in the classroom, and how accountability for student performance in reading was developed through classroom, school, local community, cluster, and district efforts. Then we describe additional types of continuous assessments intended to inform instruction during daily lessons.

Reading CBMs: Continuous Assessments in Treatment Classrooms

Although one of the key motivations for EGRA was to gauge national proficiency levels in developing countries (see Chapters 1 and 2), the door remained open to other, carefully controlled uses. The authors modified the intent of EGRA for the EGRA Plus: Liberia project, using reading CBMs to collect continuous assessment data that teachers and administrators could use to positively affect student achievement at the individual as well as the

---

4   Decodable books are books in which the majority of words are spelled with patterns (e.g., pat, mat, sat) that the children have learned so that they can easily decode the words. These are different from books such as leveled texts, which typically do not have controlled text or text that is directly linked to phonics skills being taught.

classroom level. This adjustment was based on the aforementioned and ample evidence for the validity of the use of reading CBMs to inform instruction and was used as one way to accurately indicate learning progress at the student, classroom, and school levels.

Six types of continuous assessment were employed in EGRA Plus classrooms. First, teachers in EGRA Plus schools administered reading CBMs to check individual student progress. Second, they calculated class averages and summarized both student and class progress in report cards that schools sent to parents in four out of the six usual reporting periods during the year. Third, in the least formal approach, scripted lessons incorporated procedures for teachers to check for student understanding during lesson instruction. Fourth, the coaches observed classrooms; and fifth, they occasionally conducted reading CBM assessments with randomly selected students in order to monitor individual progress and evaluate the effectiveness of instruction. Sixth, mastery checks were built into the curriculum at 4-week intervals.

The six types of continuous assessments employed in EGRA Plus: Liberia intervention classrooms are summarized in Table 4.1 and described in more detail below.

Table 4.1 Types and primary purposes of reading continuous assessments in EGRA Plus: Liberia

Types of continuous assessments	To inform daily reading instruction	To gauge student progress over time	To determine classroom/grade-level progress in reading	To inform teacher professional development	Definitions
	Primary purposes of continuous assessment measures				
Reading CBMs to check for individual student progress: Teacher-administered	✔	✔		✔	Individual student scores on letter identification, oral reading fluency, and reading comprehension for supplementary student report cards
Classroom summary: Average reading CBM score calculated by classroom teachers	✔	✔	✔	✔	Average scores of all students in a classroom on letter identification, oral reading fluency, and reading comprehension

(continued)

Table 4.1 Types and primary purposes of reading continuous assessments in EGRA Plus: Liberia *(continued)*

Types of continuous assessments	Primary purposes of continuous assessment measures				Definitions
	To inform daily reading instruction	To gauge student progress over time	To determine classroom/grade-level progress in reading	To inform teacher professional development	
Lesson-embedded instructional routines to check for student understanding	✔				Instructional routines in reading intervention that included explicit checks for student understanding
Classroom observations	✔		✔	✔	Coaches' systematic observation of teacher instruction
Reading CBMs to check for individual student progress: Coach-administered	✔		✔	✔	Letter identification, oral reading fluency, and reading comprehension subtasks randomly administered to several students by coaches
Four-week lesson-embedded mastery checks	✔	✔		✔	Tests included in the reading intervention lessons

CBM = Curriculum-based measure

Reading CBMs to Check for Individual Student Progress: Teacher-Administered Assessments

In both full- and light-treatment schools, teachers informed parents about student progress in reading by way of a simple report card indicating an individual child's progress toward the goal (a sample report card appears in Figure 4.1). The teacher obtained this benchmark of student progress by asking the student to identify letters, read a story aloud, and answer questions about the story. The project team developed a reading passage for this purpose, following EGRA standardized procedures. The teacher could then compare the student's obtained score on the indicator measures (letter identification, oral reading fluency, and reading comprehension) to the goal for that grade level, to

Figure 4.1 Early grade reading supplementary report card for parents, grade 2

Grade 2

School name: ____________

Teacher's name: ____________

Child's name: ____________

	Period 1		Period 2		Period 4		Period 6/end of year	
Your child	**Goal**	**Score**	**Goal**	**Score**	**Goal**	**Score**	**Goal**	**Score**
Letter-reading (letters per minute)	30	*33*	40	*41*	65	58	80	*81*
Story-reading (words per minute)	10	*11*	15	*20*	30	*30*	40	*42*
Story understanding (5/5, 4/5, 3/5 and so on*)	5/5	4/5	5/5	4/5	5/5	*5/5*	5/5	*5/5*
School average	**Goal**	**Score**	**Goal**	**Score**	**Goal**	**Score**	**Goal**	**Score**
Letter-reading (letters per minute)	30	*30*	40	39	65	*66*	80	*82*
Story-reading (words per minute)	10	8	15	14	30	*30*	40	*40*
Story understanding (5/5, 4/5, 3/5 and so on*)	5/5	3/5	5/5	4/5	5/5	*5/5*	5/5	*5/5*

* 5/5 means that the child was able to answer 5 questions out of 5 correctly, 4/5 that the child answered 4 of 5 correctly, and so on.

Note: Underscore (red on actual form) indicates below standard; italics (blue on actual form) indicates meets or exceeds standard.

the average classroom performance, and to the expected/standard scores and then enter this information into a report card form.

The form showed the standard performance (quantitative indicator) expected *at each reporting period* during the year (see next paragraph). Because of high levels of illiteracy among parents, the report cards used an already-familiar system of color-coding the student's scores in red ink if the student was below the standard, and in blue ink if the student met or exceeded the standard. (In the samples in Figures 4.1– 4.3 below, numbers that would be in red ink are underscored, while blue numbers are italicized.) This comparison gave parents clear and understandable student progress information. Teachers in the EGRA Plus full-intervention classrooms assessed all students during four of the six 6-week annual reporting periods, and they administered, scored, and recorded the results for each student.

As noted, an important feature of the EGRA Plus report card was the incremental goals that reflected expected student progress in performance over time. Each report card included different goals for each reporting period (see Figure 4.1). These incremental standards over time had to be explained to parents so that they could understand the meaning of the different goals. Coaches in the EGRA Plus: Liberia project worked with teachers on ways to talk with parents about report cards. Parents, in turn, could visually assess their own child's progress and use these data to ask the teacher questions about their child's rate of learning. From an accountability standpoint, parents could quickly see whether their child was on track to meet the reading goal. If the child was not progressing adequately, parents were encouraged to talk with their child's teachers to determine what could be done to improve the child's rate of learning.

Classroom Summary: Average Reading CBM Score, Calculated by Classroom Teachers

In addition to completing individual student report cards, teachers in the full-intervention classrooms kept records of student performance on the continuous assessment CBM probes (i.e., letter identification, oral reading fluency, reading comprehension). The classroom roster of student scores by report card period (see Figure 4.2), called the Student Progress Tracker, allowed teachers, principals, and other stakeholders to learn how well all students were progressing in individual classrooms across the reporting periods.

Figure 4.2 Student progress tracker, grade 2

District:
Settlement:
School/School Code:
Teacher:

Student Name	Period 1			Period 2			Period 4			Period 6		
	Letter reading Goal: 30	Story reading Goal: 10	Comprehension Goal: 100%	Letter reading Goal: 40	Story reading Goal: 15	Comprehension Goal: 100%	Letter reading Goal: 65	Story reading Goal: 30	Comprehension Goal: 100%	Letter reading Goal: 80	Story reading Goal: 40	Comprehension Goal: 100%
1. Jim	22	8	75	42	13	80	71	32	100	81	60	100
2.												
3.												
4.												
5.												
6.												

Note: Underscore (red on actual form) indicates below standard; italics (blue on actual form) indicates meets or exceeds standard.

EGRA Plus: Liberia achieved accountability for student learning at the community level by recording and distributing formative assessment data in report cards prepared for PTA members. That is, teachers distributed classroom-aggregated reading report cards to representatives of the local PTA at the end of the reporting period and also during the same periods in which they distributed the regular report cards to parents. PTA members were able to see classroom progress by reviewing a classroom report card like the one in Figure 4.3. Note that the scores on the community report card exactly matched the scores in the supplementary student report card (see Figure 4.1) in the section titled "school average." Figure 4.3 contains sample scores.

Figure 4.3 Early grade reading supplementary report card for the community

	Period 2		Period 4		Period 6/ end of year	
School average for grade 2	**Goal**	**School average**	**Goal**	**School average**	**Goal**	**School average**
Letter reading (letters per minute)	40	39	65	66	80	79
Story reading (words per minute)	15	14	30	30	40	40
Story understanding (5/5, 4/5, 3/5)*	5/5	4/5	5/5	5/5	5/5	5/5
School average for grade 3	**Goal**	**School average**	**Goal**	**School average**	**Goal**	**School average**
Letter reading (letters per minute)	80	75	80	86	80	81
Story reading (words per minute)	45	44	60	63	70	72
Story understanding (5/5, 4/5, 3/5)*	5/5	4/5	5/5	5/5	5/5	5/5

* 5/5 means that the child was able to answer 5 questions out of 5 correctly, 4/5 that the child answered 4 of 5 correctly, and so on. Underscore indicates below standard; italics indicates meets or exceeds standard.

Note: Underscore (red on actual form) indicates below standard; italics (blue on actual form) indicates meets or exceeds standard.

Lesson-Embedded Instructional Routines to Check for Student Understanding

The EGRA Plus reading intervention was structured to prompt teachers to check informally for understanding during instruction. For example, teachers were to call on students to respond to specific questions related to the skill being taught that day. The scripted instructional routines included correction procedures, to minimize student confusion and to ensure a consistent approach to giving students feedback on their answers. Teachers also asked for a thumbs up or thumbs down response from students and scanned to see whether most students understood the concept or skill being taught at that time.

Continuous Assessment Through Classroom Observations: Informing Quality of Program Implementation

Systematic classroom observation is another form of continuous assessment that can provide critical data on the implementation of a reading program. EGRA Plus: Liberia trained coaches to schedule observations of teachers implementing the reading program on a regular basis. They also completed a classroom observation checklist each month to record their updates on their visits to schools. The purpose of the checklist was to focus attention on the key features of the implementation of the reading intervention. That is, the project team could review the quality of program implementation—and especially evidence of a need for project intervention support when data suggested that implementation was not occurring according to program guidelines (e.g., if lessons were not on schedule). Because principals could refer to these data when asking teachers to modify their instruction to meet the program expectations, the data created local accountability.

Reading CBMs to Check for Individual Student Progress: Coach-Administered Assessments

Throughout the 2-year project, coaches administered oral reading fluency CBMs to students randomly and informally during monthly classroom visits. The coaches did not systematically record the results, but they provided relevant information during their debriefing sessions with teachers following the observations. If a coach discovered that none of the randomly selected students was able to demonstrate improvements in reading performance since the last reporting period, then the coach could use these data to urge the teacher to consider modifying and improving reading instruction, and could intensify support to this teacher. It was more powerful for coaches to bring data to the teacher meetings as the focus of discussion and support than to bring only their subjective impressions of the quality of instruction.

Four-Week Checks of Lesson Mastery

Periodic mastery tests yielded data that schools could use to determine student progress and instructional needs. With all that teachers were being asked to do—new lessons, new assessment, new report card system, etc.— we tried to simplify this component while making certain that the resulting data could be useful in informing instruction. Thus, we included a simple, group-administered spelling test in the lesson at the end of every fourth week. Teachers were to administer these spelling tests to ascertain whether students had mastered the skills taught. While simple spelling tests cannot capture the full complexity of reading skills, classroom observations suggested that these curriculum mastery checks were useful to assess mastery of sight words, vocabulary, and emerging fluency in word reading.

Purposes and Uses of Continuous Assessment Data

Under EGRA Plus, the primary objective of these assessments was informing and motivating student learning. The data could directly inform daily instruction at the student level; more broadly, over time they could be used to guide the professional development needs of teachers.

The data also made it possible for the education system to set standards for accountability in reading instruction. The standards assume that one does not have to be an expert in reading to know when a child is reading fluently. When the teachers and school directors informed children, families, and community PTAs of the expectations for reading achievement by grade—shown clearly in the report cards as the number of words read correctly in 1 minute in a grade-level passage—the recipients were also armed with the knowledge to evaluate both a child's and a classroom's progress toward the goal. Thus, these continuous measures were simple enough for those outside the school context to understand them easily.

Furthermore, when their students did well, communities frequently took charge of celebrating student success in reading through community and school gatherings or PTA meetings, venues at which they showcased children who strived to become successful readers. When these assessment data did not reflect adequate student progress in reading, then the principals, coaches, and project team members examined classroom-level instruction and identified appropriate types of support for the coaches to give.

Family and Community Impact on Student Learning

Most families want their children to be successful in school, and ample evidence documents that parental involvement in school is associated with positive school outcomes (Ames & Archer, 1987; Grolnick et al., 1997; Hill & Craft, 2003; Luster & McAdoo, 1996). Few studies in developing countries have addressed this issue, however. One study (Lockheed et al., 1989) examined the effects of family background and prior achievement on subsequent student achievement in Malawi and Thailand and found that family background characteristics accounted for more of the variance in student achievement than was previously thought. Family structure and parental involvement were found to be likely factors that contribute over time to increased achievement and, in some cases, a rise over time in the scores calculated as the norms for a test (Downey, 2001; Flynn, 1998). While the positive impact of parent-school involvement on student achievement in studies is well documented, we know far less about how these mechanisms work.

In the EGRA Plus: Liberia project, the primary mechanisms for parental involvement were (1) the report cards, (2) a reading-at-home tracker, a form that students took home each afternoon, and (3) information on the project disseminated through PTA community meetings. As described earlier, the report cards indicated student achievement in reading.

The reading-at-home tracker required families to support their child's reading at home by signing a form stating that the child was reading to someone at home for 20 minutes a day, 5 days a week. This form of accountability was included in the EGRA Plus program because of the findings from the smaller World Bank–funded study in Liberia in 2008 (Crouch & Korda, 2008): children who responded to interview questions that they had books at home were found to read, on average, a grade level higher than those who indicated that they did not have books at home. We believed that requiring children to read at home daily would improve their reading habits and increase their motivation to read. We also considered that children reading to parents might serve as an incentive for greater parental interest in reading, and in learning how to read.

Finally, PTA meetings became a place to explain and discuss the school reading report card, show parents how to support their child's reading at home, and tell what their school was doing to help children learn how to read. Many PTAs also became involved in organizing local reading competitions, which turned out to be a highly motivating strategy to encourage community and parent participation and to increase motivation for reading. At these competitions, usually involving an entire school cluster, children tried to earn the top prize as "best reader." Typically, four schools competed by selecting their top readers, and then they held public competitions during which each of the individual school winners read aloud for the prize.

In addition, at the same time these other mechanisms were in use, the project developed the series of local radio shows for families, narrated by reading coaches and district education officers, that emphasized the importance of children learning to read and described the EGRA oral reading fluency measure as a way for parents to gauge their children's progress in school.

End-of-project measurements of the impact of these community and family strategies yielded information that can now be used to identify alterable factors that are hypothesized to contribute to improved student achievement in Liberia. These community efforts, coupled with continuous assessments in the classroom, were integral to the success of EGRA Plus: Liberia.

Advantages and Challenges

Advantages of Using EGRA Measures for Continuous Assessment and Accountability

From among the numerous ways to approach continuous assessment, we used EGRA as the primary source of data to inform instruction and to gauge efficacy of reading instruction at the individual, classroom, school, family, and community levels. Below we elaborate on five primary advantages of using EGRA for continuous assessment and accountability.

National standards for performance, by grade level. The EGRA Plus project team established incremental growth standards or goals within and across grade levels, using estimated expected growth over time. These were the goals that teachers applied to the report cards across the four reporting periods and compared to actual performance on EGRA subtasks. Setting reading performance goals or standards was a new concept in the Liberian education system and provided a benchmark for teachers, schools, administrators, families, PTAs, and other community stakeholders to evaluate the effectiveness of classroom reading instruction. Whole communities were able to evaluate the EGRA Plus reading results against the new standards, and the public reactions were quite positive.

For example, at a local reading competition, held in conjunction with the PTA, families attended the competition and listened to children from different schools read passages aloud and answer comprehension questions. The child who performed at the highest level won a prize that was awarded by the district education officer. Families were excited about the competition and spoke to EGRA Plus staff about how pleased they were that children were learning to read successfully.

In another example, when EGRA Plus assessors arrived at a remote village to conduct midterm assessments, the village families prepared a feast for them in honor of their hard work to help their children learn to read.

Efficiency and ease of administration and scoring. RTI and Liberian Education Trust were able to train the EGRA assessors in approximately 2 days to high levels of fidelity. During the course of the intervention, coaches also trained teachers to administer reading CBM tasks that were consistent with the tasks used in the EGRA Plus: Liberia summative instrument, so that they could obtain information on individual students' learning progress and then use it to modify and improve their instruction.

Instructional utility. Just as physicians weigh and measure children to gauge their growth progress, teachers in EGRA Plus administered reading curriculum-based measures to gauge student learning progress toward a reading goal and toward proficiency. Before the reading CBM measures, classroom teachers in Liberia had to rely on written reading tests to judge whether students were learning what was taught. Unfortunately, the scores on these written tests were not useful in guiding instruction since they were not directly aligned with the content of instruction. If a student scored poorly on a standard written test, it was not clear why. The CBM measures provided a much clearer link to instruction as teachers could assume that student scores on the CBM continuous measures were directly related to the general reading outcome goal on the report card, and that increased scores meant that the reading instruction contributed to student learning. If there was no increase in student scores over time or between reporting periods, then teachers understood that they needed to modify instruction.

Scores that are easily understood, facilitating communication of results to parents and community. When a student's reading skills are indicated by the number of correct words read in a grade-level passage in 1 minute, little interpretation is required. Stakeholders can view the scores across grading periods (again, in this case, on report cards) and judge whether a student made reasonable progress from these scores. For instance, if a student did not meet the goal for that reporting period, families can begin to examine the factors that might contribute to this failure to meet the goal. If a child missed many days of school during one reporting period, a lower score might reflect frequent absences. By contrast, if a student began to read at home regularly and increased his or her rate of growth over two reporting periods, the increased time spent reading might contribute to a higher report card score for that period. Thus, the report cards described in this chapter constitute one effective way to communicate student learning progress.

The reading competitions were also effective for communicating reading achievement to local stakeholders. These reading performances did not require educators to interpret student performance to families; everyone easily understood that the students' ability to read fluently and with expression was the standard for reading performance.

Potential for information dissemination. The ease with which we established social marketing efforts within the EGRA Plus project stemmed in part from the simplicity of the scores on the measure, which also facilitated community understanding and support for meeting local schools' reading goals. Besides one-on-one communication, EGRA Plus was able to generate local support for children learning to read in the primary grades via the series of local radio shows. As noted, these shows described the EGRA Plus project and called upon families and community members to support children learning to read. In addition, EGRA Plus coaches communicated to school administrators, teachers, and villagers the importance of reading and worked with them to establish or improve local libraries, ensuring that there were books available for children to read outside of the classroom.

Challenges in Using EGRA for Continuous Assessment

Use of data to change instructional practices. One challenge that is not unique to Liberia is to make certain that teachers see the value of using data to inform instruction and then modify instruction based upon that student data when appropriate. Teachers needed support to make effective instructional decisions based on student data in the EGRA Plus: Liberia project. Coaches visited teachers at least once per month during the course of the 2-year project. During these visits, the coaches provided feedback, modeled classroom teaching, and answered teachers' questions about the implementation of the curriculum and the assessments.

Linking continuous assessment data to instructional decision making while one is learning a new program is not easy. The literature (e.g., Shepard, 2009; Stecker et al., 2005; Stecker et al., 2008; Wiliam et al., 2004) on formative/continuous assessment in the United States indicates that using formative data to guide instruction can positively affect student achievement. Too often, however, teachers lack the skills necessary to link student data to instructional decisions—and therefore to use data effectively.

Fidelity of assessments. It is important that teachers new to the EGRA instrument understand the importance of standardized assessment administration for the overall integrity of an intervention like EGRA Plus as well as for classroom continuous assessment. That is, EGRA teacher training and ongoing coaching should emphasize the need for teachers to apply EGRA consistently so that scores are meaningful in all classroom contexts.

Scaling up of EGRA use. Closely linked to the issue of fidelity, the Liberia experience confirmed that in planning to scale up from the pilot study to the randomized controlled trial, it was critical to work closely with the Ministry of Education so that the process became part of the national expectations for teachers and students. Any scaling-up plans must be included in the national goals *and* professional development for teachers.

Social marketing as a key to success in building local accountability. The plan to harness local support was clearly outlined in the EGRA Plus design, an advantage for the project. However, social marketing can be challenging if not carefully planned.

To increase local support, building strong ties with community members and families from the very beginning of a new initiative is critical. In EGRA Plus, the primary vehicle for communicating to the community was report card data. This source of continuous assessment data provided natural links among school, home, and community. Because the data were easy to interpret, student success was demonstrated to everyone through the community reading events. The challenge is twofold: first, to make certain that the data to be shared are perceived as important by community members, educators, and families; and second, to make the data easy for everyone at the local level to understand.

Other social marketing approaches for building local support were the audio and video recordings and the PowerPoint presentation. To document an actual event as it unfolded, the project team had to plan far ahead to capture the footage, sound, and still photographs needed to retell the story in a credible and compelling way.

Summary and Conclusions

The concept of continuous assessment includes a range of tasks and teacher behaviors that are designed to take stock of student learning progress. The examples from EGRA Plus: Liberia demonstrate how data gathered from a variety of continuous assessment measures can become integral components of a highly effective reading intervention. Reading CBMs were the primary source of data that informed classroom instruction as well as student, classroom, and school-level reading achievement and progress in the project. The clear goals and benchmarks for progress were key factors in motivating schools, teachers, students, and families. Engaging the local community with these simple student and classroom reading progress data, working with local villages to improve or to build new libraries, broadcasting local radio shows that emphasized the importance of children learning to read, and organizing cluster-level reading competitions resulted in communities demonstrating strong support for, and interest in, their children learning to read. These actions created a dynamic accountability context for improved student learning.

The assessment measures, both outcome and continuous measures, were relatively inexpensive at the teacher level, simple to administer, and sustainable, as they did not require any sophisticated analyses to understand. However, effectively using data from the classroom continuous measures required substantive professional development and ongoing support for teachers. This training and support depended upon a commitment of resources accompanied by social marketing efforts implemented at a local level.

The social marketing component was key to sustainability as communities began to support the common goal that all children will learn to read by the end of grade 2. They also understood that the goal was defined by children reading a minimum of 60 correct words per minute in a grade 3–level passage. The goal was measurable, observable, and meaningful to educators, parents, and community stakeholders. Evidence from interview data with community and PTA members in EGRA Plus communities (Piper & Korda, 2011) indicated that villagers would rally around a visible reading goal for children and support teacher efforts to ensure that all students in their school could celebrate the success of learning to read.

A relentless focus on examining student data regularly to determine whether they are meeting reading goals is very likely to result in an increase in the number of students who are adequately prepared to stay in school, an increase in students' academic knowledge in core content subject areas, and continuation of students' learning success beyond the primary grades so that they can contribute to building a more literate society.

We conclude that informal, continuous assessments can provide a strong foundation for accountability in student learning in all communities. With accountability and the resulting progress, countries can shift from a focus on access to education to access + achieving learning goals.

References

Ames, C., & Archer, J. (1987). Mothers' belief about the role of ability and effort in school learning. *Journal of Educational Psychology, 79,* 409–414.

Binder, C. (1996). Behavioral fluency: The evolution of a new paradigm. *The Behavior Analyst, 19*(2), 163–197.

Crouch, L., & Korda, M. (2008). *EGRA Liberia: Baseline assessment of reading levels and associated factors.* Report prepared as part of a process of collaboration between USAID and the World Bank. Research Triangle Park, North Carolina: RTI International. Retrieved September 21, 2010, from https://www.eddataglobal.org/documents/index.cfm?fuseaction=pubDetail&ID=158

Deno, S. L. (1985). Curriculum-based measurement: The emerging alternative. *Exceptional Children, 52,* 219–232.

Deno, S. L., Fuchs, L. S., Marston, D., & Shin, J. (2001). Using curriculum-based measurement to establish growth standards for students with learning disabilities. *School Psychology Review, 30,* 507–526.

Deno, S. L., Mirkin, P. K., & Chiang, B. (1982). Identifying valid measures of reading. *Exceptional Children, 49,* 36–45.

Downey, D. B. (2001). Number of siblings and intellectual development: The resource dilution explanation. *American Psychologist, 56,* 497–504.

Flynn, J. R. (1998). IQ gains over time: Toward finding the causes. In U. Neisser (Ed.), *The rising curve: Long-term gains in IQ and related measures* (pp. 25–66). Washington, DC: American Psychological Association.

Fuchs, L. S., & Deno, S. L. (1991). Paradigmatic distinctions between instructionally relevant measurement models. *Exceptional Children, 57,* 488–500.

Fuchs, L. S., & Fuchs, D. (1992). Identifying a measure for monitoring student reading progress. *School Psychology Review, 58,* 45–58.

Fuchs, L. S., & Fuchs, D. (1999). Monitoring student progress toward the development of reading competence: A review of three forms of classroom-based assessment. *School Psychology Review, 28,* 659–671.

Fuchs, L. S., Fuchs, D., & Hamlett, C. L. (1989). Computers and curriculum-based measurement: Effect of teacher feedback systems. *School Psychology Review, 18,* 112–125.

Fuchs, L. S., Fuchs, D., Hosp, M., & Jenkins, J. R. (2001). Oral reading fluency as an indicator of reading competence: A theoretical, empirical, and historical analysis. *Scientific Studies of Reading, 5,* 239–256.

Grolnick, W. S., Benjet, C., Kurowski, C. O., & Apostoleris, N. H. (1997). Predictors of parent involvement in children's schooling. *Journal of Educational Psychology, 89,* 538–548.

Hasbrouck, J., & Tindal, G. A. (2006, April). Oral reading fluency norms: A valuable assessment tool for reading teachers. *The Reading Teacher, 59*(7), 636–644. doi: 10.1598/RT.59.7.3.

Hill, N. E., & Craft, S. A. (2003). Parent-school involvement and school performance: Mediated pathways among socioeconomically comparable African-American and Euro-American families. *Journal of Educational Psychology, 95*(1), 74–83.

Hosp, M. K., & Hosp, J. (2003). Curriculum-based measurement for reading, math, and spelling: How to do it and why. *Preventing School Failure, 48*(1), 10–17.

Jenkins, J. R., & Jewell, M. (1993). Examining the validity of two measures for formative teaching: Read aloud and maze. *Exceptional Children, 59*(5), 421–433.

Lockheed, M. E., Fuller, B., & Nyirongo, R. (1989). Family effects on students' achievement in Thailand and Malawi. *Sociology of Education, 62*, 239–256.

Luster, T., & McAdoo, H. P. (1996). Family and child influences on educational attainment: A secondary analysis of the High/Scope Perry Preschool data. *Developmental Psychology, 32*, 26–39.

Marston, D. (1988). The effectiveness of special education: A time-series analysis of reading performance in regular and special education settings. *The Journal of Special Education, 21*, 13–26.

National Research Council [US]. (1999). *Testing, teaching, and learning: A guide for states and school districts.* R. F. Elmore & R. Rothman (Eds.), for the Committee on Title I Testing and Assessment, Board on Testing and Assessment, Commission on Behavioral and Social Sciences and Education. Washington, DC: National Academy Press.

Piper, B. (2011). *EGRA Plus: Liberia—Understanding the causal mechanisms: EGRA Plus's effectiveness.* Report prepared under the USAID EdData II project, Task 6, Contract Number EHC-E-06-04-00004-00. Retrieved April 27, 2011, from https://www.eddataglobal.org/documents/index.cfm?fuseaction=pubDetail&ID=298

Piper, B., & Korda, M. (2009). *EGRA Plus: Liberia data analytic report: EGRA Plus: Liberia mid-term assessment.* Report prepared under the USAID EdData II project, Task 6, Contract Number EHC-E-06-04-00004-00. Retrieved September 21, 2010, from https://www.eddataglobal.org/documents/index.cfm?fuseaction=pubDetail&ID=200

Piper, B., & Korda, M. (2011). *EGRA Plus: Liberia: Final program evaluation report.* Report prepared under the USAID EdData II project, Task 6, Contract Number EHC-E-0604-00004-00. Retrieved April 14, 2011, from https://www.eddataglobal.org/documents/index.cfm?fuseaction=pubDetail&ID=283

Quenemoen, R., Thurlow, M., Moen, R., Thompson, S., & Morse, A. B. (2004). *Progress monitoring in an inclusive standards-based assessment and accountability system* (Synthesis Report 53). Minneapolis, Minnesota: University of Minnesota, National Center on Educational Outcomes.

RTI International. (2009). *Early Grade Reading Assessment toolkit.* Prepared for the World Bank, Office of Human Development. Research Triangle Park, North Carolina: RTI International. Retrieved September 21, 2010, from https://www.eddataglobal.org/documents/index.cfm?fuseaction=pubDetail &ID=149

Santi, K., & Vaughn, S. (2007). Progress monitoring: An integral part of instruction. *Reading and Writing, 20,* 535–537.

Scriven, M. (1967). The methodology of evaluation. In R.W. Tyler, R. M. Gagné, & M. Scriven (Eds.), *Perspectives of curriculum evaluation* (Vol. 1, pp. 39–83). Chicago: Rand McNally.

Sirleaf, E. J. (2009). *This child will be great: Memoir of a remarkable life by Africa's first woman president.* New York: Harper-Collins.

Stecker, P., Fuchs, L. S., & Fuchs, D. (2005). Using curriculum-based measurement to improve student achievement: Review of research. *Psychology in the Schools, 42*(8), 795–819.

Stecker, P., Lembke, E., & Foegen, A. (2008). Using progress-monitoring data to improve instructional decision making. *Preventing School Failure, 52*(2), 48–58.

Wiliam, D. (2006). Formative assessment: Getting the focus right. *Educational Assessment, 11*(3&4), 283–289.

Wiliam, D., Lee, C., Harrison, C., & Black, P. (2004). Teachers developing assessment for learning: Impact on student achievement. *Assessment in Education, 11*(1), 49–65.

CHAPTER 5

Mother Tongue and Reading: Using Early Grade Reading Assessments to Investigate Language-of-Instruction Policy in East Africa

Benjamin Piper and Emily Miksic

Introduction

Ongoing tension exists in both the academic literature and policy contexts regarding language of instruction (LoI), particularly in sub-Saharan Africa. On the one hand, some families and communities in sub-Saharan Africa prefer literacy instruction in European languages, for quite logical reasons—including that most primary school completion examinations are in these languages, that they are the languages of broader communication, and that they are perceived to be avenues to economic prosperity. On the other hand, many experts (as well as some communities) argue that children most easily acquire reading skills in their mother tongue and that, with appropriate instruction, materials, and other supportive resources and guidance, they can successfully transfer those skills to a language of broader communication, resulting ultimately in better achievement in both languages.

As a result, many sub-Saharan African countries—including the two examined in this chapter, Kenya and Uganda—adopted LoI policies favoring mother-tongue approaches. (Mother tongue refers to the language spoken at home; local language refers to the language most commonly in use in the community.) The existence of these LoI policies in primary education, however, is incongruent with the emphasis that many of these systems place on national examinations in a European language. This mismatch between policy on paper and the incentives that parents and communities face is fundamental to the LoI difficulties in these countries.

These policy options are already difficult to navigate in many countries, and LoI issues are particularly complex in portions of the sub-Saharan African continent with long legacies of colonialism and inter- and intracountry migration. The East African countries of Kenya and Uganda are particular cases in point. Both countries' language cultures are influenced by a variety of factors, including the history of British colonialism with its disparate impact on various communities and ethnic groups across countries (Bamgbose, 2004). Moreover, Kenya and Uganda experienced differences in language diffusion between "settler"[1] and other forms of colonial endeavors in the British empire, although this is contested (Mufwene & Vigouroux, 2008). This language diffusion influenced the language choices for settler colonies like those in Kenya and South Africa. Also influential were the shifts over time among various ethnic groups' political and economic power and the ways that ethnicity has contributed to recent tensions and violence. Finally, a more recent influence has been the push-back against particular ethnic groups' dominance and the concomitant resistance to the languages preferred by those communities.

In this chapter, we explore the question of how the early grade reading assessment (EGRA) can support our understanding of LoI usage in sub-Saharan Africa and its relationship to student achievement. In 2006–2007, RTI International and the Aga Khan Foundation had implemented EGRA and a pilot intervention involving treatment and control groups in Malindi district in Kenya, using both English and Kiswahili (see Crouch et al., 2009). Based on the results, the William and Flora Hewlett Foundation funded a study that involved follow-up initiatives in Kenya and three additional countries—Uganda, Senegal, and Mali—during 2008–2010.

The Hewlett Foundation efforts serve as baseline assessments for Hewlett's activities in these countries. RTI was charged with modifying EGRA for these countries' contexts, which included further adapting it into five additional local languages in Kenya and Uganda (see Piper, 2010a, 2010b). A key component of the Hewlett-funded study was to add to the body of research on LoI and its relationship with early-grade reading outcomes. This scope made the study one of very few to produce empirical data concerning LoI policy, language use, and student outcomes in the classroom. More information about the Kenya and Uganda research designs appears later in this chapter, in the Methodology and Data section, and specific results from the study form the basis of the Findings section.

---

[1] In settler colonies, the colonial power often encouraged migration into the country and, thus, ended up with a significant segment of settlers in the country. Kenya is an oft-cited example of a settler colony in the history of sub-Saharan Africa.

Before focusing on the LoI aspects of the East Africa portion of the Hewlett study, however, we set the stage in terms of language policy and recent research regarding reading instruction in multilingual contexts.

Language History and Current Policy

Kenya

Figure 5.1 shows Kenya's eight provinces, including those discussed in this chapter, Nyanza Province and Central Province. Kenya's language diversity, like that of many countries in sub-Saharan Africa, was influenced by British colonial history (Nabea, 2009). During the colonial era, several factors shifted the relationship between languages and education. First, while the British system of colonialism provided more educational opportunities than did the alternative colonial systems on the continent (e.g., that of France and particularly Belgium), Kenyan local languages were marginalized by the demand in schools for education in English for official communication. Second, the indirect-rule method of colonial management subjugated some ethnic groups to others, which led to a relative preference for the languages of the favored ethnic groups. Third, the missionary education system in Kenya allowed for some mother tongues to be used as the language of early primary education in the small number of mission schools across the country. Graduates of these schools often formed the core of the political and technical elites who eventually took power immediately after independence in 1963, although these same elites were educated predominantly in the colonial language at secondary and tertiary levels. From the beginning of the colonial education system, however, English was the preferred language of some sub-Saharan African countries and the target language for upper primary and secondary education (Ngugi, 1986).

The "Ominde Report" (Ominde, 1964), a key educational document in post-independence Kenya, advocated for ending the segregation of the education system such that Africans, Indians, and Whites would learn in the same classrooms, unlike in the previous system. This integration policy was accompanied by a focus on English as the primary LoI. Furthermore, throughout the era of Jomo Kenyatta and Daniel Arap Moi (1963–2002), there was local resistance to mother-tongue instruction. The rationale, as articulated by communities in studies specific to Kenya (Mugambi, n.d.; Muthwii, 2004; Trudell, 2009), was that families expected the school to provide the student with what they often could not, namely, English.

Figure 5.1 Provinces of Kenya

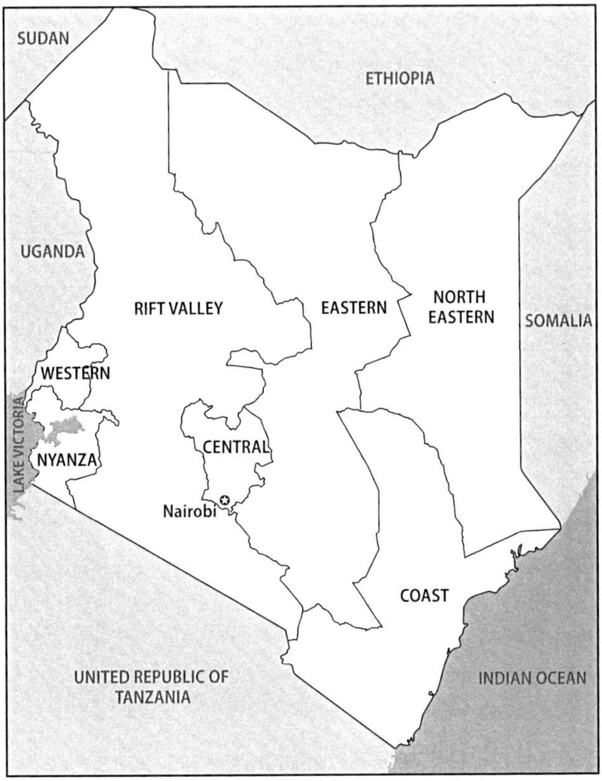

A key shift did occur after the Universal Primary Education pronounce-ments of Kenyatta in 1974, which offered free primary education from grades 1 through 4.[2] The resulting boom in primary enrollment had a limiting effect on education quality and raised concerns about the large percentages of children who struggled with English as LoI. The Gachathi Report (Republic of Kenya, 1976), therefore, advocated strongly for mother-tongue usage in early primary instruction.

The education language policy was formally established in 1976 and codified in the curriculum in 1992 (Kenya Institute of Education, 1992). It required that children be taught in the language of the catchment area—i.e., the local community. This meant that education was not necessarily provided in the mother tongue for every child, because the increasingly urbanized Kenya

---

[2] In Kenya, grade levels are called *standard* or *class*. In Uganda, the grade levels are called *P1–P7* (primary 1 through 7). For clarity, in the rest of the chapter we use *grade* to facilitate comparison.

had many locations with a broad mixture of ethnic groups. As a result, early primary education (grades 1 to 3) was to be provided in Kiswahili in towns and cities and in mother tongues in rural areas.

More recently, some people reacted to the post-election violence of 2007–2008 with heavier resistance to mother-tongue instruction. The violence was attributed in part to distrust among ethnic groups and in part to the use of local languages to incite people to violent behavior through the media, radio, and mass-mailed SMS (text) messages. Subsequent discussions in Kenya's parliament suggested that pressure for national unity might increase resistance to the language policy; some observers have noted that Tanzania's move to Kiswahili instruction under President Julius Nyerere's (1961–1985) Education for Self-Reliance initiative had modest impacts on achievement but significant impacts on national unity and the promotion of country over ethnic group (Nyerere, 1968, 1973, 1985).

In this environment, one significant factor was that the new constitution (enacted on August 27, 2010) actually provides substantial support for the development of indigenous languages as well as Kiswahili. Kiswahili is named as the national language of Kenya; the preamble recognizes the ethnic and cultural diversity of the nation, and the state is obliged to promote the development and use of indigenous languages. Most important, the power shift toward local citizens envisaged by the constitution brings with it the recognition that local languages must be part of governance and communication processes (Njogu, 2010).

Uganda

Uganda is smaller in both size and population than Kenya, but this does not mean that the language situation is less complex (Mpuga, 2003). Ethnic diversity, and with it language diversity, remains quite substantial.

During British indirect rule (1894–1962) of Uganda, particular ethnic groups were preferred. Favored ethnic groups found themselves closer to the colonial government, with the powerful Buganda kingdom (whose people spoke Luganda) particularly close (Criper & Ladefoged, 1971; Mugambi, n.d.). Language, ethnicity, and religion overlapped in the Ugandan colonial experience, with dramatic changes occurring during Idi Amin's rule in the 1970s and early 1980s. During the Amin era, a preference for Kiswahili as the dominant language surfaced in particular parts of the country, causing a language divide that still has political ramifications in Uganda (Pawlikova-Vilhanova, 1996).

The education system suffered particular neglect in the Amin era, with a confused language policy (attributable largely to the Kiswahili divide) and dramatic underachievement. Post-Amin, in 1992 the government adopted a mother-tongue policy for the public schools that was far more successful in elucidating the rationale for mother tongue than it was in ensuring mother-tongue usage (Majola, 2006; Republic of Uganda, 1992).

In the 2000s the Ugandan government undertook a curriculum review that investigated the quality of education and the question of language (Read & Enyutu, 2005). Ugandan education authorities decided to undertake a relatively quick curriculum overhaul, resulting in a curricular approach called the "thematic curriculum."

This 2007 curriculum reform had several characteristics. First, it focused heavily on a few subject areas, determining that early primary children should learn a few subjects in an integrated fashion. Reading and literacy became a much more central focus under this new thematic curriculum, with two classes per day for most children, and up to 90 minutes of literacy instruction per day. Second, the thematic curriculum was aligned with the mother-tongue policy, with strict instructions for teachers to use mother tongue across subjects for grades 1–3. Third, materials were developed to support the thematic curriculum approach.

From our conversations with officials of the Ministry of Education and Sports, we learned that these materials were only slowly distributed to the school level and were not developed in all of the mother tongues that teachers were using. For example, the Lango Subregion of Uganda's Northern Region (see Figure 5.2) assessed in the EGRA study cited here received learning materials produced in Luo (Dholuo), which is in the same language family but is not the local language for the region. The effects of these shortcomings are explored below, but it appears that, from the outset, the mother-tongue efforts under the Ugandan thematic curriculum were constrained by material (rather than language) issues. This means that some children, although being taught in a language that was recently encouraged by the thematic curriculum, often were without the requisite materials for that language. In general, the language appropriateness, content, overall quality, and availability of these materials remain relatively underresearched.

Figure 5.2 Provinces of Uganda, with Lango subregion

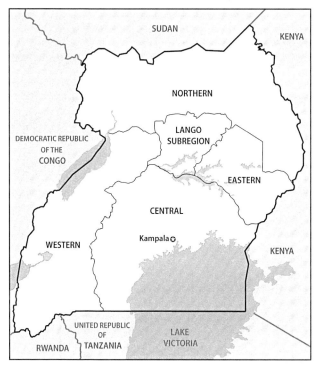

Research Questions

Although the historical background discussed above may clarify why Kenya and Uganda chose to employ mother-tongue policies, less clear are whether and how these Kenyan and Ugandan languages interact in a classroom environment beset by a variety of motivations and interests. Reading experts (local, national, and international) want children to have the opportunity to read first in their mother tongue, particularly in lower primary school. These experts include the Association for Development of Education in Africa (ADEA), an organization closely affiliated with ministers of education in sub-Saharan Africa (Alidou et al., 2006). In addition, the Association for the Development of African Languages in Education, Science and Technology (ADALEST) passed resolutions in 2000, 2002, and 2004 regarding the importance of mother-tongue education (Alidou et al., 2006).

By contrast, some communities and parents increasingly focus on the English-administered high-stakes school-leaving examinations (after grade 8 in

Kenya and grade 7 in Uganda) and the skills necessary for children to perform well on them. The point of view of many in local communities is that English language skills are key for children to do well in the primary school-leaving examinations. The rationale for some is that the route to fluency in English seems to be clearest with the early introduction of English. However, this approach diverges from the research-based point of view argued by reading experts, which holds that learning to read in one's mother tongue is the best way to literacy in that language and that with language-transfer support, learners can develop those skills more quickly in the language of broader communication—in these countries, English.

The differing points of view between language and reading experts on the one hand and some communities on the other (stylized and simplified in this example, of course) are confounded because few examples exist in developing countries of bilingual or multilingual educational structures that are of high enough quality for children to (1) learn well in their mother tongue and, even more complicated, (2) transfer the skills of the mother tongue quickly and successfully to English or other international languages. This is the very essence of the dilemma: the failure (thus far) of governments to deliver high-quality instruction in mother tongues tends to undermine the potential that researchers know exists. Notably, no examples exist of countries that have used the colonial language to deliver high-quality instruction, at least measured by early reading outcomes (Abadzi, 2011). Nonetheless, the countries implementing mother-tongue programs in sub-Saharan Africa offer few examples of systematic learning improvements on a country-wide scale.

As noted in the introduction, an RTI-led study, funded by the William and Flora Hewlett Foundation and employing EGRA, began in 2008 in four targeted countries—Senegal, Mali, Kenya, and Uganda. As of 2011, the study had produced a unique set of data for investigating some important questions. For example, focusing on Kenya and Uganda, which have somewhat similar LoI policies:

- Do the two cases differ with respect to their adherence to the LoI policies?

- How do the actual LoI observations differ with respect to matching the actual mother tongue of children? That is, do the LoI policies in practice do what they are designed to do: make it more likely that children are taught in the language that they speak at home?

- Taking it a step further, what are the relationships between the implementation of LoI and reading outcomes?

- Does higher usage of a given LoI correlate with higher reading outcomes?
- How do these LoI usage rates interact in the multilingual environments in Kenya and Uganda, where children are introduced to two or three languages in school and even more outside of school?

Literature Review

Languages and Literacy Acquisition

Research supports the point of view that teaching in a child's first language is effective for early literacy acquisition (Fafunwa et al., 1989; Heugh et al., 2006; Thomas & Collier, 2002; Yohannes, 2009). In this section, we present the various mechanisms by which mother-tongue instruction improves student outcomes and note what characteristics of literacy programs are necessary to ensure that the benefits of mother-tongue instruction accrue to students.

One influential hypothesis supporting the use of mother tongue for early learning is the interdependence hypothesis (Cummins, 1979). This hypothesis posits that the development of additional languages is partially a function of language development in the mother tongue and that a certain degree of proficiency in the mother tongue is necessary to avoid reading difficulties. The idea is that a child does not have two separate places to store language, but rather has a single underlying language proficiency. The most efficient way to influence that proficiency is in a mother tongue. This is because children can more easily be taught comprehension strategies orally, and early, in a language whose lexicon and syntax they already know and vocabulary they understand. The more comprehension and vocabulary knowledge they build, the more text they understand, which aids in fluency (accurate, quick reading, with expression).

Research has demonstrated many benefits to mother-tongue instruction. For example, studies have shown several skills that transfer across languages, such as reading comprehension strategies (Royer & Carlo, 1991) and phonemic awareness and word reading skills (August & Shanahan, 2006). Brock-Utne (2007) highlighted that mother-tongue instruction increases the potential for students to interact with parents around content. Through expanded use of the mother tongue, students integrate school-acquired knowledge with prior knowledge and develop vocabulary through interaction with peers, family, and teachers. In contrast, students use international languages such as English less frequently in informal communication outside of school.

The benefits cited above notwithstanding, other research supports the view that children learning in any language, no matter their mother tongue, can learn to read with comprehension, relatively quickly, with proper support. Research in Canada by Chiappe and colleagues (2002) showed, in a comparison of children from diverse language backgrounds receiving high-quality bilingual instruction alongside native English speakers subjected to the same instructional standards, that both groups were easily able to acquire basic literacy skills. The trajectory of growth in early reading skills was similar whether the child was a second-language learner or a native English speaker. Some abilities—such as manipulating and remembering English—were more difficult for these second-language learners.

However, "their limited exposure to English does not inhibit their acquisition of basic literacy skills…[and]… the same underlying skills, alphabetic knowledge, spelling and phonological processing were strongly related to literacy acquisition in English" (Chiappe et al., pp.111–112). For decoding and phonological awareness, which predict later reading ability, an individual's reading ability rather than status as second-language learner has been found to be more important (Chiappe & Siegel, 1999). Furthermore, a Canadian study of word reading revealed little difference between monolingual English speakers and second-language learners (Limbos & Geva, 2001).

A review of research on second-language learners by the US-based National Literacy Panel concluded that literacy instruction in non-mother-tongue languages can be successful (August & Shanahan, 2006). However, the panel reported that successful programs manifest several important features, including language-rich environments, heavy use of text, focus on oral language development, and teachers with a strong command of the language of instruction. Unfortunately, although some evidence indicates that, with proper instruction, second-language programs that do not include mother-tongue elements can be successful, all the examples cited are from Western contexts, and none is from sub-Saharan Africa.

The preponderance of the evidence suggests that mother-tongue programs bring added benefits but also that the design of those programs is important. For instance, if children are taught with methods that simply use a new language rather than teaching how that language functions in comparison with the mother tongue, children's ability to gain literacy skills can be jeopardized, and students may "never develop accurate speaking and writing" skills (Garcia, 2009, p. 231). Depending on language use, development of literacy can also take varying amounts of time. For instance, although children may develop functional language for social situations within a year, achieving academic literacy has been estimated to take 5 or more years for second-language learners (Cummins, 1979).

Transitioning to full use of second-language instruction before students have sufficient capacity in that language can block them from learning basic concepts that are key to comprehension (deep understanding that leads to the ability to use and transfer ideas). Thondhlana (2002) argued that to use English effectively, students in Zimbabwe had to reach a "threshold level," described by Cummins (1979), at which they were sufficiently fluent to be able to process new concepts and expand their understanding. The study by Thondhlana suggested that if instruction was in the second language rather than the first, *and* if pedagogy in the second language was weak, then students focused on rote memorization rather than on the cognitive processes that encourage comprehension and synthesis. This means that the children's ability to think critically and solve problems was significantly lessened in both languages.

Some of the literature goes even further to claim that there can be a negative effect on comprehension in other subject areas when teaching is not conducted in a mother tongue. In a study comparing the data from Ethiopia's 2000 and 2004 Grade 8 National Assessment examinations from four regions that had adopted mother tongue as the LoI policy and six of seven regions that had not, Yohannes (2009) found that the regions that used mother tongue in the content areas of science and mathematics outperformed the regions that used English. Interestingly, the scores on English did not differ between those regions that used it as an LoI and those that taught it as a subject. Furthermore, a study by Marsh et al. (2000) in Hong Kong showed that teaching in English as opposed to a mother tongue had positive effects on English proficiency but negative effects on other subjects, such as mathematics, history, and science.

Evaluating the quality of an LoI policy without looking at the larger learning context is difficult. Apart from the language that the teacher uses in the classroom, many other factors affect the ability of a child to learn to read. For example, both word-level skills and comprehension depend heavily on effective instruction, including method, intensity, and duration.

In that regard, Krashen's (1982) hypothetical model of second-language learning has influenced designers of effective second-language instruction. A key characteristic of this model is that students need comprehensible input (in what Vygotsky [1962] termed the "zone of proximal development") by receiving messages orally or through reading materials that they can understand, if they are to make progress in language acquisition. Another requirement based on Krashen's model is for the classroom to be a low-anxiety environment, as anxiety can act as a barrier to receiving these messages. The need for the language to be both understandable and taught in a low-stress environment implies a carefully timed, structured, and scaffolded language program and appropriate pedagogy.

The content of early literacy instruction is also critically important. The US-based National Reading Panel identified components of phonemic awareness, phonics, fluency, vocabulary, and comprehension as being essential (National Institute of Child Health and Human Development, 2000). The quality of teaching must be high—i.e., focused on learning, not simply memorization. Bunyi (2005) identified the emphasis on memorization as a problem in both mother-tongue and non-mother-tongue classrooms in Kenya.

These findings translate into a need for a carefully designed curriculum, instructional materials and lessons that use effective pedagogy, and an education system that enables teachers to spend time on reading instruction. Without this careful planning and execution, second-language teaching can fail.

Despite diverse perspectives on the importance of mother-tongue instruction, there are points of convergence. One is that if children are literate in their first language, they will find it easier to learn to read in a second language: acquiring decoding skills[3] in a first language facilitates decoding skills in learning other languages[4] (August & Shanahan, 2006). Another is that because reading is profoundly social and cognitive in nature, and situated in a particular context, the resources the child has developed prior to schooling around aspects of language such as structure, phonology, and vocabulary should be considered in any reading program (Genesee, 1994). The major difference is the degree of importance the study accords the role of the language of instruction in the effectiveness of an early reading curriculum. Unfortunately, not enough in-depth scientific research on LoI and reading performance has taken place in low-resourced environments to draw general conclusions about the degree of importance of language of instruction in relation to other factors, including teaching method and materials.

---

[3] Decoding is the act of using skills such as sound-blending and sound-symbol matching to turn letters and groups of letters into understandable words.

[4] This is with regard to alphabetic languages. For example, decoding skill in English may aid in decoding Kiswahili, but not Chinese.

Policy Versus Capacity

Language use in the classroom is clearly a central issue in reading achievement and the associated language policies. However, the realities on the ground often interfere with the stated intentions of policy. This section discusses the ability of education systems to implement various types of LoI policies and some of the barriers to successful implementation. Specifically, we present research that shows how teachers implement language policies in classrooms and how teachers' abilities and decisions make mother-tongue programs more (or less) difficult to implement. Then we provide examples of countries' capacity for the materials side of the instructional policy and conclude with an analysis of how local support influences the successful implementation of mother-tongue programs.

Teachers' Language Skills

Teachers' language ability is crucial in implementing successful language policies. Previous research has shown that teachers who are required to comply with new LoI policies, but who lack the language competencies and support to do so, are left with two choices: they can ignore the policy, or they can attempt to follow the policy at the level that their abilities permit. In either case, the LoI policy is unlikely to achieve its objective, and the result is students' limited acquisition of knowledge and skills, including literacy skills.

In a study of the effects on language policy in Kenya, Cleghorn et al. (1989) found that in attempting to comply with English-language-only requirements, teachers had difficulty explaining abstract scientific concepts. Mother-tongue instruction is not immune to this problem, however. In Kenya, Muthwii (2004) found that although teachers believed that students needed to hear the subject matter in their mother tongue (in this case, Kalenjin) to understand the concepts, the teachers often did not have local-language competency. Furthermore, in the fast-paced classroom environment, teachers were not prepared to determine when or if switching between languages or translating would be acceptable. The result was that teachers reverted to teaching in English instead of in Kalenjin.

Similarly, Pourdavood et al. (2005) studied mathematics teachers in the sixth and seventh grades in a school in South Africa. They determined that the teachers had multiple barriers to communication with students, including that their linguistic background (mother tongue) was different, and that their English language skills were also weak. This meant not only that teachers could not communicate effectively with their students, but also that they reduced their teaching methods to a central focus on computation. This effectively stripped away more complex reasoning skills and shortchanged students' ability to articulate mathematical thinking.

Moreover, mother-tongue LoI policy is subverted when teachers are deployed to regions where the local language is not their mother tongue (Miti & Monaka, 2009). Clearly, potential for difficulty arises if there is a mismatch between student and teacher language, or between policy and teacher ability.

Materials and Resources

Lack of access to learning materials and instructional aids in the mother tongue can cause a break with policy and exaggerate gaps in teachers' language capacities. Many national school systems in sub-Saharan Africa suffer from a lack of material resources. Even when resources are available, they may not be appropriate.

Several countries provide evidence of this. Miti and Monaka (2009) found that in Botswana and Zambia, most of the materials used to train teachers in African languages were in English. In Madagascar, Malagasy literacy materials were found to focus on traditional life at the expense of the types of academic and literary content found in French textbooks (Rabenoro, 2009). In undertaking qualitative research on the perceptions of Kalenjin-speaking parents, pupils, and teachers about the language policy in Kenya, Muthwii (2004) discovered a significant gap between the specifics of the policy and the capacity for implementation at the local level. Classroom materials were not printed in mother tongues, which laid the burden on teachers to translate lessons from English into Kalenjin. The phenomenon of limited access to mother-tongue materials has persisted in Kenya since Muthwii's (2004) study, as this chapter shows. Finally, even a local language used as a medium of instruction may not be the language that students speak at home, as we discuss below.

Local Support

Community support is vital for the successful implementation of mother-tongue LoI policies, as the studies reviewed in this section confirm. Trudell (2007) noted that top-down government policy mandates of African languages will not be effective if the local population does not support them. Parents' perceptions of the importance of mother-tongue instruction have an impact on students' motivation to learn as well as on schools' effectiveness, through parents' support or lack thereof (UNESCO, 2007).

In Kenya, Mali, and Cameroon, Trudell (2007) found that parents saw colonial languages (such as English and French) as the appropriate LoI. They recognized education as an investment, and they were concerned that instruction in mother tongue was harmful to learning the colonial language. Along the same lines, Kalenjin parents in Kenya who were surveyed favored English instruction over mother-tongue instruction from the beginning of primary school, save a small percentage who favored Kiswahili (Muthwii, 2004). They perceived English as providing more benefits, including increased facility with the language of the Kenya Certificate of Primary Education (KCPE) Examination, broader and better employment prospects, and increased interprovincial and interethnic communication.

In Uganda, Tembe and Norton (2008) studied parental support for local-language policies and found that 3 to 5 years after a mother-tongue curriculum had been introduced into schools, parents in the two eastern communities studied were aware of the policy and benefits of mother-tongue instruction but had mixed feelings toward its application in schools. In support of mother-tongue policies, parents expressed their belief in the importance of learning concrete subjects such as science in the local language as well as maintaining cultural identity through the language. However, those surveyed agreed that English was the most important outcome of schooling (and worthy of parents' monetary investment) in a world becoming more globalized.

Sookrajh and Joshua (2009) reported that teachers and parents in South Africa felt ambivalent toward local-language policies. They believed that the primary focus of the school should be English.

Studies have also shown that parental attitudes on language policy can change over time. Changes could come about through better understanding of the reasons behind language policy (Trudell, 2007) or through firsthand experiences. In Mali, a new model of mother-tongue instruction was not well received at first; however, over time and with an improvement in test scores, parents were gradually convinced (Canvin, 2003, as cited in Trudell, 2007). UNESCO and CARE reported a similar finding based on the introduction of a comprehensive bilingual program in a remote area of Cambodia that employed mother-tongue instruction (Middleborg, 2005). Specifically, they reported that

> through detailed information and advocacy, resistance has turned into support. A significant factor has been that the results from the pilot project on bilingual education show that it actually works and, thus, provide [sic] education opportunities for deprived indigenous minority groups. (p. 40)

The implementation of a bilingual pilot program in Mozambique won strong support from parents as well as students (Benson, 2000). Benefits stated by parents included that students could learn more easily, that the mother tongue gained in value, and that students were now literate in both languages (mother tongue and Portuguese).

Concerns about mother tongue as the LoI often create an inherent contradiction for interested researchers and policy makers. One side wishes to respect and encourage community desires (and communities often desire European languages), whereas the other sees mother-tongue instruction as supporting a more equitable and democratic society, not to mention the benefits mentioned previously in terms of learning. These contradictory positions are exacerbated by a lack of conclusive evidence regarding the most efficient policy for early reading acquisition.

Summary

In short, although some agreement can be seen in the literature as to mother-tongue instruction's potential for fostering early reading acquisition, even more congruence in the literature highlights the implementation difficulties that LoI policies face. Although the LoI literature is expanding rapidly, few of the studies provide empirical data on the actual adherence to the LoI policies in classrooms; neither do they yield evidence as to whether and how these policies match the actual mother tongues of children. Moreover, very seldom do these studies examine the relationships between language implementation and student outcomes. Using data collected with EGRA and complementary instruments, we present findings below to fill some of these gaps.

Methodology and Data

Given the focus on LoI, selecting appropriate geographic areas of study was a critical step. The aim was to ensure that the areas were relatively homogeneous, so that sampling could be done easily within languages, and that the schools used mother tongue frequently as a language of instruction. In Kenya, a panel chosen by the Ministry of Education explored the possibilities and made the final selections: Central Province and Nyanza Province. In Uganda, a technical team composed of members of the National Assessment of Progress in Education, National Curriculum Development Centre, and Directorate for Primary Education and Planning chose Central Region and Lango Subregion (within the Northern Region) as the most appropriate; these selections also answered a request from the Ministry of Education and Sports for one region with relatively sophisticated and mature language materials and one with more recently developed language materials.

We collected the data for the Hewlett study using two main instruments. First, RTI modified the Stallings snapshot tool (Texas A&M University, 2007) to obtain measurable data on the language choices used in Kenya and Uganda. This type of tool—see our version in Figure 5.3—allows the researcher to focus on measurable behavior choices pertaining to language, with particular emphasis on the language used, the person or persons using the language (teacher or student), the type of language use (speaking, writing, reading, etc.), and the target of the language (whole class, groups, or individuals). RTI's version of the snapshot tool was designed to produce 20 discrete data points during a 40-minute class; we matched it with a variety of other items, such as the languages used in the books in the classroom, the classroom materials, textbooks, wall art, and other charts, which allowed the researcher to understand the context of the classroom. Moreover, a classroom questionnaire associated with the tool allowed us to investigate the mother tongues of the majority of children in the classroom.

To determine whether the classrooms adhered to the official language policies in Kenya and Uganda, RTI analyzed data from classroom observations from both nations. The authors culled these data from 979 Kenyan classrooms and 620 Ugandan classrooms. The 979 Kenyan classrooms observed resulted in 25,496 unique observations of language usage; the 620 Ugandan classrooms observed yielded 19,806 unique observations of language usage. Thus, combined, our findings are based on more than 45,000 observations of classroom language use.

Figure 5.3 Classroom language-of-instruction instrument used in Kenya and Uganda

Legend: English = **E**; Kiswahili = **K**; Luo = **L**; Gikuyu = **G**
T+WC: Teacher speaking to entire class;
T+SG: Teacher speaking to a small group (2 or more)
T+I: Teacher speaking to individual;
S = WC: Students working in entire group;
S=SG: Students working in small group
S= I: Students working individually

Minutes from the beginning of class

6 categories of language use		2	4	6	8	10	12	14	16	18	20
T+WC	Speaking										
	Writing										
	Reading aloud										
	No language										
	Off task										
T+SG	Speaking										
	Writing										
	Reading aloud										
T+I	Speaking										
	Writing										
	Reading aloud										
S=WC	Speaking										
	Writing										
	Reading aloud										
S=SG	Speaking										
	Writing										
	Reading aloud										
S=I	Speaking										
	Writing										
	Reading aloud										
	Reading silently										

Instructions: Put the code language (E, K, L, G) in the box corresponding to the activity and the number of minutes elapsed in the lesson. For example, if the whole class is engaged in a lesson of question and answer, put a letter in the "T+WC" and "S=I" boxes indicating that the teacher poses a question to the whole class, and an individual responds. When there are interesting things that happen between intervals, or ambiguity in the coding, write a comment below. Use back of sheet if necessary.

Notes: _____

	22	24	26	28	30	32	34	36	38	40			TOTAL			
												English	Kiswahili	Luo	Gikuyu	Other

The second major tool used for the data collection and analysis was EGRA, modified to the Kenyan and Ugandan contexts, in four and three languages, respectively. Table 5.1 presents the sections included in each of the seven versions of EGRA.

Table 5.1 Sections in Kenya and Uganda EGRA instruments, by language

Country and language	Letter identification: name	Phonemic awareness	Letter identification: sound	Syllable naming	Familiar word reading	Nonword reading	Oral reading fluency	Reading comprehension
Kenya English	●	●	●		●	●	●	●
Kenya Kiswahili		●	●	●	●	●	●	●
Kenya Gikuyu		●	●	●	●	●	●	●
Kenya Dholuo		●	●		●	●	●	●
Uganda English	●	●	●		●	●	●	●
Uganda Luganda		●	●	●	●	●	●	●
Uganda Lango		●	●		●	●	●	●

EGRA and its subtasks are discussed in Chapter 1, so we do not repeat a description here. However, worthy of note in the Kenyan and Ugandan situations was the systematic process used to produce the list of letters, syllables, and words. We derived these lists by examining their frequency in the textbooks for each language. Also unique to these East African EGRAs was the syllable naming section. Because three of the languages in these countries (Kiswahili and Gikuyu in Kenya, and Luganda in Uganda) are Bantu languages that almost exclusively use open (vowel-final) syllables, we felt that an exercise with syllables in EGRA would be an important predictor in early reading acquisition. Moreover, much of the pedagogy in these languages in the early grades depends on introducing children to syllabic combinations and ensuring fluency. For that reason, determining whether children in these languages had fluency with the syllables foundational to the rest of the language was critical.

The rest of the EGRA sections represented in Table 5.1 were included (or not) based on the complexity of the task for the language and the orthography of that language.

In both Kenya and Uganda, we assessed children in more than one language to discern whether they had stronger skills in one than another that led to differences in their language usage. In urban Kenya, children in both Central Province and Nyanza Province were assessed in two languages: English and Kiswahili. In rural Kenya, children were assessed in three languages: English, Kiswahili, and Gikuyu in rural Central Province; and English, Kiswahili, and Dholuo in rural Nyanza Province. In Uganda, children were assessed in their mother tongue (either Lango or Luganda) and English.

We applied ordinary least squares (OLS) regression methods to investigate the relationships between language of instruction and reading fluency, and reading fluency in one language with that in another language. We fit these OLS regression models using the *svy* command in Stata,[5] because they were fit on weighted data. We derived the weights from the sampling frameworks for both Kenya and Uganda, which created regionally (or provincially) representative samples.

In Kenya, therefore, given the differences in LoI policies in urban and rural locales, the findings are representative first of urban and rural Central Province and Luo-speaking portions of Nyanza Province and then to Central and Nyanza provinces. In Uganda, the findings are representative of Central Region and Lango Subregion. The samples are *not* representative of Kenya and Uganda, given the regional language foci. When we discuss "Kenya" or "Uganda," then, we refer to the sampled regions together.

Findings

General Findings

Table 5.2 presents the languages of instruction, as determined by each nation's LoI policy. In Kenya, the LoI differs within province by urbanicity. That is to say—as discussed above about Kenya's LoI history—Kenya defines the LoI as the language of the "catchment area"; policies state that in urban locations, Kiswahili (rather than the local language of the province) should be used. Of course, this is regardless of whether Kiswahili is the actual mother tongue of the children in the area.

---

[5] Stata is proprietary statistical analysis software of StataCorp LP; see http://www.stata.com.

Table 5.2 Language of instruction in early primary grades in Kenya and Uganda

Country	Geographic area	Language of instruction
Kenya	Urban Central Province	Kiswahili
	Rural Central Province	Gikuyu
	Urban Nyanza Province	Kiswahili
	Rural Nyanza Province	Dholuo
Uganda	Central Region	Luganda
	Lango Subregion	Lango

The observations took place in a variety of subjects. Kenyan subjects observed included English, mathematics, Kiswahili, mother tongue, science, social studies, life skills, and Christian religious education. Ugandan subjects observed included literacy, English, mathematics, science, social studies, religious education, handicrafts, and mother tongue. In both countries, the largest number of observations occurred in subjects in which reading instruction was taking place, either in English or in the other languages relevant to the particular region or subregion. The next priority with respect to classroom observations was the subject areas, particularly mathematics, social studies, and science.

From these diverse classroom observations, we assessed the language frequency in early and upper primary school in Kenya and Uganda. Table 5.3 shows that, with respect to overall country averages, English was significantly more prevalent in Kenya (58.1 percent) than in Uganda (28.9 percent) in early primary grades. Looked at from the other perspective, mother tongue was used significantly less in Kenya (14.1 percent) than in Uganda (71.1 percent).

Table 5.3 Language of instruction: percentage uses in Kenya and Uganda, by grade level

Country and grades	English	Kiswahili	Mother tongue
Kenya (grades 1–3)	58.1	27.9	14.1
Uganda (grades 1–3)	28.9	N/A	71.1

With respect to Kenya, the issue of mother tongue makes interpreting the data by early or upper primary grades in Table 5.4 difficult. The reason is that in urban Kenyan schools, Kiswahili is nominally the mother tongue, whereas in rural areas, Kiswahili is considered a subject. In any case, mother-tongue instruction was used less in Kenya than in Uganda; Kiswahili (the "mother tongue" of urban areas) was used 31.8 percent of the time in urban Central Province and 31.1 percent of the time in urban Nyanza Province. In rural areas, mother tongue was used 18.2 percent of the time in rural Central Province and 30.5 percent of the time in rural Luo-speaking parts of Nyanza Province. Table 5.4 shows that policy adherence in Kenya was slightly higher in Central Province than in Luo-speaking parts of Nyanza Province, although both provinces had low levels of mother-tongue usage.

Table 5.4 Language of instruction: Percentage uses in Kenya and Uganda disaggregated by level, region or province, and urban/rural

Grade level	Country and grades	Region or province	Urban or rural	English	Kiswahili	Mother tongue
Early primary	Kenya (grades 1–3)	Central	Urban	66.6	31.8	1.6
			Rural	53.9	27.7	18.2
			Total	59.6	29.5	10.8
		Nyanza	Urban	64.6	31.1	4.4
			Rural	48.4	21.1	30.5
			Total	56.5	26.1	17.5
	Uganda (grades 1–3)	Central		32.4	N/A	67.6
		Lango		25.9	N/A	74.1
Upper Primary	Kenya (grades 4–8)	Central		76.2	21.0	2.8
		Nyanza		77.6	19.7	2.8
	Uganda (grades 4–7)	Central		86.6	N/A	13.4
		Lango		91.2	N/A	8.8

In Uganda, the situation is a bit simpler with respect to policy adherence because the policy does not differ by urbanicity. In Central Region and Lango Subregion, children in early primary school were very likely to be primarily taught in their mother tongue (see Table 5.4). Specifically, for early primary grades, mother tongue was used 67.6 percent of the time in Central Region and 74.1 percent of the time in Lango Subregion.

Based on these data, we conclude that the percentage of time mother tongue was used was much lower in Kenya than in Uganda. Policy adherence was both higher and more similar across countries in upper primary school (grades 4–7 in Uganda, grades 4–8 in Kenya) than in the lower primary grades. An important point, however, is that Uganda's grade 4 is supposed to be a "transition" year, with some English and some mother tongue. Instead, it is mainly an English LoI year.

Table 5.4 also shows the languages used in the observed classrooms in the two countries, aggregated for all upper primary grades, both urban and rural. This analysis shows that more English was used in the Ugandan upper primary schools (91.2 percent in Lango Subregion, 86.6 percent in Central Region) than in the Kenyan upper primary schools (77.6 percent in Nyanza Province, 76.2 percent in Central Province). This pattern was nearly the opposite of what was determined for instruction in English in *early* primary school.

These findings show that a sharp contrast exists in Uganda between language usage in early primary and upper primary grades. This is particularly an issue when the transition year (grade 4) is considered. Although some experts argue for the importance of mother tongue in its own right, some policy makers conceive of mother-tongue usage as a more effective method to ensure high-quality learning in the international language. However, without specific pedagogic strategies for ensuring that reading skills that accrue in the first few years of education in a Ugandan mother tongue are transferred to English, children in primary schools who are taught in their mother tongue might lose the benefits of the early reading acquisition, contributing to dropout or repetition.

Language of Instruction and Transition Years

Figure 5.4 presents a stark comparison between the transition periods in Kenya and Uganda. In Kenya, our data revealed that the percentage of mother-tongue instruction gradually and consistently declined between grades 1 and 7; the largest drop in percentage of mother-tongue instruction (15 percentage points) occurred between grades 4 and 5. In Uganda, by contrast, mother-tongue use was consistently above 70 percent in grades 1–3, and was highest in grade 3, at 76.8 percent. This was followed by a 63.6 percentage-point drop in mother-tongue usage between grades 3 and 4. This situation is likely to lead to a dramatic adjustment problem for many children with little exposure to written English.

To understand the Ugandan comparison between early primary and upper primary language usage, one must be aware of the rollout of the thematic curriculum, described earlier in this chapter. The thematic curriculum was in its third year in 2009 and was in its first year of rollout in grade 3. The rollout had not yet begun in grade 4, although it did begin in 2010. As a result, because of the cross-sectional nature of the data set presented here, we cannot determine the impacts of the thematic curriculum rollout on the LoI choices in Uganda. Clearly, however, the thematic curriculum has brought with it high percentages of mother-tongue usage in grades 1–3. The high dropoff observed is, to some degree, a sign of policy adherence.

Figure 5.4 Percentage use of mother tongue as language of instruction in schools in Kenya and Uganda

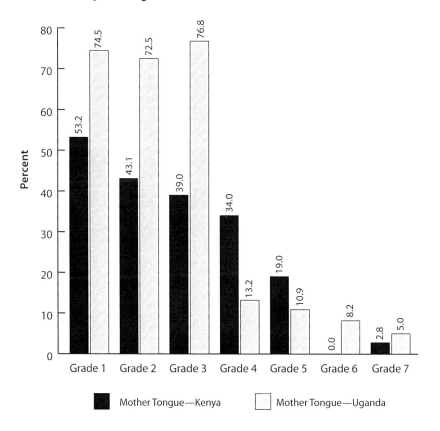

Mother-tongue usage declined throughout primary school for both Kenya and Uganda, but the pattern was very different with respect to the content areas. To reiterate, the stated LoI policy in both Kenya and Uganda is that children are to be taught content areas in their mother tongue in early primary.

Figure 5.5 shows the language use by subject in grades 1–3 in Kenya. English was used more than 70 percent of the time in all content areas, including English, of course, but also social studies, mathematics, life skills, Christian religious education, and science. Of all the content areas, science had the greatest prevalence of mother-tongue and Kiswahili usage, and combined was only about 30 percent of the instructional time. Kiswahili LoI dominated the Kiswahili class, and mother-tongue LoI the mother-tongue class. In Kenya, then, content-area instruction was taking place in English rather than in the mother tongue or Kiswahili, which was a significant departure from the policy.

In Uganda the story was quite different. Figure 5.6 shows the percentage of languages used by subject in Uganda. We observed mathematics, social studies, literacy, and English enough times to compare the language usage. The analysis showed that English was used 84.6 percent of the time in English class, but literacy class as well as the content areas (social studies and science) were taught almost exclusively in mother tongue. Instruction in Ugandan content areas, therefore, was primarily in the mother tongue, showing that policy adherence was higher in Uganda than in Kenya.

Investigating further, we wanted to determine whether the individual classrooms observed followed the LoI policy at least 75 percent of the time. To do so, we selected an analysis sample that was limited to content-area classrooms (i.e., subject-area classrooms). This removed the Kiswahili-as-a-subject classes in Kenya and the English-as-a-subject classes in both Kenya and Uganda. Excluding the language-as-subject classes allowed us to determine what percentage of each region's classrooms followed the LoI policy. Note that by the time of this data collection, the problem of Luo materials sent to Lango Subregion had been resolved, although very few classrooms had the materials.

Table 5.5 presents the percentage of classrooms in each region or province that followed the policy, the official language for the classrooms in that region or province, and the number of observed classrooms for that region or province. For Kenya, the levels of policy adherence were higher in Nyanza Province, with 40.9 percent of *urban* classrooms and 43.9 percent of rural classrooms following the policy. In Central Province, the adherence was very low, with only 37.7 percent of urban classrooms and 22.9 percent of *rural*

Figure 5.5 Percentage of instructional time used, by language and subject, in grades 1–3 in Kenya

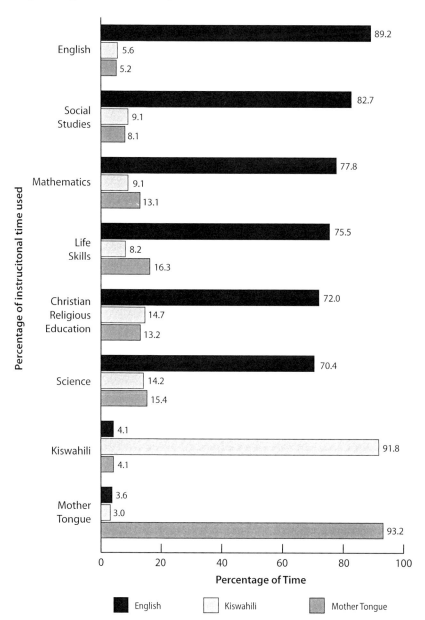

Figure 5.6 Percentage of instructional time used, by language and subject, in grades 1–3 in Uganda

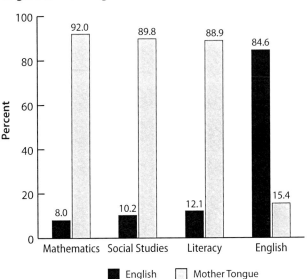

classrooms following the policy. In contrast, Ugandan policy adherence was very high in both Central Region and Lango Subregion: 87.5 percent of Central Region classrooms and 87.1 percent of Lango Subregion classrooms followed the policy (at least 75 percent of the time).

Table 5.5 shows that, similar to the findings above, LoI policies were not well followed in Kenya in either urban or rural areas. The advent of the recent thematic curriculum policy in Uganda seems to have paid dramatic dividends to LoI policy adherence across Uganda, with more than 87 percent of content-area classrooms following the policy at least 75 percent of the time.

Table 5.5 Adherence to language of instruction policies in individual classrooms

| | Kenya | | | | Uganda | |
| | Central | | Nyanza | | | |
Measure	Urban	Rural	Urban	Rural	Central	Lango
Classrooms with 75% of language use following language policy	37.7%	22.9%	40.9%	43.9%	87.5%	87.1%
Policy language	Kiswahili	Gikuyu	Kiswahili	Dholuo	Luganda	Lango
Number of classrooms	114	96	110	82	128	170

In the section that follows, we present our analysis of whether the languages used in classrooms were the same as the languages that the children said they actually spoke at home. Children were asked which language they spoke at home with their mother.[6] This information was then compared with the languages used in class. The differences were once again quite stark between Kenya and Uganda (Table 5.6).

Table 5.6 Percentages of language used in classrooms and mother tongue of children, by country and region

Language	Where used	Kenya		Uganda	
		Central	Nyanza	Central	Lango
English	Classroom	59.6	56.5	32.4	25.9
	Home	0.3	2.3	0.2	0.1
Mother tongue	Classroom	10.8	17.5	67.6	74.1
	Home	92.2	84.3	81.9	92.5
Kiswahili	Classroom	29.5	26.1	NA	NA
	Home	4.9	11.0	NA	NA
Other	Classroom	0.1	0	0	0
	Home	2.5	2.2	17.9	7.3

NA = not applicable.

Kenya's mother-tongue percentages, separated by Central and Nyanza provinces, show similarities in the levels of school–home language matches across the two provinces. The primary languages in Central and Nyanza provinces (Gikuyu and Dholuo, respectively) were spoken by 92.2 percent and 84.3 percent of the children assessed, respectively, with smaller percentages speaking Kiswahili at home. The percentage of mother tongue used as LoI in the observed classrooms, however, was quite low; mother-tongue languages were used as LoI only 10.8 percent of the time in Central Province and 17.5 percent in Nyanza Province. Kiswahili was used in the classroom more often, at a rate of 29.5 percent in Central and 26.1 percent in Nyanza.

---

6   This question was designed to account for the many multilingual families in Kenya: children are apt to speak more than one language at home, let alone in the course of their everyday life. Given that we did not allow multiple responses, the analysis here is simpler than it could have been, yet still provides an interesting picture of whether and how the school language of instruction matched the languages used at home.

More interesting are the percentages for English as the LoI. Nearly 60 percent of instruction in both Central and Nyanza provinces took place in English. This was in classrooms where very few children (fewer than 3 percent in both provinces combined) actually spoke English at home. The Kenyan language policy in practice, then, is best not termed a "mother tongue" policy, if such small percentages of children are taught in the language that they actually speak at home.

In Uganda, we also investigated the match between the mother tongue of children in each region and the LoI used in their classrooms, which is also presented in Table 5.5. In both regions, the students' self-identified mother-tongue percentages matched the predominant language of the province (Luganda in Central Region and Lango in Lango Subregion) at 81.9 percent and 92.5 percent, respectively. Unlike Kenya, the Ugandan schools had a much closer match between the language used in classrooms and the mother tongue of the children in those classrooms, with Luganda used 67.6 percent of the time in Central Region and Lango 74.1 percent of the time in Lango Subregion. One interesting comparison between countries was the greater amount of language diversity in the Ugandan sample, with 17.9 percent of Central Region and 7.3 percent of Lango Subregion students speaking a language other than either the dominant language or English.

Oral Reading Fluency: Zero Score Comparisons

To compare the reading scores of children in Kenya and Uganda, we carried out a zero-score analysis on oral reading fluency scores. Given the differences among the various languages in word length, word complexity, and orthographic transparency, comparing oral reading fluency scores at the mean level is difficult. By contrast, however, comparing the percentages of children who scored zero words correctly read on the oral reading fluency task for each language in the two countries was possible. Figure 5.7 displays our findings. Even these comparisons are tenuous given the differences between the countries, and even the regional comparisons within countries must be made cautiously. The comparisons in English are more appropriate because we used the same story in assessing the children in both cases.

We observed fewer zero scores in both mother tongue and English in Kenya than in Uganda. Because the numbers presented are simply zero scores, they demonstrate only the proportion of children who were unable to read anything, not average oral reading fluency scores. The explanation for these differences is unclear, although we discuss them further below. In our view however, LoI policy differences are likely *not* the causal factor influencing these outcomes. With those caveats, the evidence suggests that the Kenyan education system in the regions studied produced fewer nonreaders at grade 3 than the Ugandan provinces that we assessed.

Figure 5.7 Percentage of grade 3 learners with zero scores (no words read correctly) on oral reading fluency section

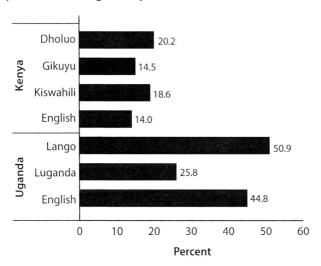

Classroom Conditions in Schools in Kenya and Uganda

Table 5.7 compares Kenya and Uganda with respect to our data on classroom conditions and materials. The Kenyan and Ugandan schools differed dramatically in two areas—attendance and percentages of classrooms with various learning materials (discussed below). Although we designed both sampling frameworks to assess the quality of schooling within regions/provinces, these analyses must be interpreted cautiously: they are only illustrative.

Table 5.7 Classroom predictors in Kenya and Uganda

Country	Attendance (percentage of enrolled)	Percentage with exercise books	Percentage with textbooks	Percentage with writing materials
Kenya	92.2	97.3	39.8	93.9
Uganda	71.4	93.8	3.2	92.6

First, we estimated attendance rates by counting the number of children actually in the classroom and comparing that figure with the number of children in the class register. On this metric, attendance rates were much higher in Kenya than in Uganda (92.2 percent vs. 71.4 percent). However, classrooms were much more crowded in Uganda, so our calculated rate of absenteeism might have been skewed by the practice of enrolling children who then do not regularly attend school. In addition, the data collection in Uganda took place a month later than in Kenya, at the end of the school year, so some children who were still on the register may have already left the Ugandan schools.

Second, the two countries were not materially different with respect to exercise books. They did, however, differ markedly in terms of the percentage of children with textbooks. In Kenya, the percentage was 39.8 percent, which was far lower than expected, given expected textbook provision in Kenya. By contrast, only 3.2 percent of children in Uganda had a textbook in their possession during our classroom observations. Given the importance of textbooks for student achievement, it is not surprising that the children did not do particularly well on reading tasks. Measured by the variables in Table 5.7, the classroom environments seem to have been more conducive for learning in Kenya than in Uganda, particularly in the areas of textbooks and other reading materials and classroom attendance.

Oral Reading Fluency Results for One Child, Multiple Languages

We demonstrated earlier the difficulty of comparing oral reading fluency scores across languages, let alone using those scores to compare the impact of LoI policies across countries. Within countries, however, we could assess a given child in more than one language and analyze that child's oral reading fluency in one language compared with another language. As described in the Methodology and Data section of this chapter, we tested each child in both Kenya and Uganda in multiple languages so that we could do this type of within-child language analysis. Our interest in fitting these multiple regression models was to determine whether children's fluency rates in one language predicted their fluency in another language.

Results for the analyses for Kenya are presented in Table 5.8, showing, by province, the outcome, the predictor, and the model estimates and R^2 (i.e., the percentage of variation in fluency scores for different languages). Our overall finding is that children's individual cross-language oral reading fluency rates were highly correlated.

Table 5.8 Multiple regression results for oral reading fluency by language in Kenya

Province	Outcome	Predictor(s)	Coefficient (correct words per minute)	Standard error	T	Significance	R²
Central	English ORF	Kiswahili ORF	1.31	0.07	18.86	<.001	.80
	English ORF	Gikuyu ORF	1.31	0.20	6.37	.02	.58
	Kiswahili ORF	Gikuyu ORF	0.99	0.11	8.94	.01	.69
Nyanza	English ORF	Dholuo ORF	1.32	0.05	25.30	<.01	.72
	English ORF	Kiswahili ORF	1.39	0.10	13.44	.001	.79
	Kiswahili ORF	Dholuo ORF	.89	0.03	25.67	.002	.78

ORF = oral reading fluency.

In Central Province, for every word children read in Kiswahili, they read 1.31 words in English (R^2 = .80). For every word read in Gikuyu, children could also read 1.31 words in English (R^2 = .58). For every word read in Gikuyu, children read 0.99 words in Kiswahili (R^2 = .69).

We also found strong predictive relationships in Nyanza Province, where reading skills transferred across all three languages. Dholuo reading explained 72 percent of the variation in English reading fluency, Kiswahili reading explained 79 percent of the variation in English, and Dholuo explained 78 percent of the variation in Kiswahili. Clearly, therefore, reading skills in one language were related to skills in the other language(s). These findings held even when we controlled for language usage rates. That is to say, in multiple regression models that controlled for language usage in classrooms, reading in one language was predictive of reading in another language.

Table 5.9 presents the regression results from Central Province demonstrating that language usage rates predicted oral reading fluency outcomes. For example, 10 percent more English used in classrooms was associated with a statistically significant 10.3 more words per minute in English oral reading fluency.[7] For Kiswahili, by contrast, oral reading fluency and the Kiswahili language usage in Central Province were not related (*p* = .46).

---

[7] This figure is derived by taking the coefficient in the first model in Table 5.9, which predicts English oral reading fluency by the English LoI usage rates. The coefficient is 103.12, which is the increase in oral reading fluency when the English LoI rate is increased from 0 to 100 percent—which is not practical as a policy recommendation. More useful, then, is to present the coefficient in terms of a 10 percent increase in English as the LoI. All results presented in the text here are thus converted to 10 percent values.

Table 5.9 Multiple regression results for oral reading fluency by language use in Kenya

Province	Outcome	Predictor(s)	Coefficient (correct words per minute)	Standard error	T	Significance	R²
Central	English ORF	% English as LoI	103.12	21.10	4.89	.02	.10
	Kiswahili ORF	% English as LoI	41.16	8.50	4.84	.02	.04
	Kiswahili ORF	% Kiswahili as LoI	-5.44	6.48	-0.84	.46	.00
	Gikuyu ORF	% English as LoI	33.45	15.15	2.21	.16	.03
	Gikuyu ORF	% Kiswahili as LoI	-27.37	6.06	-4.52	.05	.06
	Gikuyu ORF	% Gikuyu as LoI	16.37	6.21	2.64	.12	.02
	English ORF	Kiswahili ORF	1.27	0.06	20.36	<.001	.82
		% English as LoI	50.57	17.39	2.91	.06	—
	English ORF	Kiswahili ORF	1.31	0.07	18.04	<.001	.80
		% Kiswahili as LoI	-11.59	4.49	-2.58	.08	—
	English ORF	Dholuo ORF	1.32	0.05	25.30	<.01	.72
	English ORF	Kiswahili ORF	1.39	0.10	13.44	.001	.79
	Kiswahili ORF	Dholuo ORF	.89	0.03	25.67	.002	.78
Nyanza	Kiswahili ORF	% Kiswahili as ORF	27.71	11.48	2.41	.09	.08

LOI = language of instruction; ORF = oral reading fluency.

Interestingly, however, the percentage of time that *English* was used as the LoI predicted *Kiswahili* oral reading fluency. For every 10 percent more English used in Central Province, children scored significantly more more per minute—4.1—on Kiswahili oral reading fluency. This surprising finding may be attributable to wealth and other unobserved resource differences among schools that used more English in early primary. Kiswahili language usage was significantly negatively correlated with Gikuyu reading fluency, such that for every 10 percent more Kiswahili used in classrooms, children read 2.7 words fewer per minute in Gikuyu.

Finally, we posit that in the tri- (or multi-) language environments in Kenya, competition for instructional time and the resulting language decisions that were made had impacts on student achievement. For instance, for every 10 percent more that Gikuyu was used, children read 1.6 more words per minute in Gikuyu (although this was not statistically significant).

The regression results from Uganda are presented in Table 5.10. In both Central Region and Lango Subregion, oral reading fluency scores in one language were highly predictive of scores for the other language, similar to what we found for Kenya. In Central Region, for every word read in Luganda, the statistically significant relationship in English oral reading fluency was 0.77 words per minute ($R^2 = .63$). Another model showed that even when controlling for the percentage of English and Luganda used in the classroom was, Luganda oral reading fluency explained 70 percent of the variation in English.

Table 5.10 Multiple regression results for achievement on EGRA assessment in English and Luganda or Lango, controlling for language usage, in Uganda

Province	Outcome	Predictor(s)	Coefficient (correct words per minute)	Standard error	T	Significance	R²
Central	English ORF	Luganda ORF	0.77	0.08	10.07	<.01	.63
	English ORF	Luganda ORF	0.79	0.08	10.39	<.001	.70
		% English as LoI	25.68	14.67	1.75	.16	—
Lango	English ORF	Lango ORF	0.66	0.08	8.50	<.01	.56
	English ORF	Lango ORF	0.67	0.08	8.06	.001	.57
		% English as LoI	4.89	4.16	1.18	.31	—

LOI = language of instruction; ORF = oral reading fluency.

In Lango Subregion, the relationships were similarly strong. Lango fluency scores predicted 56 percent of English fluency, and every word read in Lango was associated with a statistically significant positive relationship of 0.66 words per minute in English. The other regression models showed that the percentage of language use did not predict oral reading fluency scores in either that language or other languages.[8] For any number of reasons, schools may have been using differing amounts of languages that the "percentage of language use" scores did not measure adequately.

---

[8] These models are not presented here because of space constraints.

Findings Summary

In summary, as of the time of our assessment, Kenya's adherence to its LoI policy was much looser than Uganda's with respect to the degree of mother-tongue usage in the classroom. Moreover, Kenyan children were suffering from a much greater mismatch between the LoI used and the languages that they spoke at home than was true for Uganda. We also observed that higher percentages of children in Uganda were nonreaders in both mother tongue and English. The research yielded some possible reasons: lack of textbooks, lower attendance rates, the growing pains of the relatively recent implementation of the thematic curriculum, or some combination of these factors.

The cross-national analysis does not seem to support the notion that more mother-tongue instruction automatically leads to higher outcomes on assessments carried out in the mother tongue. Neither does it offer evidence that reading skills in the mother tongue automatically transfer over into efficient reading outcomes in English, as some mother-tongue advocates argue. Rather, other factors appearing in the literature but not included in this study, such as quality of instruction and the school environment, may have a greater effect.

The research presented in this chapter shows that, regardless of instructional language, children's skills in oral reading fluency transferred across languages. This finding deserves more research attention, because we are unable to find a causal explanation for the strengths of those relationships. It appears that, even if children are instructed primarily in one language (as in the Kenyan case), they are applying the same methods to reading (decoding) words in other languages to which they have far less exposure in school. Although that is not surprising, it *is* startling how closely scores in one language were related to those in other languages, even when we controlled for classroom language use. One possible explanation is that the multilingual environment of children in East Africa makes transferring reading skills an easier process than previous research has suggested. If so, this is encouraging, given the recent increase in mother-tongue programs with elements of transition to a second language. If schools were able to teach these transfer skills systematically, then children might retain these skills across languages even better than they seem to do now.

The findings also show that in Uganda and in Nyanza Province in Kenya, language usage and reading fluency outcomes had no statistically significant relationship. However, in Central Province in Kenya, we saw a pattern of higher English LoI usage rates equating with higher oral reading fluency scores in English, which makes sense. However, the rates also equated with higher reading scores for Kiswahili and Gikuyu, even though those languages were seldom used in those schools.

As noted earlier, we can attribute this pattern mainly to unobserved factors related to the reasons that schools choose to use more or less English as LoI. Put another way, schools serving higher-income communities might offer more English instruction, causing the relationships that we identified here. Further research will need to investigate the questions brought forward by this preliminary analysis.

Research Limitations

Our analysis has produced several unique findings about the LoI policy adherence in two East African countries: the relationship between reading fluency skills within children across languages, and the relationship between LoI and reading fluency. A strength of our work is that the results are based on tens of thousands of classroom observation points and thousands of EGRA assessments. Nevertheless, the cross-sectional nature of this data set means that causal inferences are impossible.

For example, some might be tempted to state that the thematic curriculum itself, implemented in mother tongue, was the reason for the relatively high number of zero scores among Ugandan children across languages. We cannot draw this particular conclusion, however, because the single point in time makes it impossible to know the causal reasons for the achievement levels of children in either Kenya or Uganda. More research is necessary to determine whether Uganda's shift from mother tongue to English in grade 4 is successful.

Furthermore, we note that the cross-regional and cross-national comparisons are tenuous. Therefore, our conclusions are very modest. Any interregional and international comparisons must take into account a multitude of factors—such as socioeconomic status, languages used at home, linguistic complexity, and more. Our caution stems from the fact that the study, although carefully designed across languages, was not organized to make cross-national comparisons. For example, we organized by country the process for selecting and training the assessors. In addition, although we asked children in both countries basically the same socioeconomic status questions, we trained the assessors separately (albeit using the same international trainers). That is not to say that the cross-national points made in this chapter are not useful. In fact, we hope that they spur more research into the effectiveness of various national programs using mother-tongue methods.

Furthermore, this chapter focuses mainly on children's ability to read words fluently. It does not address the question of whether students comprehend what they read in either the first or second language. The data set *does* allow the complexity necessary to compare and contrast reading fluency and reading comprehension across languages, which will be addressed in future analyses.[9]

Conclusion

Neither Central Province nor Nyanza Province in Kenya was adhering to the LoI policies set out at the national level at the time we completed the EGRAs for this study. English as the LoI was dominant across regions and the urban/rural divide, regardless of the policy. By contrast, the majority of classrooms in Uganda were following Uganda's mother-tongue LoI policies. In addition, Uganda demonstrated a much closer match between the language used in classrooms and the language spoken at home. However, given the lack of language materials in classrooms and the modest training provided to teachers, the Ugandan system was not following its own LoI policy in all of its complexity. Our analysis, though, focused on language usage within larger mother-tongue policies.

A significant part of the literature we have cited shows that coherence between language at school and language at home gives children the opportunity to apply oral language skills gained at home. As a result, the literature suggests that, all things equal, children taught in their mother tongue would acquire reading skills more quickly than those taught in English. This is not what we found, in either country. Clearly, many observable differences, including availability of textbooks and other materials, influence these findings and are likely important contributors to the differences cited.

In our analysis, we found that countries with very similar LoI legislated *policies* can have quite disparate *practice*. In fact, apparently the Ugandan policy implementation under the thematic curriculum reform has been quite successful in moving toward mother-tongue instruction in the classroom, which has also increased significantly the percentage of children who speak the same language at home as they speak at school. Kenya has a particularly complex language environment—influenced by the fact that the KCPE examination is in English, by the development of Kiswahili as a regional language of commerce and communication, and by the pushback against

---

[9] Piper, B., Trudell, B. & Schroeder, L., *Oral reading fluency and comprehension in Kenya: Reading acquisition in a multilingual environment*. Manuscript submitted for publication.

ethnic-group identification (and, by extension, local languages) as a result of the 2007 post-election violence. It has chosen to deal with this complexity with a language practice that prefers English over other language options in both rural and urban areas.

Our findings showed only modest relationships between classroom language usage rates and oral reading fluency outcomes; in three of the four regions, we found no statistically significant relationship. However, the pattern identified in Kenya's Central Region merits further research: namely, how do the schools that choose to use multiple languages in multiple ways differ in their ability to teach children how to read? As we see it, what matters primarily is the overall quality of reading instruction—which, although it is a remarkably difficult construct to measure, includes the existence and use of books, time on task, and engagement of students, as well as language.

This logic suggests that both Uganda and Kenya might suffer from outside factors that muddy the understanding of whether mother-tongue policies are more successful than English-only, or what effects other LoI choices might have on student achievement in East Africa. In environments in which mother-tongue LoI policies are not being followed rigorously (with respect to time spent in Kenya, and provision of materials in Uganda), LoI may be far less important than instructional quality in predicting student outcomes.

Moreover, the research presented in this chapter shows how EGRA might be combined with other analytic questions to deepen understanding of how issues of policy relevance affect student outcomes. In particular, the existing data set could be exploited to determine whether learning in a language other than mother tongue affects reading comprehension. This is a promising area of further research, both within and outside of the field of language of instruction.

References

Abadzi, H. (2011). *Reading fluency measurements in EFA FTI partner countries: Outcomes and improvement prospects*. Washington, DC: Education for All Fast Track Initiative (EFA FTI) Secretariat.

Alidou, H., Boly, A., Brock-Utne, B., Diallo, Y. S., Heugh, K., & Wolff, H. E. (2006, March). *Optimizing learning and education in Africa: The language factor*. Paper presented at the Association for the Development of Education in Africa (ADEA) 2006 Biennial Meeting, Libreville, Gabon.

August, D. & Shanahan, T. (2006). *Developing literacy in second-language learners*. Mahwah, New Jersey: Lawrence Erlbaum Associates.

Bamgbose, A. (2004). *Language of instruction policy and practice in Africa.* New York: United Nations Educational, Scientific and Cultural Organization (UNESCO). Retrieved September 29, 2010, from http://www.unesco.org/education/languages_2004/languageinstruction_africa.pdf

Benson, C. J. (2000). The primary bilingual education experiment in Mozambique, 1993 to 1997. *International Journal of Bilingual Education and Bilingualism, 3*(3), 149–166.

Brock-Utne, B. (2007). Language of instruction and student performance: New insights from research in Tanzania and South Africa. *International Review of Education, 53,* 509–530.

Bunyi, G. (2005). Language classroom practices in Kenya. In A. M. Y. Lin & P. W. Martin (Eds.), Decolonisation, globalisation: *Language-in-education policy and practice* (pp. 131–152). Clevedon, England: Multilingual Matters.

Chiappe, P. & Siegel, L. S. (1999). Phonological awareness and reading acquisition in English- and Punjabi-speaking Canadian children. *Journal of Educational Psychology, 91*(1), 20–28.

Chiappe, P., Siegel, L. S., & Gottardo, A. (2002). Reading-related skills of kindergartners from diverse linguistic backgrounds. *Applied Psycholinguistics, 23,* 95–116.

Cleghorn, A., Merritt, M., & Abagi, J. O. (1989). Language policy and science instruction in Kenyan primary schools. *Comparative Education Review, 33*(1), 21–39.

Criper, C., & Ladefoged, P. (1971). Linguistic complexity in Uganda. Chapter VII in W. H. Whiteley (Ed.), *Language use and social change* (pp. 145–159). London, England: Oxford University Press.

Crouch, L., Korda, M., & Mumo, D. (2009). *Improvements in reading skills in Kenya: An experiment in the Malindi district.* Prepared for the United States Agency for International Development (USAID) under the EdData II project, Task 4, Contract No. EHC-E-04-04-00004-00. Research Triangle Park, North Carolina: RTI. Retrieved May 4, 2011, from https://www.eddataglobal.org/documents/index.cfm?fuseaction=pubDetail&ID=154

Cummins, J. (1979). Linguistic interdependence and the educational development of bilingual children. *Review of Educational Research, 49,* 222–251.

Fafunwa, A. B., Macauley, J. I., & Soyoya, J. A. F. (1989). *Education in mother tongue: The Ife Primary Education Research Project (1970-1978).* Ibadan, Nigeria: Ibadan University Press.

Garcia, O. (2009). *Bilingual education in the 21st century: A global perspective.* Malden, Massachusetts: Wiley/Blackwell.

Genesee, F. (Ed.). (1994). *Educating second-language children: The whole child, the whole curriculum.* New York: Cambridge University Press.

Heugh, K., Bogale, B., Benson, C., & Yohannes, M. A. G. (2006). *Final report: Study on medium of instruction in primary schools in Ethiopia.* Addis Ababa: Ministry of Education. Retrieved September 29, 2010, from http://www. hsrc.ac.za/Research_Publication-19715.phtml

Kenya Institute of Education. (1992). *Primary education syllabus: Volume one.* Nairobi: Republic of Kenya Ministry of Education.

Krashen, S. (1982). *Principles and practice in second language acquisition.* Oxford, England: Pergamon Press.

Limbos, M., & Geva, E. (2001). Accuracy of teacher assessments of second-language students at risk for reading disability. *Journal of Learning Disabilities, 34*(2), 136–151.

Majola, K. (2006, June). *Language and education in Uganda: An encounter with the National Indigenous Language Forum.* Paper presented at the Languages and Education in Africa (LEA) Conference, Oslo, Norway. Retrieved September 29, 2010, from http://www.pfi.uio.no/konferanse/LEA2006/ assets/docs/Majola_paper.pdf

Marsh, H., Hau, K., & Kong, C. (2002). Multilevel causal ordering of academic self-concept and achievement: Influence of language of instruction (English compared with Chinese) for Hong Kong students. *American Education Research Journal, 39*(3), 727–763.

Middleborg, J. (2005). *Highland Children's Education Project: A pilot project on bilingual education in Cambodia.* Bangkok, Thailand: UNESCO Asia and Pacific Regional Bureau for Education.

Miti, L. M., & Monaka, K. C. (2009). The training of teachers of African languages in southern Africa, with special reference to Botswana and Zambia. In B. Brock-Utne & I. Skattum (Eds.), *Languages and education in Africa: A comparative and transdiciplinary analysis* (pp. 213–221). Oxford, England: Symposium Books.

Mpuga, D. (2003, July). *The official language issue: A look at the Uganda experience.* Paper presented to the African Language Research Project Summer Conference, Ocean City, Maryland.

Mufwene, S. S., & Vigouroux, C. B. (Eds.). (2008). *Globalization and language vitality: Lessons from Africa*. London and New York: Continuum International Publishing Group.

Mugambi, P. J. (n.d.). *An analysis of the politics of language in Kenya: Harnessing linguistic diversity for national and regional development*. Nairobi, Kenya: Department of Kiswahili and African Languages, Kenyatta University.

Muthwii, M. J. (2004). Language of instruction: A qualitative analysis of the perceptions of parents, pupils and teachers among the Kalenjin in Kenya. *Language, Culture and Curriculum, 17*(1), 15–32.

Nabea, W. (2009). Language policy in Kenya: Negotiation with hegemony. *Journal of Pan African Studies, 3*(1), 121–138. Retrieved September 8, 2010, from http://www.jpanafrican.com/docs/vol3no1/3.1%20Kenya%20Language%20Policy.pdf

National Institute of Child Health and Human Development [US]. (2000). *Report of the National Reading Panel. Teaching children to read: An evidence-based assessment of the scientific research literature on reading and its implications for reading instruction: Reports of the subgroups*. NIH Publication No. 00-4754. Retrieved May 5, 2011, from http://www.nichd.nih.gov/publications/nrp/report.cfm

Ngugi, T. (1986). *Decolonizing the mind*. Nairobi, Kenya: Heinemann.

Njogu, K. (2010, November). *Implications of the new constitution for language policy and use in Kenya*. Presentation at meeting of the Multilingual Education (MLE) Network of Eastern Africa, Nairobi, Kenya.

Nyerere, J. (1968). *Freedom and socialism: A selection from writings and speeches, 1965–1967*. London: Oxford University Press.

Nyerere, J. (1973). *Freedom and development*. Dar Es Salaam: Oxford University Press.

Nyerere, J. (1985). Education in Tanzania. *Harvard Educational Review, 55*(1), 45–52.

Ominde, S. H. (1964). *Kenya Education Commission report* (Ominde Report). Nairobi: Kenya Education Commission.

Pawlikova-Vilhanova, V. (1996). Swahili and the dilemma of Ugandan language policy. *Asian and African Studies, 5*(2), 158–170.

Piper, B. (2010a). *Kenya Early Grade Reading Assessment findings report.* Prepared for the William and Flora Hewlett Foundation, under the Monitoring of Learning Outcomes in Sub-Saharan Africa project, Contract No. 2008-3367. Research Triangle Park, North Carolina: RTI International. https://www.eddataglobal.org/documents/index.cfm/EGRA%20Kenya%20072910%20Final.pdf?fuseaction=throwpub&ID=275

Piper, B. (2010b). *Uganda Early Grade Reading Assessment findings report: Literacy acquisition and mother tongue.* Report prepared in cooperation with Makerere University Institute for Social Research, for the William and Flora Hewlett Foundation under the Monitoring of Learning Outcomes in Sub-Saharan Africa project, Contract No. 2008-3367. Research Triangle Park, North Carolina: RTI International. https://www.eddataglobal.org/documents/index.cfm?fuseaction=pubDetail&ID=293

Pourdavood, R. G., Carignan, N., King, L. C., Webb, P. & Glover, H. (2005). Teaching mathematics in a school where the learners' and teachers' main language differs. *School Community Journal, 15*(2), 85–100.

Rabenoro, I. (2009). National language teaching as a tool for Malagasy learners' integration into globalization. In B. Brock-Utne & I. Skattum (Eds.), *Languages and education in Africa: A comparative and transdiciplinary analysis* (pp. 175–188). Oxford, England: Symposium Books.

Read, T., & Enyutu, S. (2005). *The Ugandan primary curriculum review road map: For the implementation of the curriculum reforms recommended by the primary curriculum review report and approved by the Ministry of Education and Sports.* Consultant report. Kampala, Uganda: Ministry of Education and Sports.

Republic of Kenya. (1976). *Report of the National Committee on Educational Objectives and Policies* (Gachathi Report). Nairobi: Government Printer.

Republic of Uganda. (1992). *Government white paper on the education policy.* Review commission report. Kampala: Uganda Printing and Publishing Corporation.

Royer, J. M., & Carlo, M. S. (1991). Transfer of comprehension skills from native to second language. *Journal of Reading, 34*(6), 450–455.

Sookrajh, R., & Joshua, J. (2009). Language matters in rural schools in South Africa: Are educators making the implementation of the Language in Education Policy (1997) work? *Language Learning Journal, 37*(3), 323–338.

Tembe, J., & Norton, B. (2008). Promoting local languages in Ugandan primary schools: The community as stakeholder. *The Canadian Modern Language Review/La Revue canadienne des langues vivante, 65*(1), 33–60. Retrieved May 4, 2011, from http://lerc.educ.ubc.ca/fac/norton/Tembe%20&%20 Norton%202008.pdf

Texas A&M University. (2007). *Stallings snapshot observation manual. Monograph.* College Station, Texas: Center for Collaborative Learning Communities, College of Education, Texas A&M University. Retrieved September 8, 2010, from https://www.eddataglobal.org/embedded/stallings_ snapshot.doc

Thomas, W. P., & Collier, V. P. (2002). *A national study of school effectiveness for language minority students' long term academic achievement: Final report.* Retrieved September 8, 2010, from http://gse.berkeley.edu/research/crede/ research/llaa/1.1_final.html

Thondhlana, J. (2002). Using indigenous languages for teaching and learning in Zimbabwe. In B. Burnaby & J. Reyhner (Eds.), *Indigenous languages across the community* (pp. 31–39). Flagstaff, Arizona: Northern Arizona University. Retrieved May 5, 2011, from http://jan.ucc.nau.edu/~jar/ILAC

Trudell, B. (2007). Local community perspectives and language of education in sub-Saharan African communities. *International Journal of Educational Development, 27*(5), 552–563.

Trudell, B. (2009). Local-language literacy and sustainable development in Africa. *International Journal of Educational Development, 29*(1): 73–79.

United Nations Educational, Scientific and Cultural Organization (UNESCO). (2007). *Making a difference: effective practices in literacy in Africa.* Publication No. UIL/2007/ME/H/1. Hamburg: UNESCO Institute for Lifelong Learning. Retrieved May 5, 2011, from http://unesdoc.unesco.org/ images/0015/001538/153827e.pdf

Vygotsky, L. S. (1962). *Thought and language.* Cambridge, Massachusetts: The MIT Press.

Yohannes, M. A. G. (2009). Implications of the use of mother tongues versus English as languages of instruction for academic achievement in Ethiopia. In B. Brock-Utne & I. Skattum (Eds.), *Languages and education in Africa (pp. 189–199).* Oxford, England: Symposium Books.

CHAPTER 6

Using Information and Communication Technologies to Support EGRA

Sarah Pouezevara and Carmen Strigel

Introduction

As the previous chapters of this book have shown, several factors drive the development and adoption of the early grade reading assessment (EGRA) worldwide. For example, policy makers and educators can use it as a formal, system-level diagnostic tool or as a less formal local monitoring tool. Moreover, it is accessible to national governments and to local authorities who wish to do rapid but accurate assessments of the level of reading and to repeat these often enough to analyze changes over time.

Across the different applications of EGRA, to implement the assessment in a reliable, consistent, and comparative way requires an investment of resources—both human and material. In addition to the actual data collection costs, the costs include time to train, administer, supervise, and perform high-quality data entry and analysis and then to summarize the results in a useful way for each assessment.

This chapter focuses on approaches in which assessors from outside the school arrive to assess a random subsample of students. Therefore, we discuss several "entry points" in the EGRA model that could be appropriate for applying information and communication technologies (ICT), with the aim of increasing productivity and thereby decreasing costs of the assessment. These entry points are

- test development,
- assessor training,
- data collection, and
- data management, analysis, and presentation.

We present actual cases and lessons learned—and potential applications of ICT—at two key stages of the EGRA: (1) data collection, including ongoing quality control and (2) data analysis. The first part concerns the potential for collecting data through electronic devices (e.g., portable computers, phones, personal digital assistants, or custom hardware) rather than paper-and-pencil forms. The second part discusses and presents recommendations on software to select for EGRA data management, analysis, and presentation.

We compare three commonly used applications—Microsoft Excel, SPSS, and Stata—along several dimensions. These dimensions include the nature of the research question(s), the process of data management and analysis, accessibility of support, and cost. In the Summary and Conclusions section of this chapter, we describe some potential applications of ICT—some of which involve new devices or innovative applications of existing ones—for supporting test development, assessor training, and literacy interventions as an area for further research.

Clearly, the costs and feasibility of using ICT for any of these purposes need to be explored in more detail and piloted where possible. Some of the technologies described in this chapter are only in the conceptualization or development stage and have not yet been implemented for EGRA. This is a quickly changing field in terms of available technologies, EGRA-specific products, and costs. The information in this chapter was current as of early 2011. We hope this chapter will also provoke more interest from the international community, which can contribute ideas and experiences toward making the most practicable ones a reality. The original EGRA instrument and methodology benefited from this type of open, collaborative process, and it would be natural for the evolution to ICT-supported implementation to be open as well.

Information and Communication Technologies for EGRA Data Collection

Technology can support EGRA data collection in two ways. Both aim to improve time and cost efficiency in implementing EGRA, specifically in preparing and conducting fieldwork and in managing the data. The first model is a system for collecting data electronically without changing the core parameters of the existing (externally driven) EGRA implementation methodology—that is, a sample-based assessment using trained assessors who conduct the assessment one-on-one with students in schools and submit data for processing. The second uses technology to change how EGRA is carried out altogether—for example, by using voice recognition software or recording devices to simulate test administration, which might eliminate the role of the trained assessor who visits schools one by one.

Approaches and applicable technologies are available for general electronic data collection in health and the social sciences, and handheld devices are currently being used for other reading assessments (such as Dynamic Indicators of Basic Early Literacy Skills [DIBELS], Reading 3D, or Texas Primary Reading Inventory [TPRI]). Comparable applications or approaches specifically for EGRA are emerging, and RTI, among others, is further developing and testing them. This section first discusses the overall rationale and objectives for moving from paper-based to electronic data collection, and then offers some possible implementation models.

Background on EGRA Data Collection Procedures

Before we discuss possible hardware (and its accompanying software) for EGRA data collection, we review the components of the assessment.

Content. As described in Chapter 1, the full battery of early grade reading subtasks assessed via the EGRA instrument covers multiple skills such as concepts about print, phonemic awareness, letter identification, and oral reading fluency. EGRA implementation also often features a contextual questionnaire concerning factors that may affect student outcomes, such as whether children have the school textbook, whether someone helps students with homework at home, and indicators of the child's socioeconomic background.

Implementation. The assessment is a 15- to 20-minute, individual, oral assessment involving the subject and the EGRA assessor. Assessors are trained as a group before they travel to the selected sample of schools in teams of three or four to conduct the assessment, usually with 15 to 17 students per grade, per school. Students read out the letters, words, or text passage from student prompt sheets, while assessors mark responses on a student response form. The assessors use a stopwatch for the timed exercises. Often a team supervisor verifies the completeness and clarity of the completed surveys, and harmonizes approaches from one assessment to the next.

Materials. In advance of data collection, project staff must prepare the correct number of student response forms, student stimuli sheets, school visit summary sheets, student selection sheets, and any additional instruments (such as student, teacher, or parent questionnaires) and package them by team and for each school. Project staff must check each sheet and instrument, especially the stimuli and student response forms, for copy quality, correct ordering, and stapling. They must also count and package the necessary tools for each team, including stopwatches, pencils, erasers, pencil sharpener, envelopes, bags, extra staplers, staples, and other accompanying materials, such as tape and markers. For a data collection in Mali in 2009, two international consultants and 33 team representatives required 4 days to prepare the fieldwork materials. In addition, each of the 33 teams of four assessors/supervisors needed an additional day to prepare materials by school.

Logistics and quality control. After data collection in each school, EGRA assessors must collect filled-in student response forms and questionnaires in envelopes and boxes for transportation. When the teams return from the fieldwork, local data entry specialists enter the results, sheet by sheet, into an electronic EGRA data system (some options are described in the second portion of this chapter). These data entry specialists usually receive 1 week of training by RTI staff or consultants beforehand to ensure their mastery of the process and coding rules. Furthermore, to reduce data errors and ensure quality, project staff commonly do a visual, on-screen quality check of at least 10 percent of paper questionnaires using the electronic data system. Actual data analysis often reveals anomalies that require double-checking the original hard copies of the questionnaires.

Benefits of Electronic Data Collection

A digital data collection approach could make the process described above more effective and efficient in several ways. First, and most obviously, it would reduce the amount of paper needed for EGRA data collection instruments. In that same EGRA implementation in Mali, which involved some 10,200 children, the staff needed about 156,000 sheets of paper for just the main set of instruments and accompanying documentation. Even for a simpler, single-language representative sample with only three subtasks, such as the one in Senegal referenced in Chapter 2 (national reading diagnostics), the amount of paper needed just for the tests amounted to 4,326 single-sided pages. Added to that was paper for record-keeping and supplemental research instruments, bringing the total to more than 7,000 sheets of paper.

Additional costs associated with the use of all of this paper include the labor involved in the lengthy processes of checking student sheets for copy quality, stapling individual packets, and counting instruments out by team and school in advance of data collection in the field. Furthermore, 7,000 pages of questionnaires amounts to approximately 35 kilograms (77 pounds) of weight. Although this is generally distributed among several teams traveling by car, in some cases the assessment is to be conducted in extremely rural communities where motorbike, boat, or walking is the only way to arrive. In these cases, an electronic method of data collection would significantly reduce the need for each data collection team to transport dozens of boxes of paper, exposing the paper copies to dust, inclement weather, and damage from handling, particularly where road conditions are poor. (Challenges of electronic data collection are discussed in the next section.)

Second, an electronic solution could improve the efficiency of EGRA data entry. If data were collected on a digital interface in the first place, data collection and data entry would become one and the same, because the data could be exported directly from the selected device into the database for analysis. This technique would significantly reduce the labor required for data entry specialists—both the time spent training individuals on the coding system for EGRA and the software interface, and the time needed to enter the data manually. Currently, one assessment form takes between 5 and 10 minutes to enter into a given EGRA data system. A budget analysis of two recent RTI projects (see Chapters 2 and 4) indicated that local printing and data entry costs accounted for as much as 8 percent of the budget in Nicaragua and 15 percent in Liberia.

The automatic transfer of data also would reduce the timeline for data collection, entry, and analysis. This step would thus make the assessment more accessible to a variety of stakeholders in changing circumstances, especially when they need data rapidly to make important decisions based on evidence from the study.

Third, a carefully implemented electronic approach should improve data quality, reducing potential human error introduced when the data are transferred from paper into the EGRA data system. Naturally, doing this cannot eliminate all human error, as one individual still would be responsible for marking the children's assessments; at a minimum, however, it would eliminate one redundancy that is a potential source of human error.

The system may also be designed to help reduce errors and omissions—e.g., through consistency checks—when assessors administer the test. Again drawing on actual field experience to illustrate this point, during another recent EGRA implementation using a custom-made electronic data-entry interface designed to reduce errors, a random quality control of 10 percent of the EGRA instruments revealed that more than three errors each were present in 8 of 50 schools reviewed—in other words, data from 16 percent of schools had to be reentered because of human data-entry error. One source of error was that data-entry specialists had failed to enter the sex of a dozen children into the system, although the information had been available on the paper sheets. An electronic system would prompt an assessor if such data were missing, and the test could not continue until the information was entered.

Finally, an electronic solution may also reduce measurement errors arising from problems in handling the timers and other testing materials. Field observations show that managing the student, student prompt sheets, student response sheets, and timer at the same time can be difficult for assessors, especially when conditions are poor, and there may not even be a table or chairs available for testing. Difficulties include forgetting to start the timer, setting the wrong amount of time on the timer, or leaving student prompt sheets with the student when they should have been taken away. Accurate timing is important because it allows us to create a key standard indicator of reading fluency: correct words per minute. A 1-second error in stopping or starting the timer equals a 1-word-per-minute difference in the reading score for a 60-word passage, when all other factors are the same.

Limitations and Challenges of Electronic Data Collection

Obviously, using electronic data collection would not eliminate all the limitations of print-based testing; indeed, doing so might introduce new challenges. For example, although a digital solution would eliminate the risk of environmental damage to paper forms during difficult transport situations, it might pose a great risk that all assessment data could be lost at once through loss, damage, or theft of a single device, if proper backup procedures were not in place. Likewise, handling of the new device might prove to be more challenging than handling the timer and all associated materials.

EGRA typically requires at least 2 weeks of training before assessors are fully comfortable with the assessment methodology and procedures. Adding a new technology would require learning completely new skill sets if assessors were not already familiar with computers and digital interface features such as scrolling up and down or using a stylus or touch screen.

Finally, without a paper backup, we would have no way for a different person to review or verify the accuracy of the data that were entered, especially if problems were to arise with ambiguous data. Thus, strong electronic quality control and supportive supervision during data collection would be crucial.

Finding an ideal digital solution among the technologies on the market could pose a challenge in terms of required features. First, a balance would need to be found between functionality and cost. That is, an electronic solution must be cost-effective while also being rugged, user-friendly, and reliable. A rugged device should be able to withstand regular use and transport in a variety of climates and circumstances. Furthermore, to recoup the initial investment, it should also have an extended shelf life so that the device could be used for multiple assessments over time. A user-friendly device should have a screen large enough to read comfortably and manipulate using a stylus or touch screen. A reliable device should take into account extended battery life and possibilities for creating data backups. Finding all these qualities in one, low-cost device may be a challenge, so some trade-offs might need to be considered.

Creating software that will accept multiple language fonts is another challenge. This is particularly true for two situations: use of less-common letters found in the derived and extended versions of the Latin alphabet that make use of ligatures, modified letters, digraphs, or diacritics; and use of other non-Latin writing systems, such as Arabic. Ideally, one software interface would allow local implementation teams to input the subtask items for each new instance of EGRA themselves, without having to rely on an external specialist to manipulate the programming interface. In addition to the subtask items appearing in the correct language of assessment, ideally the user interface and instructions should also be available in the language of the assessors.

Apart from the issue of language, EGRA differs from standard surveys because of its time-sensitive nature, and because assessors must enter data at the pace of the student reading the assessment, not at their own natural pace of data entry. Therefore, standard survey data software on the market is likely not appropriate for adaptation to real-time entry of responses on EGRA subtasks.

Technology-Supported Implementation Models

Education-Sector Examples of Electronic Data Collection

The EGRA process could use any number of portable technologies, such as tablet computers, handheld digital assistants, or smartphones, but a custom interface is required. In practice, mobile devices are common and have been used for electronic data collection in health (Seebregts et al., 2009; Tomlinson et al., 2009; Yu et al., 2009) and education. However, the specificity of the EGRA implementation model, as described above—particularly the timed nature of certain subtasks—presents a new challenge to existing data collection technologies. This section describes some actual experiences with electronic data collection in education and some possibilities for alternative implementation under the EGRA model.

A well-known literacy test in the United States, DIBELS, has been adapted to a handheld device for classroom use by teachers. The touch screen and stylus allow teachers to record incorrect responses to preloaded test items or texts, and the software automatically calculates scores without the need for a stopwatch. In addition to being a data collection tool, it allows teachers to use, track, and analyze student data themselves, rather than just administering tests for district or national purposes.

According to Wireless Generation, the company that produced the software for the handheld device (http://www.wirelessgeneration.com/solutions/mclass-dibels.html), using it can save teachers up to five instructional days per year (Olson, 2007). The sophisticated software also provides instant item analysis to highlight patterns and suggest areas for targeted instruction. At the school level, administrators can monitor progress over time and across grade levels; a given school can be compared with other schools or districts. The two main constraints to adapting this tool to EGRA would be the costs associated with adaptation, personalization, and setup and the need to involve the software developers for each new intervention and language.

The American Institutes for Research (AIR), with funding from the US Agency for International Development (USAID) through the Educational Quality Improvement Program 1 (EQUIP1), has conducted two studies comparing digital and paper-based data collection or data entry for education surveys (Estrada & Zimmerman, 2009; Zimmerman, 2008). In Nicaragua in 2008, the digital device was Global Relief Technology's Rapid Data Management System Ruggedized Personal Digital Assistant (PDA; http://www.globalrelieftech.com/technology/RDMS-Collect.aspx). In Honduras in 2009, the technologies were Turning Technologies ResponseCard XR (http://www.turningtechnologies.com/audienceresponseproducts/responseoptions/responsecards/responsecardxr) and EarthWalk mobile computer labs (http://www.earthwalk.com/products/mobile-labs). The research looked at flexibility, ease of use, materials, time, transportation and security, and cost to compare the electronic solutions with traditional paper-based testing. The remainder of this section describes some of the findings from the Nicaragua data collection (Zimmerman, 2008).

In terms of flexibility, using the digital device had the advantage of facilitating immediate changes to the instrument, and it reduced inefficiencies caused by photocopying too many or too few surveys for a given school. However, Zimmerman notes that the paper forms were easier to use for quickly capturing additional, qualitative information in the form of notes jotted in the margins. Similarly, for ease of use, Zimmerman (2008) cited the advantage of digital data collection over handling large volumes of paper; the report noted, however, that electronic data collection was not conducive to gathering *qualitative* data (i.e., interviews and focus groups) but only to recording responses to quantifiable or closed-ended questions. The experience showed that the learning curve with the handheld devices was overcome in a matter of hours after practicing, which is encouraging.

According to this study, digital data collection reduced the total amount of materials required. The selected technology combined several device functions into one: global positioning system (GPS) locator; photo, video, and audio capture; cellular phone; and data capture and media cataloguing. The study noted that about 4 weeks were required for paper data to be collected and processed before analysis could begin, whereas with the digital data collection it was nearly instantaneous, as data were synchronized daily so that early results could be monitored and problems identified. This also proved to be an important factor in Honduras (Estrada & Zimmerman, 2009), since previously the process of collecting test booklets to analyze data required 3 months, but for the data to be useful for education policy and teacher training, education authorities needed to have the results before the next school year began.

In Nicaragua, digital data collection facilitated both transportation and data security; data could be transmitted via satellite network nightly. Meanwhile, in the event of loss or damage to paper forms, no backup existed, and transporting the paper forms was a challenge.

Finally, the study confirmed that cost savings were considerable in terms of the time and labor involved in data entry and analysis. In the area of costs, the researchers concluded:

> An initial and high level look at both costs suggest that, at the very least, the savings in labor realized through the digital approach make up for the added costs for equipment and services to complete the project, and at best even have the potential to reduce overall costs as well as provide the other benefits described above around data security and implementation/process efficiencies…. Much of the costs associate [sic] with digital data collection are attributable to equipment. If equipment is purchased and those costs amortized over several projects then costs come down even further. This makes the cost/benefit ratio of digital very attractive compared to that of paper, particularly in light of lower vulnerability to loss which would be at significant cost. (Zimmerman, 2008, p. 7)

However, the report concluded that more research is needed in this area, including assessing the relative accuracy of the different methods.

Whereas Zimmerman (2008) reported on a sophisticated handheld device, less expensive and more widely available technologies are also a possibility for EGRA. The simplest mobile phone models are already being used for gathering school-level data and reporting information such as teacher and student attendance through SMS (text messaging). This is a technology that a great many people already have and know how to use. Low-cost or free software packages (e.g., FrontlineSMS) can capture the data sent by SMS over the mobile phone network, and they can even provide automatic SMS feedback.

In addition to saving time by combining data collection with data entry, mobile phone data collection allows schools to make information available immediately, when it is needed. For instance, parents may find it much less useful to know how many times their child was absent last week than to know that he or she is not in school right now. A simple SMS from the teacher to the parent would make this information available. The same could be done for EGRA results or other forms of advocacy and community outreach.

Potential Models of Electronic Data Collection for EGRA

In theory, one way to apply mobile phone technology to EGRA data collection would involve sending the results of each subtask, item by item, using a series of digits (e.g., 1 = correct answer, 0 = incorrect answer, 9 = no answer) in the form of a text message prefaced by a code indicating student identification number and EGRA subtask number. The database would automatically parse the data and enter them into a database. The database could also send automatic feedback, such as the number of correct words per minute, or the child's score relative to the scores of other students in the database. The main concerns in this model would be the costs of sending SMS and the reliability and coverage of national networks. It could, however, be a suitable model for informal testing, done by teachers or school inspectors at local levels.

Another conceivable use of mobile phone technology for EGRA administration would involve using the phones as audio recording devices, then scoring the tests in a central location and providing the results to parents and teachers via mobile phones. This approach would eliminate the need for experienced and trained EGRA assessors to travel to and from the schools. Instead, teachers could administer EGRA, and specialized, trained individuals could do the scoring remotely at a separate location.

This "distributed system" could improve access to the device for more learners, improve the consistency and accuracy of scoring, and possibly reduce data entry errors. Perhaps most important, however, is that this methodology might prove to be locally sustainable, as cellular technology is ubiquitous: it has achieved a maturity and cost level that has turned it from a tool for a selected few into an everyday commodity. If mobile phones could be harnessed to allow assessments to be conducted independently of location and availability of specialized human resources, it would enable experts and teachers to share observations more effectively than before and help teachers become proficient in the assessment techniques used. As a result, more schools could adopt continuous assessment and targeted interventions (see Chapter 4) as a method for improving outcomes.

For large EGRA implementations, the distributed scoring methodology enabled by phones would be time-consuming. Therefore, a phone-based application that involved automatic scoring via voice recognition would be ideal: a child could speak responses into a device that would be programmed to discern correct and incorrect answers. However, an approach based on voice recognition is not currently considered feasible except possibly in very widely used languages (such as English) for which voice recognition software has been under development and testing for some time. The reliability of this type of software is also questionable, particularly across different geographic zones with different regional variations in pronunciation.

Phones could be used in conjunction with interactive voice response (IVR) technology to capture general information automatically, such as school code, grade level, sex, and other statistical information that could be used later to analyze the scores. In this case, a recorded voice would state the information needed and would prompt assessors with the appropriate codes to enter. This would make it easier and more natural for EGRA assessors to provide the information required for remote scorers. The amount of information to be collected *a priori* would be customized centrally, after administrators had weighed the trade-offs between information collected and time taken to collect it. Such a system could be set up to allow individual children to repeat EGRA later (to assess their progress), and the key identifying information would need to be entered only once.

Finally, other technologies besides mobile phones also would be feasible, but might require a larger investment in hardware as well as development costs for custom software. RTI has developed an electronic EGRA data collection interface (Tangerine™) for touch-screen devices and is testing it on a variety of hardware models. A partner organization in Yemen has also developed a touch-screen version for use with the Apple iPad. Many models of computer-based data entry interfaces have already been designed for use with Microsoft

Excel, Access, or other custom interfaces, such as Visual Basic. Modifying these to be a direct data collection tool (rather than a mode of transcription from paper forms to the computer for analysis) is entirely feasible, but the portability and battery life of the computers required to use them will be a challenge in some field work situations. RTI will analyze whether the electronic solution produces significant gains in cost, data quality, or time (to obtain results) compared with the traditional paper-based methodology.

This chapter is by no means exhaustive in terms of potential electronic aids and EGRA. Other innovations (e.g., optical character recognition [OCR], the digital pen) and the experiences of other institutions and individuals could be applied to digital data collection for EGRA. Some technologies are

Additional Uses of ICT for Early Grade Reading Assessment and Intervention

In addition to the primary ways of using ICT with EGRA we discuss throughout this chapter, here we suggest additional supplementary technologies that can be useful for preparing the assessment items, for training assessors, and eventually for implementing literacy improvement programs.

Analysis of letter or word frequency. When an EGRA instrument is being prepared for the first time in a less-common language, developers must ensure that the subtasks accurately reflect the linguistic composition of the language (e.g., frequency of letters and sounds) and the expected level of difficulty of the grade being tested. In addition to Microsoft Excel, several innovative language-analysis software programs are capable of producing letter frequencies and word lists. They could be useful for preparing tests or for designing instructional materials and reading texts.

- Developers have used *Excel* to import a sample of text from local textbooks and then analyze the frequency and length of letters and words for different grade levels and for the language as a whole.

- *SynPhony* is a browser-based tool being developed by a researcher at the Canada Institute of Linguistics (Rennert, n.d.); it can create word lists and invented words (such as those used in the EGRA nonword reading subtask) based on parameters set by the user, such as word length, number of syllables, or beginning sound. This software is currently available in English, with pilot demonstration models in non-Latin scripts, including Devangari, Bengali, syllabic (Inuktituk), and Greek. With a few days of manual input of lists of words and letters (or graphemes—sets of letters representing a single sound), and review and pilot testing by linguists, users can create functional versions in almost any world language.

- *PrimerPro* is a software developed by SIL International to assist with the development of graded reading materials for a given language (B. Trudell, personal communication, already commonly used in health science research; for instance, Kardaun (2001) described several gains from using scanning and OCR technology for processing death certificates. Researchers in various countries have explored a range of other ICT applications (see text box). The challenge will be in determining which of these solutions is most feasible for the education sector and in low-income and low-infrastructure environments. Doing so will require carefully pilot testing, calculating cost savings, establishing the return on investment based on different use scenarios (e.g., one-time baseline versus continuous assessment), and sharing research and findings. All such information would contribute to the global knowledge base.

April 16, 2011). Like SynPhony, the software produces frequency counts for graphemes and words based on a given text, providing a suggested teaching order. These lists can aid in the development of controlled texts to ensure that they contain only material that students have learned. Once the text or story has been developed, PrimerPro can then verify that it does not contain any letters or graphemes that have not been introduced. Finally, the program can also conduct advanced searches based on parts of speech (or other language features) that may be useful in designing a primer. PrimerPro has already been used to develop reading materials in minority languages of Mali, Nigeria, Tanzania, Mozambique, and elsewhere.

Video for training assessors. ICT can be valuable to help ensure reasonable levels of interrater reliability (consistency of scoring across assessors). In Senegal, the training team pre-video-recorded actual children (during the instrument pilot testing phase) reading the subtasks. (In such cases, to protect the privacy of the child, only the student stimuli sheet was visible on the camera.) The team then used these recordings to track the consistency with which trainees watching the recording—whether individually or in a group—scored the same child on the same items. The recorded option allowed

the assessors to score the instrument under circumstances close to a real situation, as opposed to, for example, having a trainer read the instrument while everyone collectively scored the sample. In a live setting, some trainees will necessarily be at a disadvantage from being farther away, near a window, or at a different angle where sound interference or other distractions might be present.

Using the video, the EGRA team also observed a significant difference of opinion concerning the acceptable pronunciation of a certain French word, "village"; children who spoke Wolof could not pronounce the "ge" (/zh/) combination in the same manner as a native French speaker and instead pronounced a hard "z." Having a recording that allowed the assessors to rewind and listen to the pronunciation over and over again served to launch the discussion and come to an agreement about what was or was not acceptable in a test of reading.

(continued)

Additional Uses of ICT for Early Grade Reading Assessment and Intervention (continued)

Real-time data entry and analysis for training assessors. Another useful step during assessor training is to have a data entry and analysis system set up so that the training team can rapidly analyze practice tests from the same subject. The greatest benefit is quickly analyzing subtask items that might be posing a problem (as reflected in poor interrater reliability measurements). For example, in Senegal, where Wolof is a predominant mother tongue but French is the language of instruction (and in this instance, of the assessment), item analysis of practice tests demonstrated that assessors had a great deal of difficulty consistently scoring "m" and "n" sounds during the letter identification subtask. To help the assessors distinguish the sounds during administration, we placed these two items next to each other on the EGRA stimulus sheet.

ICT for reading drills and practice. Research on the process of reading acquisition highlights the importance of *automaticity*, or reaching a level of reading fluency beyond the need to focus on the mental exercise of decoding words, as a foundation skill (Sprenger-Charolles & Messaoud-Galusi, 2009; see also Chapter 1). ICT can be used to help develop this automaticity through drill and practice exercises related to letter sounds (phonemes) and vocabulary or through interactive multimedia approaches to match letters to sounds, combine sounds, and deconstruct words. Vocabulary and comprehension skills also can be encouraged through exposing children to language in general, and communicative competencies can be increased through electronic storybooks, read-aloud texts, online collaborative exchanges, collaborative story writing, and so on. For example, in August 2010, RTI introduced an interactive DVD (digital versatile disc) in Egypt to help learners—adults and children—match graphemes in Arabic to their appropriate sound.

Videos to improve classroom instruction techniques. In many countries, researchers have used model teaching videos to help teach and reinforce teaching routines for early literacy, based on the theory that video can foster certain automatic responses to key teaching situations (e.g., teaching routines, classroom management) so that teachers'

Use of Technology for EGRA Data Management, Analysis, and Presentation

There is no question about the potential of technology for data management, analysis, and presentation. Thus, rather than making a case for the use of technology, we instead address a question to be considered at the very outset of EGRA implementation: Which software package may be most appropriate for analyzing EGRA data?

We emphasize here that this chapter was written by practitioners for practitioners, not by or for statisticians. Thus, this part of the chapter reflects the experience of analyzing EGRA data from six different collections in three different countries and six languages. We offer simple guidance about avoiding cognitive resources can be freed for dealing with more complex teaching behaviors (e.g., individual feedback, continuous assessment [H. Abadzi, personal communication, 2010]). ICT can also be used to increase instructional time and to diversify instruction for learners at different levels with instructional software that is self-directed. It can also complement traditional group learning facilitated by a teacher through additional visual and audio stimuli.

Mobile phone applications offer fun and effective games and tools for literacy that may be more accessible than other technologies—or possibly even books—in many situations (Abimbola et al., 2009; Revelle et al., 2007).[1] Wagner and colleagues (2010) found that computer-assisted instruction for literacy may help motivate learners who had dropped out of school to return.

Communication and social mobilization. Another emerging area of ICT application is for communication and social mobilization related to results of EGRA studies. RTI used video for this purpose in Liberia (Chapter 4) and experimented with text messaging in Senegal (Chapter 2).

Many outstanding questions remain to be addressed through reliable, scientific research on both the effectiveness of the aforementioned technologies and the impact of ICT on literacy. Some key research questions would be: How much exposure to a given software program does it take to increase scores? Can children learn effectively from literacy software in a self-paced environment? What impact does the use of electronic literacy materials have on motivation to read and transitioning to the print-based environment? How sustainable are these efforts if costs include Internet access or recurrent mobile telephone costs?

---

[1] See, for example, the many publications of Matt Kam, PhD, and the Mobile and Immersive Learning for Literacy in Emerging Economies (MILLEE) project, Carnegie Mellon University and the University of California, Berkeley, http://www.millee.org; or the Bridges to the Future Initiative model of computer-aided instruction for literacy (Wagner et al., 2010).

pitfalls and optimizing options, based on the particular requirements for EGRA data and key indicators.

The question of the right software needs to be addressed in parallel with planning the EGRA implementation, instrument adaptation, and piloting. Answering a few strategic questions can help with the choice of the right software:

- What is the nature of the data?
- What questions does the research need to answer? (What analysis needs to be done?)
- How big will the data set be? (How many students will be assessed, and how many variables will the analysis entail?)

- How many people will be analyzing data? (Will data need to be exchanged among various people?)

- What software is commonly used in the country? (Will quick and competent help be readily available, if needed?)

- What operating system will be used? What are the system specifications?

- How much money is the funding organization willing to spend?

We compare and contrast three widely used software packages[2] on the market relative to their ability to perform the most common and useful types of EGRA analyses, as well as some of their more specialized procedures concerning sampling weights and complex sampling:

- Microsoft Excel (http://www.microsoft.com)

- Stata (http://www.stata.com)

- SPSS (http://www.spss.com)

Table 6.1 summarizes the similarities and differences among the three packages; readers are invited to refer to this table in conjunction with the comparisons that we offer in the remainder of the chapter.

Nature of the Data

Typical EGRA data types are the following:

- Continuous variables (integers and integers with decimals), e.g., for grade level, number of correct letters read, number of seconds remaining on the clock, or number of correct words per minute,

- Continuous variables (percentages), e.g., for percentage of reading comprehension questions correctly answered, and

- Dichotomous numeric variables, e.g., use of 0/1 for male/female or no/yes.

All three statistical packages compared in Table 6.1 are geared toward analyzing these types of quantitative data.

EGRA requires software that is suitable not just for data management and analysis once all data have been collected, but also for statistical analysis during instrument development and piloting. In that process, establishing the reliability of the EGRA instrument is critical. Doing so requires some

---

[2] Several other packages, such as SAS, could be applied for this purpose. To date, however, the authors have not used SAS with EGRA and thus cannot offer practical experience.

Table 6.1 Comparison of software packages for EGRA data analysis

Area	Item	Excel	Stata	SPSS
Nature of the EGRA data	Continuous variables (integers and integers with decimals)	✔	✔	✔
	Continuous variables (percentage)	✔	✔	✔
	Dichotomous numeric variables	✔	✔	✔
Analysis				
EGRA implementation approach/ Size of sample	Snapshot approach/ Below 250 variables and no more than a few hundred cases	✔	✔	✔
	National approach/ Above 250 variables and a few hundred cases	✗	✔	✔
Instrument validity	Cronbach's alpha	✔	✔	✔
	Subtask correlations	✔	✔	✔
Descriptive analysis	Frequencies	✔	✔	✔
	Descriptives	✔	✔	✔
Inferential analysis	Group differences	✔[1]	✔	✔
	Multiple regression	✗	✔	✔
	Effect size	✔	✔	✔
Survey data analysis	Proportional weighting	✗	✔	✗[2]
Analysis process and support				
Process	Individual analysis	✔	✔	✔
	Shared analysis	✗	✔	✔
Support	Access to help	✔	✔	✔
	No immediate, personal access to help	✔	✗	✗
System requirements[3]				
Operating System	Windows for PC	✔	✔	✔
	Macintosh	As Microsoft Office for Macintosh	✔	✔
	Unix/Linux	✗	✔	✔

(continued)

Table 6.1 Comparison of software packages for EGRA data analysis *(continued)*

Area	Item	Excel	Stata	SPSS
System requirements[3] *(continued)*				
Processor		500 MHz processor or higher		
Memory/ Read-access memory (RAM)		256 MB or higher	Minimum of 512 MB[4]	1 GB or more recommended
Disk space		1.5 GB[5]	Minimum of 250 MB	Minimum of 800 MB
Display/ Resolution		1024 × 768 or higher	No info	Super VGA (800 × 600) or higher
Cost[6]				
	Most basic version	US$139.99	US$1,695	US$2,248.75
	Including survey data analysis functions	Not available	Already in base package	US$1,248.75

✔ = feasible/possible to use. ✘ = not feasible/possible to use.

GB = gigabyte; MB = megabyte; MHz = megahertz; PC = personal computer; US$ = US dollar; VGA = video graphics array.

[1] Only if simple and if the sample is small.

[2] Only with add-on module for Complex Samples.

[3] System requirements are from the official product websites and for the following versions currently sold on the market: Microsoft Office 2007, Stata 11, SPSS Statistics 18.

[4] The amount of memory determines the number of variables or operations that Stata can handle.

[5] A portion of this disk space will be freed after installation if the original download package is removed from the hard drive.

[6] Prices were taken from the official vendors' websites and are provided to illustrate the relative cost of the software packages. Costs quoted are for individual license for the government/nonprofit sector, with location USA, without maintenance, and for the Windows operating system. Specific quotes are for Microsoft Excel 2010 Stand-Alone Program, Stata/SE 12, and IBM SPSS Statistics Base 19.

data analysis that is not related to the actual research questions (which are addressed below).

To explain further: whenever EGRA researchers newly create or adapt an EGRA instrument, they need to begin an instrument pilot testing phase. This phase involves running statistical procedures on results from an actual (albeit limited) field application, or pilot test, of EGRA for common aspects such as grade level, sex, or school effect. One important step is to examine carefully the results as a function of grade level to ensure that the instrument is neither so hard that all the children in the lowest grade of implementation perform very poorly nor so easy that children in the higher grades get a perfect score.

In addition, analysis is needed to establish the reliability of the instrument and its individual subtasks, such as listening comprehension. Ascertaining that the EGRA subtasks produce valid and reliable responses, should the EGRA be repeatedly administered to the same student, is critical. The appropriate operation for this type of analysis is establishing Cronbach's alpha for the instrument as a whole and for those subtasks that are scaled (e.g., the comprehension subtasks; see Table 6.2). The overall alpha of 0.80 seen here indicates a reasonably high internal consistency of the items in the test.

Furthermore, test designers should review the instruments for internal consistency (that is, how well the different subtasks within the instrument complement one another) and, at the same time, ensure that instrument subtasks are not so correlated that they measure the same thing and thus dilute the construct. Analysts typically do this by calculating the correlation between a subtask and every other subtask and the EGRA instrument as a whole. As can be seen in Table 6.3, the familiar word reading subtask in this instrument and the oral reading fluency subtask show a reasonably high correlation of 0.78. This means that higher (or lower) scores on the familiar word reading variable tend to be paired with higher (or lower) scores on the oral reading fluency variables.

Stata and SPSS can easily and very quickly conduct those procedures. Microsoft Excel also has this functionality, although it involves taking several steps and entering and calculating several formulas. Del Siegle, PhD, of the Neag School of Education at the University of Connecticut, has developed

Table 6.2 Results from the EGRA Plus: Liberia reliability analysis

Item (EGRA subtask)	Item-test correlation	Correlation of item with rest of items	Average inter-item correlation	Cronbach's alpha
Letter identification	0.67	0.53	0.37	0.78
Phonemic awareness	0.55	0.38	0.41	0.81
Familiar word reading	0.82	0.73	0.33	0.74
Nonword reading	0.60	0.44	0.39	0.80
Oral reading fluency	0.84	0.75	0.32	0.74
Reading comprehension	0.77	0.66	0.34	0.76
Listening comprehension	0.50	0.32	0.43	0.82
Overall test			**0.37**	**0.80**

Source: Adapted from Crouch & Korda, 2008, p. 5.

Table 6.3 Correlation matrix to illustrate how EGRA performs as an integrated tool

Item (EGRA subtask)	Letter identification	Phonemic awareness	Familiar word reading	Nonword reading	Oral reading fluency	Reading comprehension	Listening comprehension
Letter identification	1.00						
Phonemic awareness	0.27	1.00					
Familiar word reading	0.53	0.31	1.00				
Nonword reading	0.24	0.23	0.46	1.00			
Oral reading fluency	0.53	0.29	0.78	0.44	1.00		
Reading comprehension	0.43	0.29	0.61	0.36	0.70	1.00	
Listening comprehension	0.22	0.25	0.24	0.14	0.24	0.27	1.00

Source: Adapted from Crouch & Korda, 2008, p. 5.

an Excel spreadsheet to aid calculation of Cronbach's alpha (limits are 1,000 subjects with a maximum of 100 responses for each), which may help in those cases (Siegle, n.d.).

The Research Question(s)

As laid out in Chapter 1, EGRA can be used to answer numerous different questions that governments or other organizations pose in relation to children's abilities in early grade reading. Given the many and varied analyses that investigators can carry out on a set of EGRA data, focusing efforts on the specific question(s) under investigation is critical. At the same time, as noted earlier in this chapter, the types of analyses to be done influence what software package may be the most appropriate. This section describes the three types of research questions that most commonly drive external EGRA implementations:

1. **What is the general state of affairs regarding children's reading skills?** As demonstrated by the other chapters in this book, this type of EGRA administration can cover a small sample for a "snapshot" of a school district, a region, or an entire nation.

2. **What is the impact of an intervention?** Addressing this question involves a test/retest scenario.

3. **How do various groups differ in their performance on EGRA?**

The General State of Affairs Question

Governments and donor organizations very often want to know the general state of affairs related to core early reading skills, such as phonemic awareness or letter identification; they may want to know this across the country, in a region, or in a certain grade or grades. To simplify the discussion in this chapter, we focus on two main ways in which analysts can go about answering this question, based in part on the scope of the sample.

At one end of the spectrum is the EGRA *snapshot approach,* which involves taking a small random sample from across a limited population of interest. The snapshot is a good way to gather insights on core aspects of that population's early grade reading in a relatively cost-efficient and time-effective manner.

By contrast, at the other end of the spectrum, for some countries the national representativeness of the EGRA sample is very important. This need calls for a second EGRA implementation approach, called the *national approach* (see Chapter 2), in which appropriate sampling procedures—and later, weighting procedures (described below)—ensure that results can be generalized and reported in relation to the country as a whole, and not solely to a certain region, group of schools, or students. Taking the national approach has significant implications for data analysis and the software to choose.

Data analysis for the state of affairs research question will most likely try to extract information in three areas:

1. **the sample**—its makeup and characteristics (for either snapshot or national approach);

2. **the performance of the children** in the sample on the various EGRA subtasks chosen (for either snapshot or national approach, but usually fewer subtasks are chosen for the snapshot approach); and

3. **socioeconomic aspects** of children's home and school environment that may explain differences in their performance in early grade reading.

Describing the Sample

To describe the sample, the type of analysis most often used is to calculate frequencies and means and to cross-tabulate certain variables to show, for example, the number of male and female students in each grade. Table 6.4 shows how such data may be presented. All three software packages can produce this type of analysis and data presentation.

Table 6.4 Presentation of sample description information

| Grade | Student Sex | | Total |
	Male	Female	
2	484	442	926
3	475	423	898
4	480	395	875
Total	1,439	1,260	2,699

Source: Adapted from RTI International, 2009c, p. 7.

Analyzing Performance

The metrics for analyzing the children's performance involve numbers and percentages of items read or done correctly (in some period of time, usually 1 minute) and correlation coefficients for reading comprehension and fluency.

Final results for variables such as "correct words per minute" are usually averaged across students. The necessary procedure is a simple descriptive analysis providing the mean score, standard deviation, standard error, and confidence intervals, as shown in Table 6.5. Depending on the format of the EGRA implementation, the results may be presented for different groups defined by variables such as sex, grade, or school type.

Table 6.5 Descriptive information commonly analyzed for EGRA subtasks

| Variable | N | Mean | Standard deviation | Standard error | 95% Confidence interval | |
					Upper bound	Lower bound
Subtask 1: Number of letters read correctly in 1 minute	687	28.3	18.0	0.7	29.6	26.9
Subtask 2: Number of nonwords read correctly in 1 minute	687	9.7	11.1	0.4	10.5	8.8
Subtask 3a: Number of words in a paragraph read in 1 minute	687	18.7	20.4	0.8	20.2	17.1
Subtask 3b: Reading comprehension score (percentage of correct answers out of 6 possible)	564	22.5%	28.2	1.2	24.9%	20.2%

Source: Adapted from RTI International, 2009b, p. 2.

Results of individual EGRA subtasks can be graphically presented in many ways. The histogram, box plot, and bar chart (Figures 6.1 through 6.3) are the most commonly used, depending on focus of the presentation and the types and number of contact groups (sex, school type, grade). Both analysis and results presentation and these sorts of graphics are straightforward to do with all three software packages.

Figure 6.1 Histogram presentation of the frequency distribution of results on the variable "correct letters per minute"

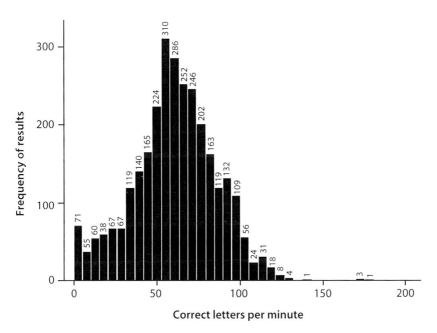

Source: RTI International, 2009a, p. 22.

Figure 6.2 Box plot presentation of results on the variable "correct letters per minute," illustrating results from students in three different grades

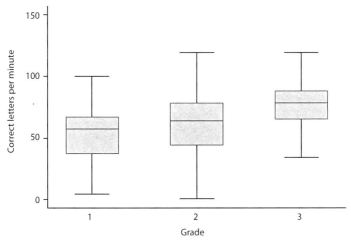

Note: The top and bottom of the box show the 75th and 25th percentile, respectively. The band inside the box indicates the median. The "whiskers" indicate the minimum and maximum of the data.

Source: Gove, 2008, p. 23.

Figure 6.3 Bar chart presentation of results on variable "correct letters (graphemes) per minute," by grades and school type, and disaggregated by sex

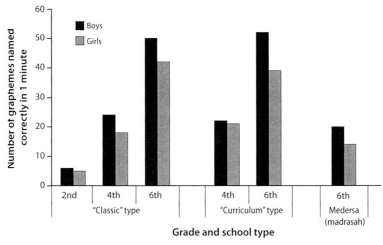

Note: This graph reports results from the EGRA application in Mali that is discussed in Chapter 3. To aid in interpretation: the letter identification subtask includes graphemes (sets of letters representing a single sound) as well as individual letters. Schools in Mali fall into three main categories: those that begin instruction with French only ("classic"), those that begin in the local language ("curriculum"), and *medersa* schools that instruct in Arabic.

Source: Ralaingita et al., 2009, p. 21 (translation from French).

To display results of the reading comprehension analysis, a correlation matrix featuring a fitted line is customarily used, as can be seen in Figure 6.4. This graphic shows the correlation between the number of correct responses in the reading comprehension subtask and oral reading fluency (correct words per minute). Again, all three software tools can do this type of analysis and produce the relevant graphics.

Figure 6.4 Correlation matrix highlighting the direction and strength of the relationship between reading comprehension and fluency

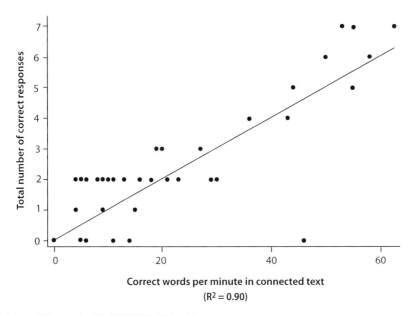

Correct words per minute in connected text
($R^2 = 0.90$)

Source: RTI International & CEPROCIDE, 2009, p. 36.

Analyzing Socioeconomic Factors

EGRA data analysts answering the general state of affairs question may want information on selected aspects of the child's home and school environment that may help explain some of the variance in students' performance on the EGRA subtasks. Such analysis may also be very helpful to inform the design of subsequent early grade reading interventions or supportive policies.

As noted earlier, an EGRA implementation often includes a set of contextual questions for students. These range from information on the age of the child, to a socioeconomic scale (possession of certain proxies of economic standing, such as radio, television, or vehicle for transport), to the availability of reading materials at home or whether somebody in the child's immediate family can read. Questions also garner more information on certain aspects of the school environment, such as whether the child has the reading textbook and whether the child's teacher gives homework.

This type of analysis and reporting is not limited to frequencies and descriptive statistics, such as the percentage of students who own the school reading textbook. Inferential statistics—specifically, regression procedures—can be applied to gain a better understanding of the factors associated with early reading skills. In other words, simple two-way correlations can tell us more about relationships of two variables, but they will not paint a comprehensive picture of the context associated with the actual EGRA results. Regressions allow a much more differentiated analysis of the associated factors, which is especially important for policy makers and intervention designers.

In theory, regression analysis is a procedure available within any of the statistical packages mentioned above. In practice, however, using Excel for this type of analysis is not convenient and therefore is not recommended for EGRA analysis. (For a step-by-step explanation of how to accomplish this task in Excel as well as more about its specific limitations in regard to doing regressions, see Miles, n.d.) Both Stata and SPSS have straightforward procedures for regression analysis, and both have been used with EGRA data. The choice of statistical analysis software for this particular task depends on the prior experience and preference of the analyst.

Analyzing Survey Data, Including Weighting

Earlier in this chapter we briefly explained two ends of a spectrum—snapshot and national approaches—in EGRA implementation. Although the EGRA instrument used may be the same in each case, data analysis will differ substantially. Most importantly, the proper analysis of EGRA data for a national approach usually requires weighting.

Weighting is necessary for estimating values such as averages or percentages when investigators cannot (for whatever reasons) draw a simple random sample of the population of students in each group of interest; this technique is also needed when some other, more complex form of sampling was used and the numbers sampled are not proportional to the population. If the sample is to drive estimates of absolute numbers in the population (e.g., estimate not simply the percentage of students who can read above a certain level, but their actual number), then analysts must always use weights.

Complex sample designs in EGRA are typically of a cluster sort, in which analysts first sample schools and then students from these schools. One reason is that, usually, no central lists of students exist from which to sample; another is that sampling just one or two students per school in hundreds of schools is too expensive. In the case in which evaluators sample a fixed number of students from each school—regardless of the total enrollment of the school—students' results have to be weighted differently, because in big schools the students sampled are "standing in" for a larger proportion of the population than in small schools.

An example might help: A country has two regions that are to be sampled, 1,000 students from each. The first region, which is poorer, contains a student population of 1,000,000. This means that each 1 of the sampled students will "stand in for" 1,000 students. The richer second region—where reading skills are better—has a total student population of only 500,000, such that each sampled student will stand in for 500 students. In this case, creating a simple, unweighted average to represent the results for both regions would overstate the nation's reading skills, because students with better reading skills would be overrepresented. That is, for poorer students to be represented appropriately relative to richer students, their scores would need to be more heavily weighted for calculating the average.

Weighting has major implications for the choice of analysis software. Mitchell (2006) discussed choice of statistical analysis packages for data analysis in general:

> Stata is far more comprehensive in its support for analyzing survey data than SAS or SPSS. Stata handles a wider variety of estimation commands and a wider variety of survey design types and/or survey aspects than SAS or SPSS. Stata provides the ability to perform survey data analysis for over 18 estimation commands (including regression, logit regression, ordinal logit regression, multinomial logit, Heckman selection models, negative binomial regression, and more). Stata supports surveys with psu/cluster/strata information as well as surveys with replicate weights.… By contrast SAS and SPSS offer extremely limited features for survey analysis. Neither can handle replicate weights, and both have a limited number of estimation commands supporting linear models and logistic regression. (p. 20)

> Stata supports four kinds of weights, frequency weights, sampling weights, analytic weights, and importance weights. Many commands support all four of these kinds of weights, while others may support a subset of these weights.… Aside from the Complex Samples module, SPSS appears to only offer one kind of weighting, frequency weights. (p. 21)

Excel may be helpful in calculating the appropriate multipliers or weights, but from what we know and have tried, *applying* the weighting multipliers for inferential analysis of the data for nationally representative samples becomes virtually impossible for anything beyond simple means (even for standard errors and confidence intervals).

Other problems with clustering arise that Excel cannot correct but that Stata can deal with even in its most basic version. These adjustments are the finite population correction and the design effect.

Finite population correction is used to estimate proper standard deviations in survey research. In a situation in which the size of the population is known (total student populations are usually known from enrollment lists) and the sample is equal to or greater than 5 percent, there is a far greater chance that the sample's data will apply to the population as a whole and not only to the sample. To show this extra confidence in the data statistically, analysts use the finite population correction factor to define both the standard error of the mean and the standard error of the proportion (Berenson et al., 2005; Pieniazek, 2007). As noted, Excel cannot account for this correction, at least not without a large amount of unpleasant manipulation.

Woods and McCurley (2004) described the *design effect* in complex samples and further noted SPSS's limitation in this regard:

> In any survey employing complex designs, clustering, stratification, disproportionate sampling, and samples with multiple stages, the standard errors are much larger than a simple random sample of the same size. Most of the standard statistical software packages, SPSS, SAS, assume a simple random sample with independent and identically distributed observations. The only exception is STATA. If the data were collected using a complex sample design, these standard packages severely underestimate the variance, resulting in too-small confidence intervals, leading to the rejection of the null hypothesis when it is true more frequently than the Type I error level would indicate. The difference between the variances produced when treating a complex sample as a simple random sample and the correct variance is called the design effect and can be calculated. (Abstract)

Thus, for any national EGRA implementation, we recommend that evaluators use Stata. It seems to be the software that is most viable and powerful among the three we have compared for the kind of analysis needed.

The Program Impact Question

Under the second research question (see page 202), EGRA serves as a tool to monitor the impact of early grade reading interventions and programs. In Mali, for example, EGRA was being used to evaluate the Read-Learn-Lead (RLL) program. As described in more detail in Chapter 3, RLL aims to demonstrate whether Mali's official curriculum, when properly implemented and supported, is a viable and effective approach to mother-tongue reading instruction and to children's acquisition of foundational reading skills in the early primary grades.

In this specific application, RTI used EGRA in 2009 to establish a baseline by gathering sample and performance information from students in both the control and the RLL program (intervention) groups. EGRA was used again in 2010 for a midterm assessment, and will be applied at the end of the intervention in 2012 to determine whether performance differed between the two groups and to explore which of these differences (if any) could possibly be explained by participation in the RLL program.

For a baseline analysis such as the one completed in 2009, the main concern in data analysis is to ensure that the two groups in the sample are similar to each other in their core characteristics, such as age, grade, socioeconomic standing, access to reading textbooks, or presence of another reader in their homes. Thus, as with the first research question, frequencies and simple descriptive analyses are presented, but they are cross-tabulated for each of the groups to highlight similarities and differences. Procedures also include tests of statistical significance (Student's t-test) to identify robust differences between groups.

Table 6.6 presents summary results of an EGRA study in this way. This table shows key characteristics of both the intervention and control group for the EGRA implementation in Mali. For each grade level, the table shows how many students were sampled for the EGRA in Bamanankan, the main national language of Mali, as well as the other languages in which EGRA was implemented in this study (Fulfulde, Songhoy, and Bomu). For each key characteristic, including grade and language, the intervention and control group were of similar size and the students in each group were of similar age.

Table 6.7 illustrates that, at baseline, the level of performance of the control group on familiar word reading did not differ significantly from that of the intervention group. The significance level used for this analysis was 95 percent—indicates that the probability of these results occurring by chance was less than 5 percent.

Table 6.6 Baseline comparison of average age of students in intervention and control schools

Grade	Language	Intervention group		Control group	
		N	Average age	N	Average age
Grade 1	Bamanankan	320	6.6	282	6.7
	Other	247	6.9	205	7.0
Grade 2	Bamanankan	298	7.7	302	7.9
	Other	374	8.1	340	8.2
Grade 3	Bamanankan	324	9.2	321	9.1
	Other	327	9.5	312	9.4

Source: Adapted from RTI International, 2009d, p. 13.

Table 6.7 Baseline sample performance of intervention and control schools: familiar word reading per minute

Subtask	Grade	Language	Contrast group	N	Mean	Standard error	Significance
Familiar word reading (correct words per minute)	1	Bamanankan	RLL	427	0.2	0.0	—
			Control	407	0.2	0.1	
		Other	RLL	438	0.3	0.1	—
			Control	419	0.3	0.1	
	2	Bamanankan	RLL	419	2.3	0.4	—
			Control	414	3.0	0.5	
		Other	RLL	538	1.3	0.2	—
			Control	523	0.9	0.2	
	3	Bamanankan	RLL	421	3.7	0.6	—
			Control	407	5.3	0.7	
		Other	RLL	445	3.4	0.4	—
			Control	449	6.6	1.9	

RLL = Read-Learn-Lead.

— The result was not significant at the 95% level.

Source: Adapted from RTI International, 2009d, p. 20.

Subsequent assessments then monitor and highlight changes in students' reading performance. This analysis is intended to establish whether the differences observed can indeed be attributed to participation in the intervention. As during the baseline, presenting descriptive analyses and reporting on analyses of significance of group differences are core procedures. Regression analysis helps illustrate and explain the context of the impact of the intervention in more detail. Further, this analysis needs to be complemented by an analysis of effect sizes—i.e., the magnitude of the difference in results between the experimental and control groups.

Table 6.8 is a simple comparison of results in absolute change and percentage. In this example, which draws on a 2008 EGRA implementation in Kenya, results for the letter identification subtask at baseline were on average 4.8 correct letters per minute. After the intervention (post-treatment), the average performance of the treatment group students on this subtask was 20.9 correct letters per minute; this represents an absolute increase of 16.1 correct letters per minute, or a percentage change of 335 percent.

Again, in theory, all three software packages—Excel, Stata, and SPSS—can support these types of analyses, although the practicality of using Excel is questionable. For guidance on how to use Excel just for calculating the effect size, see the Centre for Evaluation and Monitoring's primer on effect size and its effect-size calculator (Centre for Evaluation and Monitoring, n.d.).

Table 6.8 Results comparing performance of control and treatment schools in Kenya on four EGRA subtasks

Subtask	Group	Kiswahili Baseline Average	Kiswahili Post-treatment Average	Absolute change	Percentage change
Letter identification	T	4.8	20.9	16.1	335%
	C	4.5	20.3	15.8	351%
Familiar word reading	T	10.0	19.6	9.6	96%
	C	13.3	20.0	6.7	50%
Oral reading fluency	T	8.7	17.4	8.7	100%
	C	11.8	20.4	8.6	73%
Reading comprehension	T	0.4	0.7	0.4	106%
	C	0.5	0.3	-0.2	-40%

C = control group; T = treatment group.

Source: Adapted from Crouch, Korda, & Mumo, 2009, p. 14.

The Group Differences Question

The analysis of group differences, similar to what is described for the program impact question, can take place within a single EGRA data collection. Evaluators can compare, for example, the performance of children in one region with that of children in another region; they can also examine performance differences between, say, public and private schools. Data analysis and presentation include the following:

- sample description,
- descriptive analysis of results for each group,
- analysis of statistical significance of group differences, and
- regression analysis to identify the potential associations of several independent variables with the outcome variable of interest (e.g., the relationship between mother's ability to read and results on the oral reading fluency subtask).

The statistical analysis for this type of question is similar to that proposed above, and so is the applicability of the various statistical packages.

The Size of the Data Set (Cases and Variables)

The number of students and the number of variables included in an assessment can make a big impact on the choice of software to use for data analysis. These factors may in the end be the most decisive elements in the final choice of software.

The basic version of Stata 11 (Small Stata) has a limit of 1,200 cases and 99 variables. The more advanced Stata 11/SE can manage some 32,767 variables and a nearly unlimited number of cases (see Rodríguez, n.d.). However, the actual number of variables that can reasonably be contained and used in a data set is also limited by the computer's memory, which Stata draws on for its operations. The SPSS 18 GradPack Base has no limit on either cases or variables. The SPSS student pack is limited to 50 variables and 1,500 cases (SPSS Inc., 2009). "Unlimited," however, actually means somewhere around 2.15 billion variables or cases for either program. The Stata help website (http://www.stata.com/help.cgi?statase) explains in more detail these characteristics of the various Stata packages.

Microsoft Excel version 2003, which we have seen to be commonly available among colleagues and in the countries in which EGRA has been implemented to date, has a limitation of 256 variables (columns) and 65,536 cases (rows).

Depending on the EGRA implementation and approach, this limitation on the number of columns in a single Excel worksheet may be problematic.

The raw EGRA data may show "correct," "incorrect," and "not attempted" for every single item in the subtask (including the 100 letters, 50 nonwords, 50 familiar words, and a similar number of words in the oral reading fluency passage). Thus, it is easy to understand that 256 columns will be insufficient, especially for item-level (subtask) analysis and for EGRA implementations involving all the subtasks. Working across multiple Excel worksheets is also complicated if an analysis involves more than one variable. Although workarounds are possible (for example, one could have the 100 letters, 50 words, etc., each in a separate worksheet and only include the correct number of words or the correct number of words per minute in the main sheet), this approach is simply not practical and increases the danger of making mistakes or changing the data in ways that are not intended.

For Excel version 2007, however, the column and row limitations of previous Excel versions were lifted. Excel 2007 can include up to 1,048,576 cases (rows) and 16,384 columns (variables; see Microsoft Corporation, 2010). Excel 2010 also includes a PowerPivot function that allows for importing and analyzing millions of rows of data (Microsoft Corporation, 2011).

Again, however, this is the theory. In practice, working with EGRA data in Excel is cumbersome. In addition to the variable limitations are general limitations for any data analysis—especially those going beyond the EGRA snapshot approach. These include the following:

- **Lack of a logging feature.** No feature in Excel allows users to log and track work, as there is in Stata (log files) or SPSS (journal files). Thus, analysts have no way to see the exact point at which the analysis may have gone astray; nor can others review how the original analyst went about treating the data.

- **Lack of command/syntax feature.** Stata's "do files" and SPSS's "syntax files" are handy ways to map out analyses carefully and then effectively use earlier analyses (even from other EGRA implementations) to modify them or run the results again. This is especially valuable if more than one EGRA data collection is planned, as this means analyzing data sets with different cases but using the same variables more than once. Excel requires all analyses to begin anew with every single test or procedure to be applied.

Nevertheless, for some types of data collection, such as a snapshot version with a limited number of variables and no need for weighting, Excel may be an appropriate tool to use.

The Data Analysis Process

Whether one person will work alone on EGRA data analysis or whether several people will participate may make a big difference in regard to which software to use. Also important is who will be documenting the EGRA results, in a report or presentation, for example. If the arrangement is to have more than one person do the work, the next decision involves in what format data or results are to be shared; related to this is whether all parties can afford to have the licenses for the same statistical package. If not, then the data may need to be exported from one package to another; typically this step entails moving data from another software package to Excel, which is widely available and affordable (for cost comparisons, see Table 6.1 above).

For RTI's 2009 EGRA data analysis of the baseline data for the RLL program in Mali, one person did the actual data analysis, and a second person prepared results presentation tables and wrote the results section of an accompanying report. In this case, results were shared as raw data analysis outcomes in the form of a Stata log file (similar to the output files in SPSS), which is basically a file containing the tables and values derived from the analysis procedures. For the earlier pilot test of the instrument for this EGRA implementation, however, the same person did the analysis, produced the raw results, and created the results presentation tables and graphics. Those were then shared—as tables in a Microsoft Word file—with other staff writing the report. In yet another instance, data were first checked and cleaned in SPSS and then later imported into Stata for weighting and analysis. For EGRA data collection in Senegal in 2009 (Chapter 2), one team member did not have the Stata or SPSS software; thus, although data were analyzed using SPSS, results of the analysis were exported to Excel to facilitate sharing.

Both Stata and SPSS can store their logs/outputs as plain delimited text files. This is important, as they are easily shared with others and, given their small size, manageable for transferring via e-mail in low-bandwidth contexts. For RTI's 2009 analysis in Mali, the combined size of the "do" files for the entire data analysis was no more than 116 kilobytes. The log files themselves took up only 1 megabyte of hard-drive space. Storing log/output files as plain delimited text is the default setting for Stata, but this is not so for SPSS, which needs to be manually set.

The reality for many of the countries that have applied EGRA, including those presented in this book, indicates that pirated copies of statistical software packages are widespread—even in government entities and formal research institutions. In addition to the obvious legal issues with this situation, the versions thus available are often older and very much outdated; this problem can lead to truly distressing issues regarding compatibility of files among users of different versions (e.g., issues about length of variables, format of variables, and graphing capabilities). Furthermore, we have experienced situations in which the functionality of pirated copies did not match that of the fully licensed version. Thus, anyone who plans to work with a team of analysts and to share data and procedures should evaluate in advance not only the respective statistical software but also the versions all team members will be using.

What Software Is Already Being Used?

Another important question to consider in the choice of software is that of support. Even those who are much practiced in data analysis and have a good familiarity with analyzing EGRA data may sooner or later find themselves in need of some guidance on how to use the software to conduct a certain operation.

The learning curve for packages such as Stata and SPSS is much steeper than for Excel, and skills in Excel are far more widespread. This is one reason that we see Excel being used in most EGRA data collections for some stage of the process, despite the drawbacks mentioned earlier.

From a very practical point of view, reviewing and cleaning data are easier tasks in Excel, given its sorting and cell editing features, than in the other packages. For this reason, EGRA staff may do data entry or management in Excel and then export the data to either Stata or SPSS for data analysis.

Both Stata and SPSS have built-in menu navigations that allow users to conduct most analyses without knowing any of the syntax or command coding. Some researchers prefer using either software package entirely on the basis of coding rather than menu navigation. Graphing wizards, available for both Stata and SPSS, however, can considerably facilitate presentation of results in appealing formats.

For all three software tools, plenty of online resources are available for further information and help:

- The Stata website (http://www.stata.com/links) contains a wealth of links leading to additional resources provided by Stata itself and by other providers, including sample operations, tutorials, videos, frequently asked questions (FAQs), forums, mailing lists, and more. We have found especially helpful Stata's own help manual and the website of Academic Technology Services of the University of California, Los Angeles (http://www.ats.ucla.edu/stat/stata) for both Stata and SPSS.

- For SPSS, similarly, the SPSS website (http://www-947.ibm.com/support/entry/portal/Forums_communities) provides links to its own training materials and resources and to those of other providers. A good selection of links to SPSS resources can be found also on the website of California State University at San Marcos (http://courses.csusm.edu/resources/spss). Furthermore, Pallant (2007) has been very helpful for many of our EGRA data analysis activities.

- Microsoft's website offers a multitude of tutorials and other learning resources for using Excel for data analysis. For instance, a 50-minute tutorial (http://office.microsoft.com/en-us/excel-help/excel-statistical-functions-RZ001091922.aspx?CTT=3) starts with the basics of using Excel for data analysis. Excel solutions to data analysis and related procedures are also topics of numerous forums and listservs.

Given bandwidth limitations and Internet access costs in many of the EGRA implementation countries, we strongly suggest that the availability of local, in-person support also be considered during planning of data entry, management, and analysis.

Finally, other questions remain. What operating system will be used? What are the system specifications? How much money is the funding organization willing to spend? Table 6.1 (pages 199 and 200) offers a direct comparison of these points across the three software packages.

Summary and Conclusions

Summary

In this chapter we discussed two main areas of ICT use in EGRA implementation: data collection and management, and data analysis. For the former, we addressed several entry points at which ICT could be used to enhance the efficiency and quality of EGRA data collection. Benefits include

- reducing the consumption of paper and number of copies to be made and avoiding issues with using paper in adverse environments,

- combining the tasks of result recording and data entry into a single activity to enhance efficiency and timeliness of the assessment,

- improving data quality by reducing human error introduced when data are transferred from paper into an electronic data management system, and

- reducing measurement errors secondary to handling timers.

At the same time, however, the use of technology for EGRA implementation also introduces new challenges. These challenges, which have to be carefully weighed against the benefits, include the following:

- danger of data loss where proper backup procedures are not in place,

- assessor difficulties in handling the technology,

- cost-effectiveness, ruggedness, user-friendliness, availability, and reliability of the devices, and

- flexibility of the data recording platform, especially in dealing with various languages, symbols, and scripts.

The use of software for EGRA data analysis has become near universal, given the numerous benefits of automating high-level calculations and dealing with thousands and sometimes millions of data points. Important here, however, is the choice of software to facilitate data management and the desired analysis and presentation.

We reviewed three software packages—Excel, SPSS, and Stata—along a number of dimensions. These included the nature of the data and the nature of the research question(s) driving the EGRA implementation; the EGRA implementation approach and related size of the data set (number of cases and variables); the planned process of data management and analysis (individual or collaborative); accessibility of local support; and cost and system requirements.

All three software tools can be used for EGRA data management, analysis, and presentation, albeit to varying extents of practicability and not for all types of EGRA implementation approaches. Excel is recommended especially for tasks related to data management and cleaning, and where little locally accessible support exists for either SPSS or Stata; Excel can be used for EGRA snapshot approaches, especially when the size of the data set is limited and few or no inferential statistics are required.

SPSS and Stata are recommended especially to assess national EGRA implementation approaches, which aim to generalize predictions and relationships as the basis of policy decisions and interventions, or to analyze intervention impacts. These two packages are thus recommended for large data sets. In addition, they are better suited for collaborative data analysis processes, where data manipulation and analysis procedures should be logged and replicable.

Stata is the only one among the three software tools that is suitable should simple random sampling not be an option for a national EGRA implementation approach (which is usually the case). Even with Stata, EGRA data need to be weighted for analysis results to be generalizable to the entire student population.

Finally, cost, sustainability, and system requirements are also important considerations in the choice of the appropriate software. System requirements are especially important when data analysis would be done on older computers or processes may involve sharing data between computers or even operating system platforms. Cost may play a significant role in the choice of software. In absolute terms, Excel is the least costly and SPSS is the most costly. However, the question of cost-effectiveness needs to be analyzed carefully in light of each package's specific limitations, many of which have been discussed in this chapter.

Conclusion

Although this chapter deals with the use of technologies—some of them still quite new—for supporting EGRA, we do not mean to imply that they are a requirement. EGRA was meant from the outset to be a simple and accessible tool, particularly for developing countries or low-resource contexts. Therefore, every effort is made to ensure that it remains as such. Nonetheless, as the approaches mature and we acquire new lessons, we can expect an ongoing tension between improving the technical quality of the instrument and maintaining its original intention to be a simple, accessible approach to assessment.

The equipment, software, and techniques mentioned in this chapter may have an impact on overall labor productivity in implementing EGRA, but for some of its applications, even data analysis can be performed using pencil and paper. Early literacy assessments such as Pratham's annual surveys of reading and arithmetic skills (see http://www.pratham.org/M-20-3-ASER.aspx) in India are evidence that such assessments done at community levels with minimal resources can be effective drivers of change (Pratham, 2009). EGRA is also being implemented in very simplified contexts at the school and community levels without reliance on any sophisticated technologies, and we encourage these experiences just as much as innovation and experimentation with new technologies. The key consideration is that certain trade-offs may need to be made in costs and rigor depending on the approach chosen.

As noted in the opening section of this chapter, practical and collaborative input from EGRA users regarding ICT-supported implementation could benefit the entire community of practice.

References

Abimbola, R., Alismail, H., Belousov, S. M., Dias, B., Dias, M. F., Dias, M. B., et al. (2009, August). *iSTEP Tanzania 2009: Inaugural experience.* Technical Report CMU-RI-TR-09-33. Pittsburgh, Pennsylvania: Robotics Institute, Carnegie Mellon University. Retrieved November 5, 2010, from http://www.ri.cmu.edu/pub_files/2009/8/iSTEP%20Tanzania%202009%20Final%20Report.pdf

Berenson, M. L., Levine, D. M., & Krehbiel, T. C. (2005). Course topic 7.3: Sampling from finite populations. Student CD-ROM for *Basic business statistics: Concepts and applications,* 10th ed. Upper Saddle River, New Jersey: Pearson Prentice Hall. Retrieved September 30, 2010, from http://courses.wcupa.edu/rbove/Berenson/10th%20ed%20CD-ROM%20topics/section7_3.pdf

Centre for Evaluation and Monitoring, Durham University. (n.d.). *Effect size resources.* Retrieved August 25, 2010, from http://www.cemcentre.org/evidence-based-education/effect-size-resources

Crouch, L., & Korda, M. (2008). *EGRA Liberia: Baseline assessment of reading levels and associated factors.* Prepared for the World Bank under Contract No. 7147768. Research Triangle Park, North Carolina: RTI International. Retrieved August 24, 2010, from https://www.eddataglobal.org/documents/index.cfm?fuseaction=pubDetail&ID=158.

Crouch, L., Korda, M., & Mumo, D. (2009). *Improvements in reading skills in Kenya: An experiment in the Malindi District.* Prepared for the United States Agency for International Development (USAID)/Kenya under the EdData II Project, Task 4, Contract No. EHC-E-04-04-00004-00. Research Triangle Park, North Carolina: RTI International. Retrieved August 25, 2010, from https://www.eddataglobal.org/documents/index.cfm?fuseaction=pubDetail&ID=154.

Estrada, M., & Zimmerman, R. (2009). *Pilot of digital data collection options for Honduras' education assessments.* Prepared for USAID under the Educational Quality Improvement Program (EQUIP1), Cooperative Agreement No. GDG-A-00-03-00006-00. Washington, DC: American Institutes for Research (AIR). Retrieved February 11, 2011, from http://www.equip123.net/docs/e1-HondurasDigitalDataCollectionPilotTest.pdf

Gove, A. (2008). *EGRA/Arabic in Egypt: Summary and pilot results* [PowerPoint presentation]. Prepared for USAID/Egypt under the Girls' Improved Learning Outcomes (GILO) project, Contract No. 263-C-00-08-00010-00. Washington, DC: RTI International.

Kardaun, J. (2001). Poster 1: Scanning and OCR as aid for the cause-of-death statistic. In A. M. Minino & H. M. Rosenberg (Eds.), *Proceedings of the 2nd International Collaborative Effort on Automating Mortality Statistics, volume II* (pp. 195–199), Bethesda, Maryland, September 7–10, 1999. Hyattsville, Maryland: National Center for Health Statistics. Retrieved September 30, 2010, from http://www.cdc.gov/nchs/data/misc/ice01_acc.pdf

Microsoft Corporation. (2010). *Excel specifications and limits.* Retrieved August 25, 2010, from http://office.microsoft.com/en-us/excel-help/excel-specifications-and-limits-HP010073849.aspx

Microsoft Corporation. (2011). *PowerPivot add-in.* Retrieved May 13, 2011, from http://office.microsoft.com/en-us/excel-help/sql-server-powerpivot-add-in-HA101811050.aspx?CTT=5&origin=HA010369709

Miles, J. (n.d). *Regression with Excel/Multiple regression with Excel.* Web page adapted from Appendix 2 of J. Miles & M. Shevlin, Applying regression and correlation: A guide for students and researchers. Thousand Oaks, California: Sage. Retrieved August 25, 2010, from http://www.jeremymiles. co.uk/regressionbook/extras/appendix2/excel/

Mitchell, M. N. (2006). *Strategically using general purpose statistics packages: A look at Stata, SAS and SPSS.* Technical Report Series, No. 1, Statistical Consulting Group, UCLA Academic Technology Services. Los Angeles: University of California (UCLA). Retrieved August 25, 2010, from http:// www.ats.ucla.edu/stat/technicalreports/Number1/ucla_ATSstat_tr1_1.0.pdf

Olson, L. (2007, May 2). Instant read on reading: In palms of their hands. *Education Week,* 26(35): 24–34. .

Pallant, J. (2007). *SPSS survival manual: A step-by-step guide to data analysis using SPSS for Windows (Version 15)* (3rd ed.). Crows Nest, Australia: Allen & Unwin.

Pieniazek, A. (2007, April 24). Finite population correction factor. [Web log post]. Retrieved from http://adamp.com/statistics/finite-population-correction-factor/

Pratham. (2009). *Pratham India Education Initiative: Annual report 2008–09.* New Delhi: Pratham Resource Center. Retrieved October 5, 2010, from http://pratham.org/file/Pratham%20Annual%20Report.pdf

Ralaingita, W., Spratt, J., & Strigel, C. (2009). *Report on Milestone 1: Baseline data collection and analysis using the adapted "EGRA-plus" in French.* Prepared for the Ministére de l'Education, de l'Alphabétisation et des Langues Nationales [Ministry of Education, Literacy, and National Languages] and USAID/Mali under the Mali Programme Harmonisé d'Appui au Renforcement de l'Education (USAID/PHARE) [Unified Program for Strengthening Support to Education], Contract No. EDH-I-00-05-00031-00. Research Triangle Park, North Carolina: RTI International.

Rennert, N. (n.d.). *SynPhony: A multi-lingual synthetic phonics literacy project.* Website of Computer Assisted Language Learning (CALL), Canada Institute of Linguistics. Retrieved August 25, 2010, from http://call.canil.ca/english/SynPhony2.html

Revelle, G., Reardon, E., Green, M. M., Betancourt, J., & Kotler, J. (2007). Persuasion via mobile phones. In Y. de Kort, B. J. Fogg, W. IJsselsteijn, C. Midden, & B. Eggen (Eds.), *Persuasive technology: Proceedings of the 2nd International Conference on Persuasive Technology 2007, Palo Alto, CA [California], USA, April 26–27, 2007. Revised selected papers* (pp. 253–258). Berlin and New York: Springer-Verlag.

Rodríguez, G. (n.d.). *Stata tutorial.* Princeton, New Jersey: Office of Population Research, Princeton University. Retrieved August 25, 2010, from http://data. princeton.edu/stata/dataManagement.html

RTI International. (2009a). *Data analytic report: EGRA Plus: Liberia baseline assessment.* Prepared for USAID/Liberia under the EdData II project, Task 6, Contract No. EHC-E-06-04-00004-00. Research Triangle Park, North Carolina: RTI International.

RTI International. (2009b). *EGRA Senegal 2009: Final report summary.* Prepared for the William and Flora Hewlett Foundation under Grant No. 2008-3367. Washington, DC: RTI International.

RTI International. (2009c). *Guyana Early Grade Reading Assessment: October 2008 results.* Prepared for the World Bank under Contract No. 7146794. Washington, DC: RTI International. Available from https://www. eddataglobal.org/documents/index.cfm?fuseaction=pubDetail&ID=267, retrieved August 24, 2010.

RTI International. (2009d). *International independent evaluation of the Institut pour l'Education Populaire's "Read-Learn-Lead" (RLL) Program in Mali: Baseline report.* Prepared for the William and Flora Hewlett Foundation under Grant No. 2008-3367. Research Triangle Park, North Carolina: RTI International.

RTI International & Centre de Promotion de la Citoyenneté pour le Développement Durable à la Base (CEPROCIDE) [Center for Promotion of Citizenship for Basic Sustainable Development]. (2009). *Evaluation des compétences fondamentales en lecture des élevés de 2eme année des écoles Bamanankan, Bomu, Fulfuldé et Songhoï du premier cycle de l'enseignement fondamental* [Evaluation of basic skills in reading for students of 2nd year of school, in Bamanankan, Bomu, Fulfulde and Songhoi, first cycle of basic education]. Prepared for the William and Flora Hewlett Foundation under the Monitoring of Learning Outcomes in Sub-Saharan Africa project, Grant No. 2008-3367. Washington, DC: RTI International.

Seebregts, C. J., Zwarenstein, M., Mathews, C., Fairall, L., Flisher, A. J., Seebregts, C., et al. (2009). Handheld computers for survey and trial data collection in resource-poor settings: Development and evaluation of PDACT, a Palm Pilot interviewing system. *International Journal of Medical Informatics,* 78(11): 721–731.

Siegle, D. (n.d.). *Reliability.* Retrieved September 30, 2010, from http://www. gifted.uconn.edu/siegle/research/Instrument%20Reliability%20and%20 Validity/Reliability.htm

Sprenger-Charolles, L., & Messaoud-Galusi, S. (2009). *Review of reading acquisition and analyses of the main international reading assessment tools.* Report prepared for the International Institute for Education Planning, United Nations Educational, Cultural and Scientific Organization (IIEP– UNESCO). Paris, France: Laboratoire Psychologie de la Perception, Centre National de la Recherche Scientifique, Université Paris Decartes. Retrieved May 13, 2011, from http://lpp.psycho.univ-paris5.fr/abstract.php?id=2673

SPSS Inc., an IBM Company. (2009). *Teaching and learning licensing options.* Retrieved August 25, 2010, from http://www.spss.com/media/collateral/ spss-for-instruction-software.pdf

Tomlinson, M., Solomon, W., Singh, Y., Doherty, T., Chopra, M., Ijumba, P., et al. (2009). The use of mobile phones as a data collection tool: A report from a household survey in South Africa. *BMC Medical Informatics and Decision Making, 9,* 51.

Wagner, D. A., Daswani, C. J., & Karnati, R. (2010). Technology and mother-tongue literacy in southern India: Impact studies among young children and out-of-school youth. *Information Technologies & International Development,* 6(4): 23–43.

J. Walk & Associates, Inc. (2010). The 256-column limitation. *The spreadsheet page: For Excel users and developers.* Retrieved August 25, 2010, from http:// spreadsheetpage.com/index.php/oddity/the_256_column_limitation/

Woods, J. A., & McCurley, C. J. (2004, April). *Design effects in complex sampling designs.* Paper presented at the annual meeting of the Midwest Political Science Association, Palmer House Hilton, Chicago, Illinois.

Yu, P., de Courten, M., Pan, E., Galea, G., & Pryor, J. (2009). The development and evaluation of a PDA-based method for public health surveillance data collection in developing countries. *International Journal of Medical Informatics,* 78(8): 532–542.

Zimmerman, R. (2008). *Digital data collection demonstration white paper—A comparison of two methodologies: Digital and paper-based.* Prepared for USAID under the Educational Quality Improvement Program (EQUIP1), Cooperative Agreement No. GDG-A-00-03-00006-00. Washington, DC: American Institutes for Research (AIR). Retrieved August 24, 2010, from http://www.equip123.net/docs/e1-DigitalDataCollection.pdf

CHAPTER 7

Motivating Early Grade Instruction and Learning: Institutional Issues

Luis Crouch

Most of the previous chapters in this volume have focused on applications of the early grade reading assessment (EGRA) as case studies, or have explored certain technical aspects of such applications and methods. Some also have indicated, however, that the purpose is not just to assess but to mobilize opinion toward improvement. That is, once a country's education leaders have in their hands empirical evidence from an assessment of early grade reading, what happens next? What factors might dispose that country to mobilize itself for improvements, and what institutional qualities are most likely to encourage a movement from assessment to use of assessment results for improvement? The aim of this chapter is to offer interested actors some suggestions as to how to move the agenda forward toward actual change in instructional practice.

In what follows, I first provide background, then use several country examples to explain and illustrate some critical concepts. What is meant by "early" in the concept of early adopter? Does "early" mean "early start but normal process"? or "normal start but fast process"? What actual amounts of time, in any case, are we talking about? There may be lessons here for other cases.

Next I offer hypotheses, setting out some suggested reasons why the countries in question were either fast or early. Some discussion of each case illustrates the factor or reason in question. I conclude with a summary of drivers that motivate reforms to encourage early grade instruction and learning.

Background and Assumptions

Several countries, or regions within countries, have moved relatively quickly to adopt EGRA—or some similar tool—to drive instructional improvements in early grade reading. South Africa, Liberia, and Kenya are cases in point, and certain aspects of their experience are discussed in other chapters in this book (Chapters 3, 4, and 5). Other countries, such as Peru, have used various approaches to start an improvement process, but it was some EGRA-like tool that generated sufficient policy discussion to motivate change in the first place. Either way, in these countries there is now an emerging base of experience in moving beyond measurement and awareness and toward improvement.

This chapter draws on patterns from the early adopters of instructional improvements and evaluation to lay out some of the institutional and technical factors that should be considered in moving from assessment to action. On the way toward that goal, I also present hypotheses suggesting why tools such as EGRA—or similar ones such as Pratham's annual surveys of reading and arithmetic skills (see http://www.pratham.org/M-20-3-ASER.aspxASER)— seem to spur action in poor countries.[1]

Several points that underlie the arguments in this chapter are presented below.

Experience in Scaling Up

None of the countries discussed in this chapter has yet truly gone to full scale in implementing improvements in reading instruction and evaluation. These countries *have* progressed from carrying out an awareness-raising and research assessment of early grade reading to piloting some serious projects to gather on-the-ground evidence of how to improve, under the auspices of an international partner.

Moreover, some have incorporated the idea or intent of "going to national scale"—that is, to improve reading instruction, not just to complete assessments—into education sector plans and investment projects. Going to national scale to implement improvements in reading instruction most likely would entail

- institutionalizing teacher- or district-level monitoring of reading, using instruments such as EGRA,
- offering better and more in-service training of teachers in reading,
- specifying lesson plans and the yearly scope and sequence of instruction (overview of goals and order in which lessons are taught),
- ensuring there is enough time in the school programs for reading, and

---

[1] Some other comparable tools, such as Progress in International Reading Literacy Study (PIRLS) and Trends in International Mathematics and Science Study (TIMSS) have tended to be used in middle- or high-income countries. For more about both, see the website for Boston College's TIMSS & PIRLS International Study Center, http://timss.bc.edu.

- making sure parents and communities understand that children can and should read by a fairly early point in their school career, such as grade 2 or 3.

Other possible changes might be revamping certain aspects of the curriculum or the curriculum-based syllabus or lesson plans, improving the coverage of reading instruction in preservice training, and using outreach and communication techniques for social marketing of reading.

Even after policy makers have decided on reforms, changes may take considerable time and effort to implement. For example, improved training of teachers requires a reorientation of university and teacher training college staff, who may resist new techniques. As part of system-wide adoption, such changes may be challenging and slow.

As previously stated, none of the countries discussed in this chapter has yet truly gone to full scale with processes to improve reading instruction. Thus, this chapter refers only to the factors to be considered in going from assessment to serious pilots to a statement of national ambition to go to full scale.[2] The weight of evidence is not yet available to take the argument forward to factors that drive the actual carrying out of *national*-scale implementation of programs to improve early grade reading.

Technical Aspects of EGRA

The technical aspects discussed here are brought up largely because they have institutional, economic, or bureaucratic implications, not because the points made will further the state of technical knowledge involved in the assessment of early grade reading. The focus is on the interaction between the technical and the institutional or motivational.

Experience of Early Adopters

Trying to reason from the experience of early adopters (of which the sample is small) presents several challenges. Some factors make such experiences easier, and other factors make them harder, than might be the case with later adopters. These favorable/unfavorable forces may balance each other out. If so, one might wonder, why bring them up at all? The reason is that *whether* they balance, and how, will likely vary from country to country. Knowing what these factors were, and how they played out, can help other countries—and providers

---

[2] National ambitions may also be influenced by a growing global focus on primary learning and literacy indicators (see, among others, Chapter 1 of World Bank: Independent Evaluation Group, 2006; and Hanushek & Woessman, 2009). These influences are not investigated in this chapter.

of advice and assistance to those countries—decide how to proceed. It can also speed things up or, more importantly, reveal how much speed can be expected, from which countries. Both the implementing countries and their international partners will then have a better grasp of priorities and expectations.

Favorable Factors

It is possible to enumerate favorable aspects that are related to being an early adopter. For example:

- These countries may have had a general predisposition to early adoption of any interesting ideas.
- There may have been a crisis environment where new ideas were welcome.
- Personalities could play a role; early adopters may simply have been blessed with top-level officials who happened to care about these issues.

The early adopters described in this chapter are not a random sample but a group of countries in which I played a role in advising and motivating early grade reading assessments. However, this does not invalidate the lessons learned. As countries and their international partners start to move forward, they need to think about features that favor early adoption. If the features are not present, those interested in change should bring them into existence if possible, or use them to moderate the country's ambition as to the pace of change. If it is not possible for stakeholders to stimulate these favorable factors into being, knowledge of that fact can at least affect the choice of countries to be the next generation of adopters.

Unfavorable Factors

Among the unfavorable factors is simply the fact that early adopters cannot benefit from the experience of others. They essentially invent their approaches by themselves, without much support from the international community. This applies in two ways, one technical and one emotional:

- Early adopters face a dearth of models of technical approaches, evidence of what works, and documented evidence on *how* it works. This factor is not entirely negative, however. Having to think through the steps very carefully does force an early adopter to make sure the approach fits the possibilities to an extent that later "cookie cutter" approaches cannot. (This subaspect should be tallied among the *advantages* of being an early adopter.)

- Much of what happens in education, whether in developing or developed countries, needs to have society's approval. This is why there is such a thing as fashion (some would say faddishness) in educational development, or indeed in any area of social and institutional improvement. This is also the reason that it is harder to get going than to keep going, with any new idea. Later adopters of the process of going from early grade reading assessment to early grade improvement will be able to benefit from the emotional or psychological "cover" provided by the early adopters.

Early Start—or Fast Process?

The fact that some of the countries that this chapter examines were early adopters might suggest that they were also fast adopters. However, they may have already been working on the issues for a long time—that is, they may have *started* earlier than anyone else. In any case, some sense of precisely how long it took these ideas to mature is instructive as one considers expanding the effort to other countries. Keep in mind that if these countries were not just early in adoption, but also fast in implementation, and if they are not a random sample, then they may have been more motivated than others. That would also explain why things proceeded so speedily.

Liberia

The speediest case—by comparison with South Africa and Kenya, at least—was Liberia (refer to Chapter 4 for a more detailed discussion of EGRA in Liberia). The entire cycle from an idea that RTI International floated to donors and the Ministry of Education to a full-fledged, funded, and fairly large-scale randomized trial took only about 20 months. This is quite remarkable. The factors that made it possible suggest caution as to whether such an undertaking could easily be accomplished elsewhere. Nevertheless, education leaders and international partners can work to bring about these factors, or to take advantage of them (or similar ones).

Which institutional factors seem to have helped speed things up? First, in coming out of a deep conflict, Liberia had a clear need to be seen as innovative and forward-looking. Liberia was applying for Education for All–Fast Track Initiative (FTI) status;[3] its education officials had attended a basic education reform course at the World Bank in Washington, DC; and these officials had

---

[3] For more information about FTI, see http://www.educationfasttrack.org/about-fti.

gotten to know key actors at the World Bank and RTI who were interested in reform and quality. At the same time, Liberia was not participating in any form of external learning assessment. Thus, in Liberia's FTI application, as early as March 2007, it proposed to do some form of rapid reading assessment in the early grades.

Relatively little happened for a few months, but conversations ramped up toward the end of that year. By early 2008, an agreement had been reached among the Ministry of Education, the World Bank, the United States Agency for International Development (USAID), and RTI that it would be convenient to develop some form of baseline measurement that same year, with the goal of starting a well-evaluated pilot project in reading improvement in the early grades by the beginning of the 2008–2009 school year if possible.

Second, the leaders in the ministry were open-minded and inquisitive, and some happened to have a track record of interest, training, and activity in early-grade reading, including authoring children's books. By June 2008, RTI and its consultants and collaborators had carried out a nationally representative study (for the report of results, see Crouch & Korda, 2008). The implications for designing an improvement strategy were sorted out over the summer and early fall of 2008, and the World Bank, USAID, and RTI held policy discussions with the ministry in August 2008. USAID then followed up by funding a randomized controlled trial in some 180 schools (described in Chapter 4), which got started in late 2008. Thus, the period from initial discussions in documents to start-up of a serious pilot was 18 to 20 months.

Note also that the 180-school pilot required a similar amount of time from initial planning to start-up. The implementation team expected that by mid-2010, enough lessons would have been learned from the project that donors and the ministry could design and start a separate full scale-up. In fact this did happen, with a gradual process of national scale-up. As of late 2010, interventions were under way in some 2,000 schools, and plans were in place for gradual dissemination to a national scale through in-service and pre-service training starting in 2011.

An important lesson from Liberia is that in all situations and circumstances, the government was willing to move faster than the international agencies. Most of the delays were caused by coordination problems between and within the groups external to the government of Liberia, by the difficulties in getting clarity and agreement among the external actors, and by the length of time required to procure experts to supply technical assistance.

South Africa

In South Africa (see Chapter 3), the process of going from initial discussion to a serious pilot project with fully specified lesson plans and a serious evaluation took a little longer than it did for Liberia. The most likely reason was that although by 2005 the first post-apartheid curriculum had been roundly criticized for lack of specificity, and a new curricular framework had been put into place, the midlevel functionaries or academics available to the Department of Education may not have been fully on board with the need for a curricular approach that was simpler, more focused, more linear, and more centrally directed. Further, those who were on board may simply have lacked the specific knowledge of how to set up a clear and simple scope and sequence and a package of lesson plans that teachers could implement, particularly if they felt themselves to have weak instructional skills.

At a key conference in late 2008 on the Foundations for Learning, the South African system was still offering many ways to teach reading. The guidance then consisted of a set of numerous options and approaches that teachers and schools could mix and match, rather than one or two clear approaches that teachers could follow, lesson by lesson, over a year and that could more or less guarantee that at the end of the year all children in the classroom could read.

In short, the Department of Education had clarified and systematized the curricular goals, but still had not made available at least one specific approach that a teacher could simply follow and that could lead to proven results. In 2009 the department engaged in what seems to have been the first officially sanctioned experiment with a structured, planned-lesson approach. In fact, by 2009, the highest authorities in the country had become quite impatient with progress, creating (at least from the top-down point of view) a fertile ground for the notion of going to scale, as discussed below.

Kenya

In Kenya, RTI first held discussions about an experimental reading improvement trial not with the government, but with the Aga Khan Foundation—an international development organization—in mid-2006. Discussions took some time, but by early 2008 a serious pilot with control and treatment groups was under way under the auspices of USAID's Education for Marginalized Children in Kenya (EMACK II) project. Thus, the time from idea to pilot was 18 months or so. RTI and Aga Khan Foundation evaluated the pilot at the end of 2008 (see Crouch et al., 2009) and disseminated results in early 2009, at which point key government officials showed interest in the possibility of scale-up. Larger-scale efforts, supported by USAID, are underway in 2011.

Summary

In all, taking an average for these countries, the period from formal introduction of the idea to starting a pilot was about 18 months. Another year or so can produce results that a Ministry of Education then might show interest in taking to scale.

Factors Hypothesized to Determine Early Adoption

In this section, I use the cases of Kenya, Liberia, and South Africa to illustrate three major factors that seem to have contributed to early adoption. However, the formulation of the hypotheses was informed by various other cases, so I bring in Peru as a contrast. The three key factors were (1) a preexisting curriculum that was conducive or receptive to the introduction of both EGRA-type assessments and instructional changes, or at least would not prevent them outright; (2) a predisposition to use data and assessments to assist with instruction; and (3) a sense of national concern, which may already have existed but at least was easily made obvious by the baseline application of EGRA.

Preexisting Curricular Receptivity

One factor common to Kenya and South Africa in all likelihood helped increase initial receptivity and motivated early adoption of the ideas: the prior existence of a curriculum that was inherently "friendly" to the improvement ideas that flow naturally from the EGRA assessment.

EGRA, as noted elsewhere in this book, tends to focus on big skill areas: phonological awareness, alphabetic principle, fluency, and comprehension. EGRA interventions have frequently worked some on vocabulary as well, even though EGRA as an assessment has not focused on assessing vocabulary. In any case, if a curriculum in a country does not even mention any of these topics as important early skills or, worse, is actively or implicitly opposed to them, then it is unlikely that such a country will move quickly. At best, such a country might engage with a smallish pilot, but progressing to national scale, or even to large pilots, would be difficult because doing so would require creating openness first.

This statement is not a declaration or even implication that groups interested in reading improvement (or at least early-grade competencies associated with EGRA) should avoid working with such countries. It simply means that work in such countries could be slower and might require more initial steps, involving lengthier discussions around curricular issues and the approach to reading.

This "friendliness" toward improvements has to be fairly specific in terms of the content and goals of a given curriculum. If these countries had already had a way to operationalize and assess their curricular goals, they might not have been as open to EGRA. The curricula in these countries did contain conceptual elements regarding certain skills, which resonated with the EGRA approach; at the same time, however, the countries possessed no practical instruments that could assess whether teachers were working on those skills (and hence, whether students were developing them).

Peru poses an interesting contrast (see Chapter 1 as well as Abadzi et al., 2005, and Alvarado Pérez, 2006). It did not have a specific curriculum primed to introduce enhancements in reading instruction, and therefore EGRA or EGRA-related approaches to improvement (e.g., an emphasis on oral and early skills) did not progress much or as quickly.

Kenya

The case of Kenya (some aspects of which are covered in Chapter 5) is instructive. Using the 2002 version of the curriculum, or "syllabus" (the one that was official and operational at the time of start-up [Ministry of Education, Science and Technology, Kenya, 2002]), I note the following.

The Kenyan syllabus is detailed in terms of the basic skills upon which EGRA touches. As early as Standard 1—the first year of primary school—learners are expected to "recite and recognize the letters of the alphabet" (Objective 1.2.a). EGRA focuses on recognition and fluency (but not *recitation* as such, because ability to recite the letters, in sequence, and without visual cues, is not a very good predictor of later skills). The ability to recognize and name letters fluently from a randomized list—like the EGRA letter identification subtask—is a good way to assess letter recognition and naming and/or sounding skills.

By Standard 2, students are expected to "read simple sentences/passages related to greetings and polite language" (Objective 1.2.d) as well as colors

(2.2.f), numbers (4.2.e), time (5.2.e), position and direction (6.2.e), home and home activities (7.2.e), shopping (8.2.c), their bodies (9.2.e), health and hygiene (10.2.c), travel (11.2.f), clothes (12.2.c), food (13.2.d), wild animals (14.2.c), weather (15.2.c), the farm (16.2.c), and home equipment (17.2.c and d). In many of these cases, the child is also expected to "answer comprehension questions." For applying assessment methods that line up with the objectives, the syllabus (on page 31, for example) recommends oral (and silent) reading and answering comprehension questions (among many others). EGRA added the notion of fluency to give more specific meaning to the notion of "reading" and also made a contribution as a clearly defined assessment method.

The Kenyan syllabus is even more specific about reading skills when it comes to reading in mother tongues.[4] It notes that students even in Standard 1 are expected to "read and understand graded reading materials" (42.1.c). In this area, reading skills include naming the letters of the alphabet. In Standard 2 students are expected to read books in their mother tongue (5.2.1.a).

The concept of fluency, which EGRA handles because of its acknowledged importance, is introduced in Kenya only in the context of mother tongue. For example, Objective 5.2.1.e refers to "read a range of materials with some independence, fluency, accuracy, and understanding." Even in this case, however, the syllabus does not specify standards for either fluency or accuracy. EGRA seems to have helped Kenyan educators by specifying both, with the concept of fluency as measured by correct words per minute. The EGRA assessment exercise began to lay some benchmark concepts such as fluency, albeit as part of a baseline for a specific project.

Many key Kenyans who were involved in adapting and codesigning the application of the first EGRA to their country were familiar with debates around the curriculum. They weighed in thoroughly during an adaptation discussion and pilot that lasted five days in April 2007, before a baseline measurement was taken in August 2007.

South Africa

The situation in South Africa is similar to Kenya's but with some nuances. In this case, even a decade or so after the end of apartheid and the coming of democracy, South Africa has continued to score last on international comparative assessments. This is true even for the early grades—that is, with

---

4   A possible factor impeding EGRA adoption may be the post-colonial tendency in some countries to prioritize reading in the official language rather than a student's mother tongue (see Chapter 5). Additional research is required to explore this possibility.

children who came into schooling many years after the advent of democracy and a new curriculum. Much discussion has ensued about these issues, and it would not be an exaggeration to label the discussion as reflecting consternation, and perhaps even a sense of real crisis.

In the search for culprits, a favorite "usual suspect" for commentators on the South African scene is curricular reform. Reforms were introduced and implemented almost immediately after democracy, and the subsequent discussions have been intense and convoluted (for example, see Cross et al., 2002; Jansen, 1998; Muller, 2000; Rogan, 2007; Taylor et al., 2003). That these reforms are responsible for the low quality of South African education seems extremely improbable, however, because most evidence suggests that quality, at least for the majority, has always been extremely poor. Nevertheless, the reforms likely have not helped the situation.

Shortly afterward, in reaction to the perceptions that the curricular reforms were not helping, South African education officials set in motion reforms within reforms, in fairly rapid succession. The reforms adapted fairly rationally to impact evaluations—albeit impact as assessed theoretically and qualitatively rather than via deeply rigorous and quantitative evaluations. Influential commentators (although hardly unanimously), and eventually the Department of Education itself, converged on two key ideas: (1) the post-apartheid curriculum and curricular execution were unclear and underspecified; and (2) classroom instruction was in general unplanned, poorly conceived in terms of scope and sequence, lax in its use of time, unstructured and vague, etc. (Department of Education, South Africa, 2009). Awareness was growing among stakeholders that the problems started in the earliest grades, or that schools failed to address environmental poverty and lack of school readiness right from the beginning. As a result, education leaders have since attempted to imprint greater specificity onto curricular materials and lesson plans, and provide these to teachers, along with coaching on how to use them.

One could argue that even those attempts are insufficiently focused or specific. Nonetheless, by the time RTI and USAID had discussed the notion of EGRA-like tools with South Africa, the curricular statement had many aspects that were "friendly" to the concepts in EGRA (or at least more so than the earliest post-apartheid curricular statements, which were rather vague), but the education authorities did not have any way to operationalize them. Thus, for example, the curriculum statement for English language in the foundation phase, or preschool through grade 3 (Department of Education, South Africa, 2002), says that it is important to

> help learners to discover techniques and strategies that unlock the "code" of the written word, for example:
> - the development of various word recognition and comprehension skills such as phonemic awareness (sensitivity to the sounds of language),
> - knowledge of letter-sound correspondences (phonics), and
> - knowledge of blending (the putting together of two or three letters to make a sound). (p. 10)

In addition, as assessment standards, the curriculum statement helpfully proposes factors such as

> Recognises and makes meaning of letters and words in longer texts:
> - reads with increasing speed and fluency;
> - reads aloud and uses correct pronunciation and appropriate stress;
> - uses phonic and other word recognition and comprehension skills such as phonics, context clues, and making predictions in order to make sense of text;
> - uses self-correcting strategies such as rereading, pausing, practising a word before saying it out loud. (p. 35)

As of 2006, however, when I first discussed these matters with the Department of Education, South African officials had no real way to operationalize these issues, either in assessment or in lesson plans. In a sense, South Africa was a fairly ideal application of EGRA because the curriculum contained similar concepts, but few, if any, instruments were available to assess curricular coverage or achievement. Even then, as noted above, going from initial discussion to a real pilot project took about 2½ years.

Peru

Again, the contrast with Peru is enlightening. In the mid 2000s, the World Bank undertook a process of policy dialogue with Peru of which one of the early predecessors of EGRA was a part (Cotlear, 2006). In sessions on social marketing and policy dialogue, the World Bank recommended that Peru engage in some form of universal fluency assessment in an early grade. This exercise would serve as a form of stocktaking and as a proxy for improvements in reading performance, within communities, on a school-by-school basis.

Peru at that time did not have any form of universal learner assessment, although it did have a sample-based assessment. However, in Peru the idea of assessment-driven changes in reading instruction did not progress well. The curricular approach to reading did not recognize or explicitly address basic skills that can be precursors to comprehension. "To read," in Peru's curricular vision, meant essentially to comprehend, to analyze critically, and so on. This expectation started as early as grade 2, without any specification of the preceding steps and without any grade-specific statement of reading goals prior to grade 2:

> [The learner] Constructs the comprehension of the text being read by:
> - Anticipating the type of text and the purpose of the writing, according to context (situation, motive circumstances and the means whereby the text arrives at his hands).
> - Reads individually and silently; identifies signals and cues such as: title, subtitles, shapes, known words.
> - Formulates hypotheses (suppositions) about the meaning of the text.
> - Tests his or her hypotheses against those of classmates and draws conclusions.
> - Creates a synthesis on the meaning of the text.
> - Confronts the constructed meaning with the reading of the text, as carried out by the teacher.
>
> (Ministerio de Educación del Perú, 2000, as translated and cited in World Bank, 2007, p. 104)

The backdrop for these statements was a situation in which perhaps one-third of grade 2 students were not mastering even the most elementary aspects of the mechanics of reading.

Even the precursor to EGRA used in Peru emphasized the skills that learners needed as a foundation for the competencies outlined in Peru's curricular statement at the time. (Subsequent curricular specifications still appear to be too demanding of the first grades, while at the same time being vague regarding earlier constitutive steps; see Ministerio de Educación, Perú, 2005.) Nevertheless, the ideas and approaches associated with the precursor to EGRA were simply too different from the vision implicit in the curriculum. In the end, Peru did develop a universal reading and mathematics assessment in grade 2, but the reading assessment attempts to measure only comprehension, and it is not oral.

In short, application in Peru of some of the principles noted in this book did lead to action, and fairly speedily at that. For example, the policy dialogue process did lead to presidential pronouncements and, as noted, to universal measurement (Alvarado Pérez, 2006). Nevertheless, the resulting improvement ideas seem unlikely to boost learning outcomes measurably.

A Predisposition to Using Assessment Data

The case of Kenya demonstrates the predisposition to using assessment data as a factor in adopting reading performance measures such as EGRA.

The Kenyan education system is said to be somewhat exam-driven. Many Kenyans and some outside observers decry this situation. However, even if the

Figure 7.1 Kenya's status as a country whose education system adds relatively high value

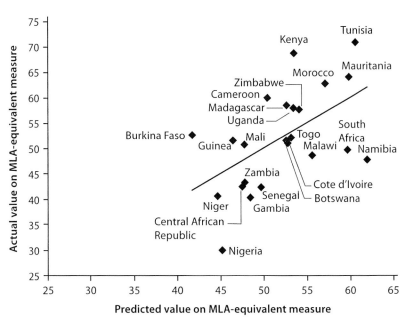

Source: Calculated by the author from the World Bank Education Statistics (EdStats) (retrieved April 6, 2010, from http://ddp-ext.worldbank.org/ext/DDPQQ/member.do?method=getMembers&queryId=189&userid=1) for gross domestic product, gross enrollment, and expenditure data; and from Mingat et al. (2004) for Measuring Learning Achievement (MLA)–equivalent learning outcomes data. Note truncated axes.

assertion is true and the criticism warranted, this behavior may nonetheless be serving Kenya well.

Figure 7.1 shows a set of African countries' predicted and actual scores on a Measuring Learning Achievement (MLA)–equivalent measure of quality created by Mingat and colleagues (2004). The predicted score is based on a simple regression of the scores against gross domestic product (GDP) per capita, the gross enrollment ratio at the primary and secondary levels, and the share of education expenditure in GDP. The latter two are factors that sometimes are said to "advantage" countries. In that sense, the score predicted by those three factors can be said to constitute a sort of "index of advantage." Graphing actual scores against these predicted scores, or index of advantage, illustrates how much "value added" a country's education system produces.

Figure 7.1 shows that Kenya produced the biggest deviation between real and predicted scores, in either absolute or percentage terms.[5] In that sense, Kenya arguably possesses a relatively efficient education system, and its tendency to be driven by examinations accounts for some of this efficiency or value added.[6]

Of course, one could also counterargue that this apparent greater efficiency is somewhat definitional. On the one hand, countries in which students have a great deal of experience with exams may simply tend to do well on exams. On the other, a focus on exams may create some measure of accountability—

---

[5] The slope of the regression line is not statistically significant, but that makes our assertion more, not less, conservative. If one dismisses the slope and simply considers an average, Kenya appears even more efficient. Many would argue that Kenya has a higher income per capita than most of the rest of the countries in the list, spends more on education, and has somewhat lower enrollment, and that these factors "allow" Kenya to do relatively well. The graphic shows that even controlling for those factors (albeit if the controls are not statistically significant), Kenya does well.

[6] For suggestive evidence that proficient use of examinations or assessments can lead to improved outcomes, see Woessman (2000). For detailed analyses of how Kenya's examination system has in fact been intentionally engineered to produce those results, see Wasanga (2010) and Somerset (1974 and 1987). Kenyan system managers and teachers seem to have a fairly highly evolved view of how assessments can inform instruction and feed accountability. An argument could be made that exams serve as selection mechanisms, however, rather than as a means of gaining insight into pupil learning. Whether the Kenyan system is too exam-driven, and whether it is ultimately a good thing or not, is beyond the scope of this chapter. The fact remains that the Kenyan system is a proficient user of assessments. I have visited many schools in Kenya, for instance, and cannot think of one that did not prominently display school-specific information on assessment results to the community. Perhaps because of the pressure of the exams system, teachers in Kenya, to an unusual degree, develop and set mock exams at the local level, and in grades earlier than those at which the exit exams are set. In short, both the examinations and the dissemination of results appear to be taken fairly seriously.

which appears to be the case. Anecdotal evidence does suggest that teachers, communities, and the bureaucracy all take the public exam system in Kenya seriously. Also important is that the exam system is used to assess curricular coverage and to provide feedback to teachers on areas in which their curricular coverage is lacking.

Figures 7.2 and 7.3 are photographs of public displays in a not-atypical primary school in Kenya.[7] Figure 7.2 shows key input measures—funding for Free Primary Education—reported to the community by general purpose account and Simba account (the current account for direct teaching-learning materials).

Figure 7.2 Communication for accountability: a display on education finances at a Kenyan primary school

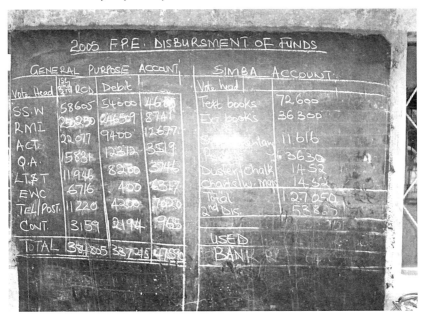

Source: Photograph by Luis Crouch.

Also publicly reported (Figure 7.3) are one "output" measure with internal efficiency implications, namely enrollment by grade and one "outcome" measure, namely results on the Kenyan Certificate of Primary Education exams (bottom panel of Figure 7.3). In addition, results for the school-based exams are shown (see top panel of Figure 7.3).

---

[7] The photographs, which are from 2005, are intended to illustrate a particular practice of communicating for accountability rather than to present the most current data.

Figure 7.3 Communication for accountability: enrollment figures and examination results at a Kenyan primary school

Source: Photograph by Luis Crouch.

This is a fairly simple and effective reporting system—some key inputs, some key outputs, and some key outcomes. In any case, the point is that in Kenya's system, measurement is valued, is not seen as threatening, and is seen instead as a goad to improvement.

System-Wide Awareness and Drive for Going Beyond Pilots

As pointed out previously, none of the early adopters under discussion in this chapter has yet gone fully to national scale with an approach to reading improvement that is highly focused, directed, and truly implemented. Any that do will become early adopters of a national scaled-up approach. South Africa and Liberia are traveling along this path in terms of strong and widespread interest in moving beyond pilot programs for reading improvement.

South Africa

In South Africa, exasperation with poor results from the education system has manifested itself at the highest possible point in the society, namely the President's office, and in extremely sharp and basic terms. The language in President Jacob Zuma's 2010 State of the Nation address (Zuma, 2010) was quite stark; gone were expressions of education's role in lofty pursuits such as democracy, development of a critical citizenry, or nation building. The President called instead for at least getting children to acquire some basic skills:

> In our 2010 programme, we want to improve the ability of our children to read, write and count in the foundation years. Unless we do this, we will not improve the quality of education. Our education targets are simple but critical. We want learners and teachers to be in school, in class, on time, learning and teaching for seven hours a day. (Zuma, 2010)

Two points are particularly salient in this portion of the address. First, he emphasized *counting*, not mathematics. Second, rather than laying out complex goals on school governance and democracy, he simply expressed the desire for the actors be at school and working "for seven hours a day." The wisdom of such a narrow path could be criticized, but it is unarguable that this approach reflects desperation at the current situation.

At the South African Department of Education, the same attitude seems now to prevail. Gone is a focus on a curricular approach that is vague about means and hence appears to many, including teachers, to be unteachable and that overplays the nature of teacher as "mere" facilitator. Also gone is the earlier, idealistic, and hopefully progressive notion that teachers could draft their own learning materials. Instead:

> For learning outcomes and educational experiences of the majority to improve we need focused attention to dedicated, inspired teaching based on a curriculum that is teachable…. Teachers said that development of learning materials is not the core business of teachers. It also erodes teaching time. The textbook is the most effective tool to ensure consistency, coverage, appropriate pacing and better quality instruction…. The Programme establishes the 'non-negotiables'–of resources, teacher planning and effective teaching. The focus is on reading, writing and mental maths each day, and regular, standardised assessment of learner performance. (Motshekga, 2009)

Again, some observers may quibble about the specifics, but they cannot quibble about the clear tone of impatience with vague overambitiousness and overcomplexity, or about the need to focus on students' acquiring measurable skills.

Arguably, then, among the early adopters, South Africa is the closest to instituting a scaled-up program in reading that is simple, direct, and focused. Among the key desired actions are the following (Q. Moloi, Department of Education, South Africa, personal communication, April 7, 2010):

- Issuing high-level (ministerial) directives on minimum expectations for (1) the time to be allocated to reading in daily school timetable, (2) the reading resources and materials for every classroom, and (3) assessment.

- Providing detailed lesson plans on what to teach in reading (deliberate focus on core skills) to teachers who need this kind of assistance. Some teachers may have more effective alternatives and so may not need the centrally developed plans.

- Creating print-rich environments by giving schools storybooks for children to practice reading, and by directing the materials to the most resource-poor schools.

- Piloting simple EGRA tools in mother tongues to start a process of (1) monitoring progress in reading and (2) setting oral reading standards. The process to roll out the use of the "draft tools" to more schools on a trial basis is under way, and nongovernmental organizations that provide reading services are showing increasing interest as well.

- Initiating a randomized controlled experiment on the efficacy of mother-tongue instruction and well-planned lessons for teaching reading in the early grades. (This stipulation led to further refinement of the EGRA tools in the languages that were used in the experiment.)

- Advocating (1) the benefits of early-grade reading, (2) how and why South Africa needs to assess early-grade reading (particularly reading fluency and comprehension), and (3) promotion of reading for enjoyment as a whole-school activity.

- Providing reading kits to grade R (pre–grade 1) centers for laying solid reading foundations for school readiness.

- Having the President and the Minister of Education prioritize literacy and numeracy for significant measurable improvements in the medium-term framework (2009–2014). To monitor the achievement, annual national assessments will be conducted at the critical transition grades (grades 3, 6, and 9).

Whether these actions *already* constitute an effective, implemented, integrated, and direct approach is something history will judge, however, as it is still early days. At any rate, these multiple intentions have not yet merged into a seamless system that is actually applied, and such a system might even be seen as overbearing in a country with South Africa's (recent) democratic and somewhat decentralist traditions. However, compared with other countries and with earlier stages in South Africa's post-democracy history, one could say the country is "almost there."

Liberia

Liberia provides evidence of willingness for immediate systemic or systematic stocktaking. Indeed, when the World Bank, USAID, and RTI originally proposed the notion of the baseline assessment, the Ministry of Education showed healthy impatience, telling international partners, in effect, that they knew the situation would be dismal. They understood the need to have a scientific baseline and establish some correlates of poor performance but wanted urgently to design remedial pilots and think about how to go to scale as quickly as possible.

As noted earlier in this chapter, discussions started in mid-2007, the baseline had been done by mid-2008, and the pilot was under way in late 2008. By 2009 the Ministry of Education was more and more anxious to learn from the pilot by, for example, expanding the number of ministry personnel who could shadow teacher trainers in the pilot projects so as to speed up the learning process. Furthermore, even as the pilot proceeded, sectoral planners took note of the baseline and the experiment: "All of these findings have serious policy implications and it is hoped that appropriate actions proposed in this document will be taken" (Ministry of Education, Liberia, 2009, p. 161). These are all encouraging signs for future progress.

Conclusions

The countries covered in this chapter—namely Liberia, Kenya, and South Africa (with Peru in contrast)—progressed from a discussion of issues related to early-grade reading to implementation of serious pilot experiments to introduce improvements, and they did so in about 18 months. Further, the pilot programs yielded sufficient evidence of impact to warrant some national interest in going to scale in about another year, or about 2½ years from the initial discussions. Experience suggests this is fairly fast for development work, particularly in education.

Three main factors helped impel speedy action. The first was an existing national **curriculum that was predisposed to the particular form of assessments and interventions** associated with EGRA. Without this element, getting "permission" to work around the existing curriculum can slow things down, at least when it comes to directed and simplified lesson plans. The second factor was a **willingness to use measurement and evidence**, and to base assistance and support to teachers on evidence. The final element was **national concern over the quality of teaching and learning**. This concern within the countries examined as cases in this chapter may have predated the application of EGRA, but the results also contributed to the concern and prompted action.

This chapter's qualitative approach does not permit generalization as to which of these factors may have been the strongest. Having observed several countries at length and over time, I and others at RTI working in this area have found these three factors to be at work. The one factor missing in South Africa was the second: a tradition of or predisposition to using learning assessment data to drive specific instructional improvement. Although we cannot argue that Liberia held this *tradition*, the predisposition certainly existed in the leadership of the ministry. The experimental pilot provided the experience.

References

Abadzi, H., Crouch, L., Echegaray, M., Pasco, C., & Sampe, J. (2005). Monitoring basic skills acquisition through rapid learning assessments: A case study from Peru. *Prospects, 35*(2), 137–156.

Alvarado Pérez, B. (2006). *Success in implementing education policy dialogue in Perú*. EdData II Working Paper No. 1. Retrieved April 8, 2010, from https://www.eddataglobal.org/documents/index.cfm?fuseaction=showdir&pubtype=5&statusID=3

Cotlear, D. (Ed.) (2006). *A new social contract for Peru: An agenda for improving education, health care, and the social safety net*. Washington, DC: International Bank for Reconstruction and Development and the World Bank. Retrieved August 23, 2010, from http://siteresources.worldbank.org/INTPCENG/Resources/A_New_Social_Contract_for_Peru.pdf

Cross, M., Mungadi, R., & Rouhani, S. (2002). From policy to practice: Curriculum reform in South African education. *Comparative Education, 38*(2), 171–187.

Crouch, L., & Korda, M. (2008). *EGRA Liberia: Baseline assessment of reading levels and associated factors*. Report prepared as part of a process of collaboration between USAID and the World Bank. Research Triangle Park, North Carolina: RTI International. Retrieved September 21, 2010, from https://www.eddataglobal.org/documents/index.cfm?fuseaction=pubDetail&ID=158

Crouch, L., Korda, M., & Mumo, D. (2009). *Improvements in reading skills in Kenya: An experiment in the Malindi district*. Prepared for the United States Agency for International Development (USAID) under the EdData II project, Task 4, Contract No. EHC-E-04-04-00004-00. Research Triangle Park, North Carolina: RTI International. Retrieved May 4, 2011, from https://www.eddataglobal.org/documents/index.cfm?fuseaction=pubDetail&ID=154

Department of Education, South Africa. (2002). *Revised national curriculum statement grades R–9 (schools), languages: English – home language*. Pretoria: Department of Education. Gazette No. 23406, Vol. 443, May 2002. Retrieved June 1, 2011, from http://www.education.gov.za/LinkClick.aspx?fileticket=DA61L1i6%2f4U%3d&tabid=266&mid=720

Department of Education, South Africa. (2009). *Report of the Task Team for the Review of the Implementation of the National Curriculum Statement*. Final report presented to the Minister of Education, Ms. Angela Motshekga. Pretoria: Department of Education.

Hanushek, E. A., & Woessmann, L. (2009). *Do better schools lead to more growth? Cognitive skills, economic outcomes, and causation*. Working Paper 14633. Cambridge, Massachusetts: National Bureau of Economic Research.

Jansen, J. (1998). Curriculum reform in South Africa: A critical analysis of outcomes-based education. *Cambridge Journal of Education, 28*(3), 321–331.

Mingat, A., Rakotomalala, R., & Kengne, V. (2004). *La dynamique des scolarisations au Niger: Evaluation pour un développement durable* [The dynamics of enrollment in Niger: Evaluation for sustainable development]. Working Paper No. 32805. Washington, DC: World Bank, Africa Region, Human Development Department. Retrieved August 23, 2010, from http:// www-wds.worldbank.org/external/default/WDSContentServer/IW3P/IB/ 2005/07/06/000160016_20050706130522/Rendered/PDF/ 328050NG0Scolarisations0AFHD0no40.pdf

Ministerio de Educación [Ministry of Education], Perú. (2005). *Diseño curricular nacional de educación básica regular: Proceso de articulación* [National curriculum design for regular basic education: Formulation process]. Lima, Peru: Ministerio de Educación.

Ministry of Education, Liberia. (2009). *The Education Sector Plan of Liberia, 2010–2020*. Monrovia, Liberia: Ministry of Education.

Ministry of Education, Science and Technology, Kenya. (2002). *Primary education syllabus, Vol. 1*. Nairobi: Kenya Institute of Education.

Motshekga, A., Minister of Education, South Africa. (2009). *Statement to National Assembly by the Minister of Basic Education on curriculum review process, 5 November 2009*. Retrieved April 8, 2010, from http://www. education.gov.za/dynamic/dynamic.aspx?pageid=306&id=9148

Muller, J. (2000). *Reclaiming knowledge: Social theory, curriculum and education policy*. London: Routledge/Falmer.

Rogan, J. (2007). An uncertain harvest: A case study of implementation of innovation. *Journal of Curriculum Studies, 39*(1), 97–121.

Somerset, H. A. C. (1974). Who goes to secondary school? Relevance, reliability and equity in secondary school selection. In D. Court & D. Ghai (Eds.), *Education, society, and development: Perspectives from Kenya* (pp. 149–184). Nairobi: Oxford University Press.

Somerset, H. A. C. (1987). *Examination reform in Kenya*. Discussion paper, Education and Training Series, EDT65. Washington, DC: World Bank.

Taylor, N., Muller, J., & Vinjevold, P. (2003). *Getting schools working*. Cape Town: Pearson Education South Africa.

Wasanga, P. (2010, April). *Users and uses on national assessment results: The Kenyan experiences.* Presentation delivered at the Workshop on Africa–Alliance for Learning and Education Results (Africa–Alert), Cape Town, South Africa.

Woessman, L. (2000). *Schooling resources, educational institutions, and student performance: The international evidence.* Working Paper 983. University of Kiel, Germany: Kiel Institute of World Economics.

World Bank. (2007). *Toward high-quality education in Peru: Standards, accountability, and capacity building.* Washington, DC: World Bank. Retrieved August 23, 2010, from http://siteresources.worldbank.org /INTINDIA/4371432-1194542322423/21542208/ TowardhighqualityeducationinPeru.pdf

World Bank: Independent Evaluation Group. (2006). *From schooling access to learning outcomes—An unfinished agenda: An evaluation of World Bank support to primary education.* Washington, DC: World Bank.

Zuma, J., President, Republic of South Africa. (2010). *State of the Union Address, South African Parliament, 11 February 2010.* Retrieved April 8, 2010, from http://www.info.gov.za/speeches/2010/10021119051001.htm

Early Grade Learning Community of Practice Members

The Early Grade Learning Community of Practice is a group of educators, government officials, and development practitioners working together, with varying degrees of affiliation, toward the common goal of improved learning in the early grades in low-income countries. Members of the Community of Practice include government officials of more than 40 countries, university researchers in the United States (California, Massachusetts, South Carolina, Texas, Utah, and Washington, DC), Chile, Egypt, France, South Africa, Spain, the United Kingdom, and the United Arab Emirates, as well as individuals associated or working with the following institutions and initiatives:

- Academy for Educational Development (AED)
- Aga Khan Foundation
- American Institutes for Research (AIR)
- Amigos de Patzún (ADP)
- Bangladesh Rural Advancement Committee (BRAC)
- CARE
- Catholic Relief Services (CRS)
- Centre de Promotion de la Citoyenneté pour le Développement Durable à la Base (CEPROCIDE)
- Centro de Investigación y Acción Educativa Social (CIASES)
- ChildFund International
- Creative Associates International
- UK Department for International Development (DFID)
- East African Development Consultants (EADEC)
- Education Development Center (EDC)
- Education Sector Support Programme in Nigeria (ESSPIN)

- Fast Track Initiative (FTI)
- Focus Africa
- Fundación Centro de Estúdios en Políticas Públicas (CEPP)
- Fundación para el Desarrollo Agrario (FDA)
- Grupo de Análisis para el Desarrollo (GRADE)
- Graded, The American School of São Paulo
- L'Institut pour l'Éducation Populaire (IEP)
- International Reading Association (IRA)
- International Rescue Committee (IRC)
- Johns Hopkins University Center for Communication Programs (JHU/CCP)
- Liberia Education Trust (LET)
- Makerere Institute of Social Research (MISR)
- The Molteno Institute for Language and Literacy
- Plan USA
- Pratham
- Room to Read
- RTI International
- Save the Children
- School to School
- UNESCO Institute for Statistics (UIS)
- United Nations Educational, Scientific and Cultural Organization (UNESCO)
- United States Agency for International Development (USAID)
- Uwezo Initiative
- Volontaires pour l'Intégration Educative (VIE)
- The William and Flora Hewlett Foundation
- The World Bank

EGRA Subtask Examples

This appendix provides examples in English for most of the EGRA subtasks summarized in Chapter 1. The only subtasks for which there are no examples are syllable naming and maze/cloze. The former subtask has not been used in English; interested readers may refer to the Kiswahili instruments on the website of the Education Data for Decision Making (EdData II) project sponsored by the United States Agency for International Development (www.eddataglobal.org). The maze/cloze subtask is under development for inclusion in future EGRAs. As none has been tested to date, we do not include an example here. For a cloze example from another literacy assessment, see subtest 16 in Navas et al. (n.d.).

The examples are excerpts from instruments used in Guyana, Kenya, Liberia, and Rwanda. Readers are reminded that EGRA subtasks need to be adapted to the linguistic structures of local languages and cultural contexts; these examples should therefore be thought of as illustrative and should not be assumed to be applicable in any future assessments without further adaptation.

For each example, the subtask title refers to the general terminology used in this book. Within some examples, a different subtask name reflects the terminology that was used locally.

For the full instruments from which the examples are drawn, please see www.eddataglobal.org. Additional examples and details on adaptation and implementation are available in the EGRA toolkits (RTI International, 2009).

References

Navas, A.L., Linan-Thompson, S., & Siegel, L. (n.d.). *Reading readiness assessment: Recording booklet*. Pembroke Pines, Florida: Association of American Schools in South America Emergent Literacy Project. Retrieved May 12, 2011, from http://www.aassa.com/literacy/assessmentdocs/RecordingBooklet.pdf

RTI International. (2009). *Early Grade Reading Assessment toolkit*. Prepared for the World Bank, Office of Human Development, under Contract No. 7141961. Research Triangle Park, North Carolina: RTI International. Retrieved August 23, 2010, from https://www.eddataglobal.org/documents/index.cfm?fuseaction=pubDetail&ID=149

Concepts About Print
SUBTASK EXAMPLE

Source: USAID, EGRA Plus: Liberia, EdData II, 2010

Task 1. Orientation to Print

Show the child the paragraph segment on the last page of the student assessment (Section 6).

Tom wakes up very early. Today is the first day of school. His little brother Robert is awake, too. Robert gets his shoes and tells Tom he is ready to go. Then, Tom walks Robert to school to meet his new teacher. The teacher sees Robert and says hello. Tom and Robert are very happy to be at school today.

Read the instructions in the gray boxes below, recording the child's response before moving to the next instruction.

I don't want you to read this now. On this page, where would you begin to read? Show me with your finger.

[Child puts finger on the top row, left-most word]   ○ Correct   ○ Incorrect   ○ No Response

Now show me in which direction you would read next.

[Child moves finger from left to right]   ○ Correct   ○ Incorrect   ○ No Response

When you get to the end of the line, where would you read next?

[Child moves finger to left-most word of second line]   ○ Correct   ○ Incorrect   ○ No Response

Phonemic Awareness: Phoneme Segmentation
SUBTASK EXAMPLE

Source: USAID, EdData II, Kenya, 2007

Section 5. Phoneme Segmentation

Instructions: There is no student sheet for this, as they read nothing. They only listen to the word the assessor reads. The assessor will say:

"I am going to say a word. After I say it, tell me all the sounds in the word. If I say "Hen" you would then say / h //e/ /n/? Now you try it. Let's another word "hat". Tell me the sounds in "hat".

If the child responds correctly say: **Very good, the sounds in "hat" are /h/ /a/ /t/.**

If the child does not respond correctly, say: T**he sounds in "hat" are /h/ /a/ /t/. Now tell me the sounds in "hat"**

The child should be allowed two minutes to finish as many items as possible. Pronounce the word twice. Allow 10 seconds for the child to respond. Provide the number and sounds of the words, mark it incorrect and move on. Score both the number of sounds (correct / incorrect).

Section 5 Marking Sheet: Phoneme Segmentation

Put a slash (/) through incorrectly said phonemes

shop /sh/ /o/ /p/ _____/3

stand /s/ / t/ /a/ /n/ /d/_____/5

thank /th/ /a/ /ng/ /k/ _____/4

bat /b/ /a/ /t/ _____/3

seen /s/ /ea/ /n/ _____/3

should /sh/ /uu/ /d/ _____/3

up /u/ /p/ _____/2

at /a/ /t/ _____/2

top /t/ /o/ /p/ _____/3

if /i/ /f/ _____/2

Count and write down the total number of correctly pronounced Phonemes _____

Phonemic Awareness: Identification of Onset Sounds
SUBTASK EXAMPLE 1

Source: USAID, EGRA Plus: Liberia, EdData II, 2010

Task 3. Phonemic Awareness

This is **NOT** a timed exercise and **THERE IS NO STUDENT SHEET.** Read aloud each set of words once and have the student say which word begins with a different sound. Read these instructions to the child:

This is listening exercise. I'm going to say THREE words. ONE of them begins with a different sound, and you tell me which word BEGINS WITH A DIFFERENT SOUND

1. For example:

   "lost", "map", "like". Which word begins with a different sound?

   [If correct:] **Very good, "map" begins with a different sound.**

   [If incorrect:] **"lost", "map", "like". "map" begins with a different sound than "lost" and "like."**

2. Now try another one: "train", "trip", "stop". Which word begins with a different sound?

   [If correct:] **Very good, "stop" begins with a different sound.**

   [If incorrect:] **"train", "trip", "stop". "stop" begins with a different sound than "train" and "trip."**

Do you understand what you are supposed to do?

Pronounce each set of words **once slowly** (about 1 word per second). If the child does not respond after 3 seconds, mark it no response and move on.

Early stop rule: If the child gets the **first 5 sets** of answers **incorrect or no response**, draw the line through each of the 5 first rows, discontinue this exercise, check the box at the bottom of this page and go on to the next exercise.

Which word begins with a different sound? [repeat each set ONCE]						
1 boy	ball	cat	[cat]	☐ Correct	☐ Incorrect	☐ No Response
2 man	can	mad	[can]	☐ Correct	☐ Incorrect	☐ No Response
3 pan	late	pin	[late]	☐ Correct	☐ Incorrect	☐ No Response
4 back	ten	tin	[back]	☐ Correct	☐ Incorrect	☐ No Response
5 fish	fat	cat	[cat]	☐ Correct	☐ Incorrect	☐ No Response
6 boat	bit	coat	[coat]	☐ Correct	☐ Incorrect	☐ No Response
7 day	bag	dot	[bag]	☐ Correct	☐ Incorrect	☐ No Response
8 can	girl	cold	[girl]	☐ Correct	☐ Incorrect	☐ No Response
9 run	race	sand	[sand]	☐ Correct	☐ Incorrect	☐ No Response
10 leg	make	lay	[make]	☐ Correct	☐ Incorrect	☐ No Response

☐ Exercise was discontinued as child had no correct answers in **the first five
sets** of words.

Phonemic Awareness: Identification of Onset Sounds
SUBTASK EXAMPLE 2
Source: USAID, EdData II, Kenya, 2009

Section 2. Initial Sound Identification

*This is NOT a timed exercise and **THERE IS NO STUDENT SHEET**. Read aloud each word twice, and have the student say the initial sound. Remember to model the "pure" sounds: /p/, not "puh" or "pay." Say:*

This is a listening exercise. I want you to tell me the beginning sound of each word. For example, in the word "pot", the first sound is "/p/". In this exercise, I would like you to tell me the first sound you hear in each word. I will say each word <u>two times</u>. Listen to the word, then tell me the very first sound in that word.

Let's practice. What is the first sound in "mouse"? "Mouse."
  [If the child responds correctly, say]: **Very good, the first sound in "mouse" is /mmmmm/.**
  [If the child does not respond correctly, say]: **Listen again: "mmmouse". The first sound in "mouse" is /mmmmm/."**

Now let's try another one: What is the first sound in "day"? "Day".
  [If the child responds correctly, say]: **Very good, the first sound in "day" is / d / ".**
  [If the child does not respond correctly, say]: **Listen again: "day". The first sound in "day" is / d / ".**

Do you understand what you are to do?
  [If the child says no, say]: **Just try your best.**

Read the prompt and then pronounce the target word a second time. Accept only as correct the isolated sound (without a schwa). If the child does not respond after 3 seconds, mark as "No response" and say the next prompt. Enunciate clearly, but do not overemphasize the beginning sound of each word.

Early stop rule: *If the child responds incorrectly or does not respond to the first five words, say "**Thank you!**", discontinue this exercise, check the box at the bottom of the page, and go on to the next exercise.*

What is the first sound in "_____"? "_____"? *[Repeat the word twice]*						
Map	/mmmm/	○ Correct	○ Incorrect	○ Don't know	○ No Response	
Say	/ssssss/	○ Correct	○ Incorrect	○ Don't know	○ No Response	
Up	/uh/	○ Correct	○ Incorrect	○ Don't know	○ No Response	
Go	/g'/	○ Correct	○ Incorrect	○ Don't know	○ No Response	
Now	/nnnn/	○ Correct	○ Incorrect	○ Don't know	○ No Response	*(5 words)*
Can	/k'/	○ Correct	○ Incorrect	○ Don't know	○ No Response	
Fish	/ffffff/	○ Correct	○ Incorrect	○ Don't know	○ No Response	
Pig	/p'/	○ Correct	○ Incorrect	○ Don't know	○ No Response	
Run	/rrrrrr/	○ Correct	○ Incorrect	○ Don't know	○ No Response	
Look	/llllll/	○ Correct	○ Incorrect	○ Don't know	○ No Response	

Check this box if the exercise was discontinued because the child had no correct answers in the first five words :

Oral Vocabulary
SUBTASK EXAMPLE

Source: USAID, EdData II, Rwanda, 2011

Section 2. Common Vocabulary Words

You will ask the pupil to show parts of the body and objects in the environment, and to check comprehension of spatial terms. Note the answers in the manner indicated :

- *Error:* Slash (/) each item for which the pupil gave an incorrect answer
- *Self-correction:* If the pupil gave an incorrect answer but corrected the response thereafter (self-correction), circle the item that you already slashed. Count this answer as being correct

Materials needed: Put a pencil, the "Big Cow" book, and an eraser/rubber side by side in front of the pupil.

A. Ibice by'umubiri:

> **Ndakubwira amwe mu magambo agaragaza ibice byawe by'umubiri.**
> **Ujye unyereka icyo gice ku mubiri wawe iryo jambo rigaragaza.**
> **Nk'urugero ni : « izuru ryawe », « ijisho ryawe». Reka dutangire**

your arm -	your foot -	your chin -	your knee -
your shoulder -	your elbow -	your face -	your hair -

Number of correct answers | /8 |

B. Amagambo avuga ku bidukikije :

> **Ndavuga amagambo amwe. Wowe uratunga urutoki aho ibyo bintu biri.**

a pencil   a paper book   a wall   the floor   an eraser/rubber   a chair

Number of correct answers | /6 |

C. Spatial Terms:

Amagambo ajyanye n'ahantu:

Put the pencil:

on the book	behind you	on the floor
under the book	in front of you	beside the book

Number of correct answers	/6

TOTAL CORECT	**/20**

Listening Comprehension
SUBTASK EXAMPLE

Source: USAID, EdData II, Kenya, 2009

Task 7. Listening Comprehension

This is **NOT** a timed exercise and **THERE IS NO STUDENT SHEET**. The administrator reads aloud the following passage **ONLY ONE TIME**, slowly (about 1 word per second). Say,

> I am going to read you a short story aloud ONCE and then ask you some questions. Please listen carefully and answer the questions as best as you can.
> Do you understand what are you supposed to do?

Every day Sam walks to school with his friend Tom. On their way to school, the boys like to have a race to see who runs the fastest. It is Tom!

1. Who does Sam like to walk to school with?

[Tom]   ☐ Correct   ☐ Incorrect   ☐ No Response

2. What do they do on their way?

[they race/run]   ☐ Correct   ☐ Incorrect   ☐ No response

3. Who runs faster?

[Tom]   ☐ Correct   ☐ Incorrect   ☐ No Response

Letter Identification: Names
SUBTASK EXAMPLE

Source: USAID, EGRA Plus: Liberia, EdData II, 2010

Section 2. Letter Name Knowledge

Show the child the sheet of letters on the first page of the student assessment. Say,

> **Here is a page full of letters of the alphabet. Please tell me the NAMES of as many letters as you can--not the SOUNDS of the letters, but the names.**
> **1. For example, the name of this letter** [point to O] **is "OH".**
> **Now you try: tell me the name of this letter** [point to V]:
>   [If correct:] **Good, the name of this letter is "VEE."**
>   [If incorrect:] **The name of this letter is "VEE."**
>
> **2. Now try another one: tell me the name of this letter [point to L]:**
>   [If correct:] **Good, the name of this letter is "ELL."**
>   [If incorrect:] **The name of this letter is "ELL."**
>
> **Do you understand what you are supposed to do? When I say "begin," name the letters as best as you can. I will keep quiet and listen to you, unless you need help. Ready? Begin.**

Set the timer on 1 minute. Start the timer when the child reads the first letter. *Follow along with your pen and clearly mark any incorrect letters with a slash (/). Count self-corrections as correct.* **Stay quiet,** *except when providing answers as follows: if the child hesitates for 3 seconds, provide the name of the letter, point to the next letter and say* "**Please go on.**" *Mark the letter you provide to the child as incorrect.*

WHEN THE TIMER REACHES 0, SAY, "stop." *Mark the final letter read* **with a bracket ( ]).** *If the learner finished in less than 60 seconds, enter the remaining time.*
Early stop rule: *If the child does not give a single correct response on the first line, say* "**Thank you!**", *draw a line through the letters in the first row, discontinue this exercise, check the box at the bottom, and go on to the next exercise.*

(continued)

L	i	h	R	S	y	E	O	n	T	10
i	e	T	D	A	t	a	d	e	w	20
h	O	e	m	U	r	L	G	R	u	30
g	R	B	E	i	f	m	t	s	r	40
S	T	C	N	p	A	F	c	a	E	50
y	s	Q	A	M	C	O	t	n	P	60
e	A	e	s	O	F	h	u	A	t	70
R	G	H	b	S	i	g	m	i	L	80
L	i	N	O	e	o	E	r	p	X	90
N	A	c	D	d	l	O	j	e	n	100

Time left on stopwatch if student completes in LESS than 60 seconds: _____
☐ Exercise was discontinued as child had no correct answers in the first line.

Letter Identification: Sounds
SUBTASK EXAMPLE
Source: World Bank, Guyana, 2008

Section 3. Letter Sound Knowledge

Show the child the sheet of letters in the student stimuli booklet. Say:

> **Here is a page full of letters of the alphabet. Please tell me the SOUNDS of as many letters as you can--not the NAMES of the letters, but the SOUNDS. For example, the sound of this letter** *[point to A]* **is "AH" as in "APPLE" or "AAAA" as in "AGE".**
> **Let's practise: tell me the sound of this letter** *[point to V]:*
> > *If the child responds correctly say:* **Good, the sound of this letter is "VVVV."**
> > *If the child does not respond correctly, say:* **The sound of this letter is "VVVV."**
> **Now try another one: tell me the sound of this letter [point to L]:**
> > *If the child responds correctly say:* **Good, the sound of this letter is "LLL."**
> > *If the child does not respond correctly, say:* **The sound of this letter is "LLL."**
> **Do you understand what you are to do?**
> **When I say "Begin," please sound out the letters as quickly and carefully as you can. Tell me the sound of the letters, starting here and continuing this way.** *[Point to the first letter on the row after the example and draw your finger across the first line].*
> **If you come to a letter sound you do not know, I will tell it to you. Otherwise I will keep quiet and listen to you. Ready? Begin.**

🕐 *Start the timer when the child reads the first letter. Follow along with your pencil and* **clearly** *mark any incorrect letters with a slash (/). Count self-corrections as correct. If you've already marked the self-corrected letter as incorrect, circle the letter and go on.* **Stay quiet,** *except when providing answers as follows: if the child hesitates for 3 seconds, provide the sound of the letter, point to the next letter and say "**Please go on**." Mark the letter you provide to the child as incorrect. If the student gives you the letter name, rather than the sound, provide the letter sound and say: ["**Please tell me the SOUND of the letter**"]. This prompt may be given only once during the exercise.*

AFTER 60 SECONDS SAY, "stop." Mark the final letter read with a bracket ( ]).

*Early stop rule: If you have marked as incorrect all of the answers on the first line with no self-corrections, say "**Thank you!**", discontinue this exercise, check the box at the bottom, and go on to the next exercise.*

Example :   A   v   L

(continued)

	1	2	3	4	5	6	7	8	9	10	
	L	i	h	R	S	y	E	O	n	T	(10)
	i	e	T	D	A	t	a	d	e	w	(20)
	h	O	e	m	U	r	L	G	R	u	(30)
	g	R	B	E	i	f	m	t	s	r	(40)
	S	T	C	N	p	A	F	c	a	E	(50)
	y	s	Q	A	M	C	O	t	n	P	(60)
	e	A	e	s	O	F	h	u	A	t	(70)
	R	q	H	b	S	i	g	m	i	L	(80)
	L	i	N	O	e	o	E	r	p	X	(90)
	N	A	c	D	d	l	O	j	e	n	(100)

Time remaining on stopwatch at completion (number of SECONDS): ☐

Check this box if the exercise was discontinued because the child had no correct answers in the first line. ☐

Nonword Reading
SUBTASK EXAMPLE

Source: USAID, EGRA Plus: Liberia, EdData II, 2010

Task 5. Simple Unfamiliar Nonword Decoding

Show the child the sheet of nonwords on the third page on the student form. Say,

---

**Here are some made-up words. I would like you to read me as many made-up words as you can (do not spell the words, but read them).
For example, this made-up word is: "ut".**

1. **Now you try:** [point to the next word: "dif' and say] **please read this word**
              [If correct]: **"Very good: dif"**
              [If incorrect]: **This made-up word is "dif."**
2. **Now try another one:** [point to the next word: mab and say] **please read this word.**
              [If correct]: **"Very good: mab"**
              [If incorrect]: **This made-up word is "mab."**
Do you understand what you are supposed to do? When I say "begin," read the words as best as you can. I will keep quiet and listen to you, unless you need help. Ready? Begin.

🕐 **Start the timer when the child reads the first word.** Follow along with your pencil and clearly mark any incorrect words with a slash (**/**). Count self-corrections as correct. **Stay quiet**, except when providing answers as follows: if the child hesitates for 3 seconds, provide the word, point to the next word and say "*Please go on.*" Mark the word you provide to the child as incorrect.

WHEN THE TIMER REACHES 0, SAY, "*Stop.*" Mark the final word read with a bracket (⌐). If the learner finished in less than 60 seconds, enter the remaining time.

*Early stop rule: If the child gives no correct answers on the first line, say "**Thank you!**", discontinue this exercise, draw the line through the words in the first row, check the box at the bottom of the page, and go on to the next exercise.*

(continued)

loz	ep	yat	zam	tob	5
zom	ras	mon	jaf	duz	10
tam	af	ked	ig	el	15
tig	pek	dop	zac	ik	20
uf	ral	ep	bab	vif	25
lut	sig	zop	zar	jaf	30
ruz	huf	wab	ak	jep	35
wub	dod	ik	vus	nux	40
pek	zel	bef	wab	hiz	45
wof	ib	dek	zek	vok	50

Time left on stopwatch if student completes in LESS than 60 seconds: _____

☐ Exercise was discontinued as child had no correct answers in the first line.

Familiar Word Reading
SUBTASK EXAMPLE

Source: USAID, EGRA Plus: Liberia, EdData II, 2010

Task 4. Familiar Word Identification

Show the child the sheet of words on the second page of the student assessment. Say,

> **Here are some words. I would like you to read me as many words as you can (do not spell the words, but read them).**
> **For example, this word is: "CAT".**
> **1. Now you try:** [point to the word "mat" and say] **please read this word:**
>   [If correct]: **Good, this word is "mat."**
>   [If incorrect]: **This word is "mat."**
> **2. Now try another one:** [point to the word "top"] **please read this word :**
>   [If correct]: **Good, this word is "top."**
>   [If incorrect]: **This word is "top."**
>
> **Do you understand what are you supposed to do? When I say "begin," read the words as best as you can. I will keep quiet and listen to you, unless you need help. Ready? Begin.**

⏱ **Start the timer when the child reads the first word.** Follow along with your pencil and clearly mark any incorrect words with a slash (**/**). Count self-corrections as correct. **Stay quiet**, except when providing answers as follows: if the child hesitates for 3 seconds, read the word, point to the next word and say "**Please go on**." Mark the word you read to the child as incorrect.

WHEN THE TIMER REACHES 0, SAY, "*stop.*" *Mark the final word read with a bracket* (**⌐**). If the learner finished in less than 60 seconds, enter the remaining time.

Early stop rule: If the child gives no correct answers on the first line, say, "***Thank you!***", *discontinue this exercise, draw the line through the words in the first row, check the box at the bottom of the page, and go on to the next exercise.*

(continued)

but	time	in	the	also	5
make	no	its	said	were	10
came	very	do	after	long	15
water	as	all	for	even	20
her	was	three	been	more	25
that	must	can	around	it	30
another	words	back	called	work	35
could	an	him	on	see	40
than	get	not	where	what	45
you	if	their	through	when	50

Time left on stopwatch if student completes in LESS than 60 seconds: _____

☐ Exercise was discontinued as child had no correct answers in the first line.

Oral Reading Fluency (Paragraph Reading)
with Comprehension
SUBTASK EXAMPLE

Source: USAID, EGRA Plus: Liberia, EdData II, 2010

Task 6. Passage Reading and Comprehension

Show the child the story on the last page of the student form. Say,

> Here is a short story. I want you to read this aloud. When you finish, I will ask you some questions about what you have read.
>
> Do you understand what are you supposed to do? When I say "begin," read the story as best as you can. I will keep quiet and listen to you, unless you need help. Ready? Begin.

🕐 **Set the timer on 1 minute. Start the timer when the child reads the first word.** Follow along with your pencil and clearly mark any incorrect words with a slash (**/**). Count self-corrections as correct. **Stay quiet**, except when providing answers as follows: if the child hesitates for 3 seconds, provide the word, point to the next word and say "**Please go on**." Mark the word you provide to the child as incorrect. **WHEN THE TIMER REACHES 0, SAY,, "stop."** Mark the final word read with a bracket (**]**). If the learner finished in less than 60 seconds, enter the remaining time. If the child gets the entire first line incorrect, discontinue this exercise – both reading and comprehension questions -, check the box below and go on to the next exercise.

STOP THE CHILD AT 0 SECONDS AND MARK WITH A BRACKET ( ]). Take **the text away** from the child after they read it. Read instructions to the child. Then read each question slowly and clearly. After you read each question, give the child at most 15 seconds to answer each question. Mark the answers to the questions as correct or incorrect.

(continued)

Now I am going to ask you a few questions about the story you just read. Try to answer the questions as best as you can.		
Tom wakes up very early. Today is the first day of	11	**Why did Tom wake up early?** [it's the first day of school, school day] ☐ Correct ☐ Incorrect ☐ No Response
school. His little brother Robert is awake, too.	20	**What is Tom's little brother's name?** [Robert] ☐ Correct ☐ Incorrect ☐ No Response
Robert gets his shoes and tells Tom he is ready to go.	31	**What does Robert do after he wakes up?** [puts on his shoes, gets ready] ☐ Correct ☐ Incorrect ☐ No Response
Then, Tom walks Robert to school to meet his new	41	**Who will Robert meet today?** [his teacher, new teacher] ☐ Correct ☐ Incorrect ☐ No Response
teacher. The teacher sees Robert and says hello.	50	**How are Tom and Robert feeling today?** [happy, they feel good] ☐ Correct ☐ Incorrect ☐ No Response
Tom and Robert are very happy to be at school today.	60	

Time left on stopwatch if student completes in LESS than 60 seconds: _____

☐ Exercise was discontinued as child did not read a single word correctly in the first line.

Dictation
SUBTASK EXAMPLE

Source: USAID, Core Education Skills for Liberian Youth (CESLY), 2010

[From assessors' instructions on reading sheets and student booklet]

Section 5. Dictation

Turn to the next page; it is a lined page for learners to write on. Put it in front of the learner. For yourself, turn to the last page of the Learners Reading Sheets, where you will find instructions for yourself.

By now, your learner should have a lined page in front of them. Follow instructions carefully. Say,

> I am going to read you a short sentence. Please listen carefully. I will read the whole sentence once. Then I will read it in parts so you can write what you hear. I will then read it again so that you can check your work. Do you understand what you are to do?

Read the following sentence ONCE at about one word per second.

The girls wanted to go and ride their bikes.

Then, give the child a pencil, and read the sentence a SECOND time, grouping the words as follows:

The girls wanted /wait 5 secs/ to go and /wait 5 secs/ ride their bikes.

Wait 15 seconds and read the whole sentence.

The girls wanted to go and ride their bikes.

Wait 5 seconds and then retrieve the instrument from the learners. Leave the pencil with the child and tell them to keep it safe because they will need it again.

The girls wanted / to go and / ride their bikes.

(continued)

Evaluation Criteria		Correct = 1 Incorrect = 0
Wrote 'the' correctly	The	
Wrote 'girls' correctly	girls	
Wrote 'wanted' correctly	wanted	
Wrote 'to' correctly	to	
Wrote 'go' correctly	go	
Wrote 'and' correctly	and	
Wrote 'ride' correctly	ride	
Wrote 'their'	their	
Wrote 'bikes' correctly	bikes	
Use appropriate direction from left to right		
Used capital letter for word "The"		
Used full stop (.) at end of sentence		

Glossary

automaticity/fluency The bridge between decoding and comprehension. Fluency in word recognition means that the reader is no longer aware of or needs to concentrate on the mental effort of translating letters to sounds and forming sounds into words. At that point, the reader is decoding quickly enough to be able to focus on comprehension.

baseline, midterm, endline In impact evaluation, assessments are usually conducted at the very beginning of the project (baseline) midway through the project (midterm) and at the end of the project (endline).

ceiling effect A statistical term to denote an artificial upper limit on the possible values for a variable, causing the distribution of scores to be skewed. For example, the distribution of scores on an EGRA ability test will be skewed by a ceiling effect if the test is much too easy for most children in the early grades to allow for analysis.

civil society The arena, outside of the family, the state, and the market, where people associate to advance common interests.

continuous assessment Ongoing, classroom-based assessment conducted by the teacher to inform instruction.

criterion-referenced assessment Assessment that refers back to standards and criteria developed external to the classroom, typically at the district, state, or national level.

decodable books Books in which print can be easily deciphered into the sounds that correspond to each letter.

decoding The act of relating the print read to the corresponding sounds of each letter.

floor effect A statistical term to denote an artificial lower limit on the possible values for a variable, causing the distribution of scores to be skewed. For example, the distribution of scores on an EGRA ability test will be skewed by a floor effect if the test is much too difficult for most children in the early grades to perform at a sufficient skill level to allow for analysis.

fluency, fluent The ability to read text accurately and quickly.

grapheme The most basic unit in an alphabetic written system. Graphemes combine to create phonemes (see *phoneme*). A grapheme might be composed of one or more than one letter (such as ph or gh for the phoneme /f/) or of a letter with a diacritic mark (such as "é" vs. "e" in French).

interrater reliability The degree of agreement among raters or assessors. If the assessors do not agree to the required level, either the assessment needs to be improved or the assessors need to be retrained.

legal syllables Syllables that adhere to the orthographic rules of a given language.

language of instruction The language in which content is conveyed in the classroom.

logograph A single grapheme that also forms a word or morpheme, for example, "a" in Spanish or "I" in English.

maze/cloze A technique in which words are deleted from a passage according to a word-count formula or various other criteria. The passage is presented to students, who insert words (maze includes three possible choices for student selection; cloze does not provide any options) as they read to complete and construct meaning from the text.

mother tongue Language spoken by a child's mother in the home; usually the first language the child learns.

morphograph Smallest unit of meaning in a word.

onset The first consonant or consonant cluster that precedes the vowel of a syllable; for example, *spoil* is divided into "sp" (the onset) and "oil" (the rime).

orthography The art of writing words with the proper letters according to the spelling and construction rules of a language.

phoneme The smallest linguistically distinctive unit of sound allowing for differentiation between two words within a specific language (e.g., "top" and "mop" differ by only one phoneme, but the meaning changes).

phonemic awareness The ability to focus on, manipulate, and break apart the smallest units of sounds (or phonemes) in words.

phonological awareness A general appreciation of the sound structure of language, as demonstrated by the awareness of sounds at three levels of structure: syllables, onsets and rimes, and phonemes; the ability to hear and manipulate sounds and sound segments.

rime The part of a syllable that consists of its vowel and any consonant sounds that come after it; for example, *spoil* is divided into "sp" (the onset) and "oil" (the rime).

scaffolding Supportive instruction. In reading, scaffolding is the act of pushing students to learn just beyond their developmental level by using verbal or written prompts to guide students through texts.

About the Authors

Amber Gove is the team leader for Teaching and Learning with RTI's International Education Group. Much of her recent work has centered on the development of the Early Grade Reading Assessment (EGRA), which has been used in more than 50 languages and countries to inform policy and improve teaching and learning. She has worked closely with government counterparts in Latin America, Africa, and South Asia in project design and evaluation, research and data analysis, and policy dialogue. Her research and policy interests include measurement and improvement of student learning, education finance, conditional cash transfer programs, and factors affecting achievement, enrollment, and attendance. Dr. Gove received her PhD in international comparative education and her MA in economics from Stanford University and will complete a Certificate in Literacy Instruction from George Washington University in 2011.

Anna Wetterberg, a postdoctoral researcher in RTI's International Development Group, has more than 10 years' experience working on research and operations in international development. In Indonesia, she managed a research and training program at the Ministry of Agriculture, led research on local-level institutions for the World Bank, and contributed to the monitoring and evaluation framework for the country's largest poverty alleviation and participatory planning program. Dr. Wetterberg's current research interests include state-society relations, corporate social responsibility, and international labor standards. Dr. Wetterberg received her PhD in sociology from the University of California, Berkeley and her MA in international development policy and BA in economics from Stanford University.

Luis Crouch recently (March 2011) joined the Education for All Fast-Track Initiative Secretariat as head of its Global Good Practice team. Previously he worked at the World Bank and for many years at RTI International. Dr. Crouch is an education economist (PhD, University of California, Berkeley) specializing in policy, decentralized finance (e.g., funding formulas) and decentralization, political economy of reform, education statistics, and projections. He has become interested in early grade reading to improve education systems' response to the quality imperative. He has worked closely on South Africa's funding reforms and more recently Egypt's decentralization experiments.

Marcia Davidson is a senior education analyst with RTI International and the senior advisor to the Early Grade Reading/Math component of the Liberia Teacher Training Program. She was the reading consultant for the EGRA-Plus Liberia project from 2008 to 2010. Her research focuses on reading acquisition, teacher professional development, and assessment. Dr. Davidson was a professor in both special education and elementary education, teaching courses in reading and assessment for 12 years. In 2009, she served as a Fulbright Scholar in the Slovak Republic. Her doctorate is from the University of Washington in Seattle.

Medina Korda, a research policy analyst at RTI International, has over 11 years of experience in development policy. Ms. Korda's experience pertains mainly to policy and planning activities and early grade reading and assessments. She has been involved in project design and evaluation, research and data analysis, and policy dialogue and has provided input on early grade assessments for many education projects. She managed the USAID-funded EGRA Plus Liberia pilot (designed as randomized controlled trial) that led to significant improvements in student reading in just 2 years. She is currently the home office technical manager for a USAID-funded scale-up of this pilot that will reach more than 1,200 Liberian schools nationwide. Ms. Korda has an MA in international development policy from Duke University.

Benjamin Piper is a senior research education analyst with RTI International. He currently investigates the impact of a variety of language-of-instruction educational policies on student outcomes. His previous research investigated an Ethiopian in-service teacher professional development program's effect on teacher and student outcomes. He has experience in quantitative research and mixed methodological research designs.

Dr. Piper completed a master's in school leadership, a master's in international education policy, and a doctorate in international education, the last two from Harvard University.

Carmen Strigel is team leader for information and communication technology (ICT) for education and training in RTI's International Development Group. Her expertise is in pedagogic integration of ICT into teaching and learning and content development, teacher training, organizational development, and ICT policies. In 2007, she co-developed the first EGRA in French and Wolof in Senegal. Since then, she has contributed to several EGRA efforts, mainly in data analysis and report writing. She also oversees the development of Tangerine™, an electronic system for EGRA data collection. Ms. Strigel received a master's in education from the University of North Carolina at Chapel Hill.

Emily Miksic is a research education analyst at RTI International with a master's degree in international educational development. She has over 9 years of experience that includes work in seven countries in Africa, South America, and the Caribbean. Her work focuses on early grade reading and math assessment (EGRA/EGMA), reading intervention, and professional development for teachers. She manages and provides technical assistance on projects, collaborates with multiple stakeholders in program design, and conducts research and training. Ms. Miksic holds a master's in international educational development from Teachers College, Columbia University, in New York.

Jessica Mejía is a research education analyst at RTI International. Her recent work has centered on the implementation of EGRA and has assisted in the deisgn and implementation of EGRA in Egypt, Kenya, Nicaragua, Honduras, Peru, Malawi, Zambia, and Ethiopia. She has also designed and implemented teacher-training modules in Nicaragua and Malawi. She has more than 7 years of experience in research in classrooms and reading, including development and implementation of intervention curricula in English and Spanish. She received her master's degree in education from the University of Texas at Austin, the Language and Literacy Department, in curriculum and instruction.

Sarah Pouezevara has worked with RTI since 2006. She specializes in eLearning and the use of technology for education and training. She is supporting RTI in finding or developing custom digital learning materials for literacy, numeracy, and teacher training, as well as applying technology to improve EGRA processes. Ms. Pouezevara has also worked as an instructional designer, program evaluator, and technical writer for international organizations including UNAIDS, WHO, IRC, World Bank, and Open Society Foundation. Her master's degree is in international educational development from Teachers College, Columbia University (2001), with a specialization in information and communications technology for education and development.

Wendi D. S. Ralaingita is a research education analyst at RTI International with over 15 years' experience in education and international development. Her work focuses on school-based research, instruction, and teacher learning and professional development. Dr. Ralaingita is the lead evaluator for the evaluation of the effectiveness of the Institut pour l'Education Populaire (IEP's) "Read-Learn-Lead" Program in Mali. In addition, she has led multiple EGRA and EGMA (Early Grade Mathematics Assessment) efforts in Mali and Rwanda and provided technical advising and training for EGRA and EGMA efforts in the Democratic Republic of the Congo. Dr. Ralaingita also leads RTI's work in early grades mathematics assessment and instruction. She holds a PhD in international education policy from the University of Maryland.

Ollie White is senior director of Reading and Math on the Liberia Teacher Training Program II project in Liberia. In 2008, she coordinated the Early Grade Reading program that supported the effort of USAID and the Ministry of Education to improve reading in Liberia. As a result of the success, USAID scaled up the reading program through the Liberian Teacher Training Program for national impact. Ms. White holds a master's in educational ministries from Gordon Conwell Theological Seminary, South Hamilton, Massachusetts, and a bachelor's in religious education from the Baptist Theological Seminary, Monrovia, Liberia.

Index